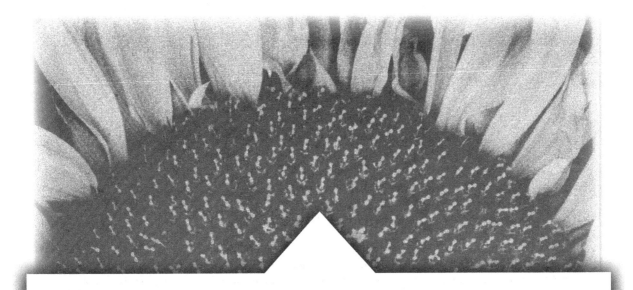

THE ACTS OF CREATION

a workbook for adults who work or live with children and young adults, to teach them intuitive, psychic and spiritual science skills

DON ELLISON

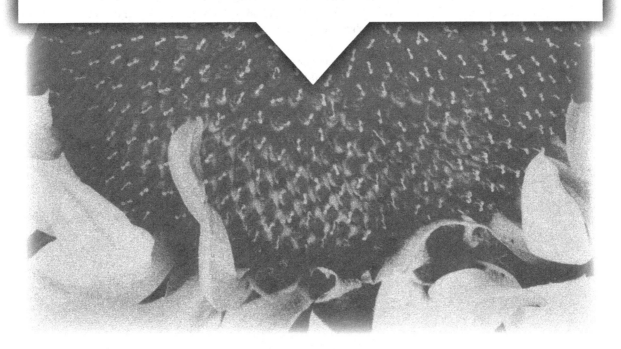

iUniverse, Inc.
Bloomington

The Acts of Creation
a workbook for adults who work or live with children and young adults,
to teach them intuitive, psychic and spiritual science skills

Body, Mind & Spirit / Parapsychology

iUniverse books may be ordered through booksellers or by contacting:

iUniverse
1663 Liberty Drive
Bloomington, IN 47403
www.iuniverse.com
1-800-Authors (1-800-288-4677)

ISBN: 978-1-4759-4022-0 (sc)
ISBN: 978-1-4759-4023-7 (e)

Library of Congress Control Number: 2013904758

Printed in the United States of America

iUniverse rev. date: 3/12/2013

"There is more in Heaven and Earth than in your philosophy"

—Shakespeare

"Attention to radiance must be an intense feeling and that, in its turn, must depend on a clear experience. Man cannot love something he does not know. Hence, the belief spoken of implies knowledge."

A heartfelt thanks to the Mill Valley Program for its existence; to Dr. Francis Coelho, for his untiring dedication and help with the entire publication and his philosophical clarity and friendship; to San Francisco Community School; to Ross and his enlightened children of the 5th and 6th grade, who started a journey into the unknown; to Synergy School and their enlightened and truly uninhibited sense of exploration, for which I am truly grateful; to La Conte School and a small group of 5- and 6-year-olds for their enthusiasm in a new area of experience; for Diane Sundberg for her relentless dedication; to Duke, for his many efforts in the printing process; and, finally, to all the others, seen and unseen, for their help and guidance on my life's path.

"When you change the way you look at things…the things you look at change."

TABLE OF CHANNELS (CONTENTS)

Foreword		1
Introduction		19
I.	Psychotronics/Radionics	23
II.	The Pendulum	45
III.	Chakras	61
IV.	Concentration, Meditation, Contemplation And Visualization	71
dreams		75
V.	Mandalas	93
chanting		101
VI.	The Aura	109
VII.	E.S.P.	141
precognition		162
clairvoyance		164
VIII.	Numerology	181
IX.	Pyramid Energy	197
X.	Appendix	217
About The Author		219

AGE RELATED PROJECTS
AND EXERCISES

	Age Construction	Age Use	Page
RADIONICS			
Energy Feeling Task	5 to Adult	5 to Adult	26
Bio-plasmic Energy Generator	8 to Adult	5 to Adult	30
PENDULUMS			
Homemade Pendulums	8 to Adult	6 to Adult	50
Resin Cast Pendulums	8 to Adult	8 to Adult	51
CHAKRAS			
Chakra Meditation		5 to Adult	63
Eye Mirror Energy Transfer		5 to Adult	64
CONCENTRATION, MEDITATION AND CONTEMPLATION			
Dreams			
Waking Dreams		8 to Adult	75
Concentration, Meditation, Contemplation			

	Age Construction	Age Use	Page
VISUALIZATION EXERCISES			
Sun Visualization		5 to Adult	77
Sun to Aura Visualization		8 to Adult	78
Astral Body Meditation		8 to Adult	79
Crystal Guide Visualization		8 to Adult	80
Over Soul Visualization		8 to adult	82
MANDALAS			
God's Eye	6 to Adult	6 to Adult	92
Looking for Mandalas in Nature	5 to Adult	5 to Adult	94
Mandala Meditation		8 to Adult	94
Group Mandala	5 to Adult	5 to Adult	95
Color Wheel Meditation		6 to Adult	96
CHANTING			
OM Chant		6 to Adult	98
AURAS			
Color Chart	7 to Adult	7 to Adult	114
Color Chart Math	8 to Adult	8 to Adult	122
Colors Game	8 to Adult	5 to Adult	123
Peripheral Vision Exercise		7 to Adult	123
Electric Color Wheel	7 to Adult	7 to Adult	124
LIGHT EXPERIENCE			
Light Box		9 to Adult	125
Flashlights		8 to Adult	126
Sun Reflectors		8 to Adult	127
L-ROD Meter		9 to Adult	128

	Age Construction	Age Use	Page
ESP			
Relaxation Exercise		7 to Adult	137
Remote Viewing		7 to Adult	146
Telepathic Exercise		7 to Adult	149
Creative Telepathy		6 to Adult	152
Telepathy Flasher		6 to Adult	152
NUMEROLOGY			
Numerological Chart		13 to Adult	172
PYRAMIDS			
Constructing a Pyramid		9 to Adult	195
Pyramid Experiments		6 to Adult	196
King's Chamber	9 to Adult	6 to Adult	199
APPENDIX			
Coil Winding Device		8 to Adult	207

FOREWORD

The intuitive sense is an underlying theme of this publication, manifesting itself in each exercise and subject, giving an unlimited potential to the universal creative process.

I'm sure you have heard the old adage, "Read between the lines, and you will understand." This saying may turn out to be more than just an insignificant common saying. Words do express concepts which become mental pictures. The understanding of what one reads is channeled through the intuitive sense. Without intuitive sense, understanding would be considerably limited; the brain would translate information like a computer with little conscious understanding. Understanding comes from the higher mind; and misunderstanding may result from a lack or blockage of the intuitive sense, the creative connection with the higher mind.

Creativity is expressed throughout the history of the human race as the ultimate expression and fulfillment that has stimulated man's progress. Nothing would change, and everything would stay the same, without the intervention of creative thought. To say that creativity is an important aspect of being human is quite an understatement.

Creativity is the connection between the higher mind (super conscious mind) and the lower (intellectual) mind. The process by which we change our consciousness is the ability to tune our intuitive sense to various frequency levels inside and outside the electromagnetic spectrum. We all have the ability to develop our intuitive sense by utilizing creativity.

Exercises are woven into this book on how to develop these intuitive abilities. I decided to call each chapter a channel because this more effectively describes the nature of the book's content sections. You are invited to think about "channels" as they relate to this book and I present some key relationships as a beginning interpretation:

- Process (1) effect

- Suggest (2) movement

- Makes (3) connections

The relationship between channels and chapters is vastly different. Chapter is a concept, which, for some people, denotes a confined body of information limited to a particular space designation in a book or in the context of a speech. Chapter denotes an ordinary reality perception where the written sentence or paragraph and its basic meaning are retrieved through the process of comprehension. Channel, on the other hand, is a process, a pathway, by which ideas and concepts are realized. Channeling is a tuning procedure, which allows a person to focus on information, retrieve it and use it.

When we read a story by a well-known author, we intuitively realize more information than is actually written into the text of the story. A truly great artist can write in such a way that he/she stimulates the reader to experience extraordinary types of perception. Telepathically, the reader may become part of the story the author is writing or actually observe future or past events through the process of reading the story.

The structure and process of poetry gives us some indication of the ways words may affect how we translate meaning and context. Words become passageways of experience, tuning in on a concept or group of concepts, setting off the mechanism of visual pictures called "memory." Knowledge is inferred by words in poetry communicating a thought or feeling.

Reading "Yes" from poet James Merrill's book, The Changing Light of Sandover; Scripts from a Pageant, a particular passage created images for me. These poems were written partly through Merrill's fascination for the ouija board.

> The cup had moved so dreamily at first,
>
> We thought we were losing him –
>
> until he spoke of Earth. Mes Enfants from
>
> the past a moment naturally reveals
>
> in comparison comes back (so like Maria
>
> to explain the miracle as if it were mundane).

The first images that come to mind in the first sentence are the picture of the cup (a plastic, heart-shaped object with little stubbly round feet) with sixteen fingers holding it to a board with an arch of upper case letters from the English alphabet. This object, of course, is a ouija board pointer with two men (J.M. and D.J.) holding it down with eight fingers on one side and eight fingers on the other side. (The two men were interpreted from reading the passage preceding this one.)

The second sentence brings messages of a being with whom, J.M. and D.J. were communicating through the ouija board, and the pointer stopped moving for some time. J.M. and D.J. thought the being had broken off the communication. As it turns out, the being started moving across the pointer, again communicating a message about the planet Earth.

The third sentence, the message itself, takes somewhat more concentrated thought to ascertain its meaning. This sentence has the possibility of triggering the mind below its focus within the mundane world and focusing it in dimensions outside the time space continuum. It is very possible to contact this being's level of consciousness clairvoyantly by following the key phrases (images) with which this person is communicating. This may be a reason we can understand poetry or how an individual may understand the depth of poetic meaning. The more we read and contemplate the meaning of poetry (depending on the writer's use of words and concepts), the greater our ability to bridge the gap between dimensions. Although the mechanics of intuitive senses have not been worked out yet, I feel we will bridge that gap soon. An interesting book called Seth Materials by Jane Roberts gives some general information about these precious senses.(refer to Bibliography)

Of course, we can refer to the author's breakdown of characters in this poem "Yes"...and we find a list of beings. This poem spans God, biology and Nature (creation), psyche and chaos with all its lofty characters, from Michael (the Archangel to Gautama the Buddha and to other great beings of ordinary history—Pythagoras, Gertrude Stein and Alice B. Toklas are listed) and also some mundane characters like Maria. So we find ourselves searching for a lofty, historical goal to picture on high as we contemplate what the prophets have foretold over the centuries.

The breakdown of this message, in my understanding, is first of all that Mes, is short for message. Enfant means children. "A message from the children of Earth's past is a moment trivial to the present period of time but has come back as a message nevertheless." Maria is obviously the being speaking through the ouija at the time.

The more information one has about the subject, the easier it is to fill in the missing pieces. When I read the passage, "mes enfants from the past a moment naturally trivial in comparison came back;" I recalled historical accounts I had learned about living in the 20th and 21st centuries—as one of the most important periods in spiritual history. In a channeling by Kevin Ryerson, one of his spiritual beings spoke about the Aquarian Age as a time that all incarnated souls have worked so hard for over centuries. It will bring the next shift in man's consciousness arising from the over-dominant left brain function (logical/linear) to the integration of the right brain (intuitive/creative) function. That is said to be taking place at this time, culminating around the year 2500 AD.

The important point here is to attain an even flow of thoughts so that it becomes easier to enter a "meditative state." This state will free up the mind of left-brain concerns and open up whole new avenues of understanding. This understanding, has been explored by individuals in the Radionics (psychotronics) field. Tuning devices have been developed for the purpose of intuitively linking persons with medical problems. Numbers on rotating dials are used to calibrate frequencies between the people under observation. More and more information is becoming available on these devices, so that their accuracy will inevitably increase, culminating as we have seen in the integration of Radionics devices with portable computers, like the SE-5. Accuracy will inevitably increase "because every organ in our bodies has a frequency, and for that matter, everything in the universe has a particular frequency, often translated into color & sound frequencies.

Michael Kay, a New Age researcher, states that the capability now exists to supply total energy for a house or car through free energy devices, perpetual motion or zero point gravity devices, energy which he hopes this will become accessible to a great number of people in the near future. Based upon my understanding of the behavioral history of the established corporations, the competition, which this new technology will bring will also cause developmental problems. In other words, though established corporations may make it difficult for these new technologies to flourish, the values in these new technologies will surely prevail.

I have just attended the "Co-Tech Conference" and understand that other individuals have developed similar devices that extract energy from the universe. Michael assured us these devices were already built and are being tested by individuals across the United States to Canada.

Free energy devices are another approach to connecting with other levels of consciousness. Around the turn of the century, Henry Moray, after doing research on extracting electrical energy from the earth, determined that a new unlimited source of energy could be extracted from the universe. He built a device with 15-20 100-watt light bulbs that would light up when Moray would bring this energy into play.(more of this discussion in Radionic Channel).

Moving forward in time we see that zero-point gravity, energy from a vacuum, has taken on a concrete manifestation in 2002. The first-ever patented device has graced our presence. If you go to the US patent office online and put in the #6, 362, 718 "The Motionless Magnetic Generator" (MEG), you will see the patent and you can download it for yourself. Now, to get a better understanding of what you are reading and the patent, you can go to Bill Morgan's email-(wmorgan@nycap. rr.com) and ask him for synopses of this patented device; or one of the authors Tom Bearden –(http://jnaudin.free.fr) for a more in-depth look at the principles behind the apparatus. And if you want to go further in your quest, you can access the Aero Inc. website (info@theorionproject.com) for a look at what Dr. Steven Greer M.D. and Dr. Theodore C. Loder, PhD have compiled as breakthroughs in energy technologies, (along with electrogravitic systems) for President Osama and the U.S. Congress in 2009.This energy, it is said , is the same energy that UFO's fly on and it may turn out to be the energy that our natural ability to telepathally communicate with other individuals even other life forms, manifest its self.

In Itzah Bentov's book, Stalking the Wild Pendulum, his theory of objective/subjective time may also shed some light on the mechanics of intuitive connection with others. Basically, he says our consciousness blinks in and out of our time-space reality so many times a second. "In our altered states of consciousness, we expand our subject time greatly, " he says. This allows us to observe the action of others "at a leisurely pace and bring back useful information. This is done without much objective time." It is similar to a technique used in television whereby an image is flashed on the screen so fast our conscious minds do not see the image; yet it is picked up by our subconscious and filed away in our computer banks. We move in and out of our ordinary reality so fast that we don't realize we have left it.

The type of connection made with another person's thoughts determines communication. This connection is a channel to other fields of information, whether in written or spoken form.

Frequently, one gains understanding of an author by intuitively reading between the lines, following the writer's thoughts far past their written words.

This experience in alterative consciousness may suffice to point out the tremendous creative variety in alternative communication. As I mention, a little further on with a similar experience, I was pulled out of meditation this second time to reveal 7 of my spiritual personalities stretched out over the planet. I want to focus on one personality because I am able to find some collaboration in waking reality, with this character. This being was, as I found out latter, was name Great Bear of the Iagala Sioux Tribe; (I found his name with the help of the Ouija board and a good friend). He had a full feathered headdress down to his ankles; a chieftain. I decided to contact the U.S. Department of Interior Bureau of Indian Affairs to see if there was even a Great Bear in Indian history. To my surprise they sent me back a Treaties about Kernal McLaughen speaking to Chief Red Cloud about relocating to a reservation in 1871. Part of the dialog was stated, "Red Cloud was talking to Great Bear about the relocation". The interesting thing is that all the individuals present at the meeting were chronicled in the document with the exception of Great Bear.

I searched my intuition to ascertain an answer for this discrepancy. The answer fired back through my intuitive consciousness that Great Bear was in spirit form and Red Cloud was speaking to his spirit guide "Great Bear" (I do not think this was an oversight because every line of dialog was recorded specifically in the treaties). So we have another example of spirit consciousness & our intuitive understanding, coming together as well as aspects of myself that I previously wasn't aware of up to this time.

In this publication, a parallel is drawn between radio channels and concepts or groups of concepts. We tune into different concept patterns as if tuning into alternative radio stations or Radionic frequencies. Concepts can be recognized as energy frequencies easily broken down into individual harmonics, thereby making it simpler to study thought communication scientifically.

The ability to tune in intuitively to other fields of information will become useful in many areas of society. A few of these might be as follows: helping law enforcement officials find criminals; predicting probability futures (individuals will understand prediction in the context of probability and synergistic experiences); healing the sick; and counseling individuals about future plans and past mistakes.

Channeling is a tuning procedure, which allows a person to focus on information, retrieve it and use it. If you did not understand this process, you would be unable to retrieve this information; however, understanding it can lead to the following processes:

- Identify: feel something

- Focus: define it

- Retrieve: integrate it into your cognitive structure

- Use: express yourself in some form

Let us take each of these functions and look at them in more depth.

Identify. In the process of identifying we need to focus on the intuitive sense to decode the characteristics of the light vibration. My experience with the intuitive sense of feeling bioenergy (the 6th sense) involves the sensing of a particular emotional light cord level that we human beings or animals are expressing; filtered throughout the solar plexis chakra.

Focus. This initial contact opens a window for decoding emotional light vibrations in the context of contemporary metaphysical understanding. Extending this discussion a bit further, joy, fear, depression, etc., can be determined by an individual's behavior, but also are decoded by individuals (quite naturally) on different energy light levels. On a normal level, the decoding of a particular pattern is accomplished on an unconscious level. On the other hand, individuals who have been conscious of energy patterns and their particular meanings and functions are able to define synergistic patterns in the context of colors, sound, texture or form.

Retrieve. At this level of awareness, information is integrated into cognitive structures: moving simultaneous information through the chakra levels and the brainwave networks, stimulating areas of the brain associated with colors, sight, sound, body functions, hormonal systems, creative and analytical processing; memory retrievably and storage over the neuro net. As this information is digested, one can see individuals from a more holistic perspective. One now has a holistic avenue for communication (on a conscious level, rather than just an unconscious level, a perspective one may not have had before). One can choose to discuss the perspective or act on it as one would choose. These four qualities signify a functions phenomenon.

There is always the other side of a picture, with this enlightened form of communication that brings additional responsibility for one's own actions. To manipulate another with this power of perception is an ultimate sin that is all too neatly recorded in the cosmic records (Akashic Records)—karma—(I dislike this term karma as there is so much misunderstanding surrounding its definitions)—is piled high for such transgressions against the soul. As a consequence, a sound grasp of ethics is necessary prior to our spiritual quest and enlightenment. As the common saying expresses it, "what goes around, comes around."

The single most important aspect or should I say responsibility of this author is to impress upon the reader that this information, especially for children, brings with its lessons of integrity. Opening up these abilities in all of us will shape our ideas & perceptions for the rest of our lives. We are hatchlings in the process of consciousness expansion & we should take care that we use our potentials in ways that up-lift our humanity rather than become involved in the manipulation of other's consciousness. Emphasize with your children the need for fairness, respect for others rights, honesty & unconditional love that we have with each individual soul. Discuss with the children concrete ways that they can realize each of these goals; brain storm possible solutions.

More than likely the last of these goals, unconditional love, is the most difficult. Unconditional love for each individual person you meet is of course a tall precept to live up to. There are so many sick, homeless and misguided people in the world today that it is difficult to even acknowledge these individuals at all. It is easier to turn away & walk on by. But, sometimes, it is a random act of kindness that is the thing that may give them the courage to live on one more day. It may not solve their problem, but it will give them a lift to meet their destiny head on one day at a time. And I'm not saying you should let your children interact with strangers but teach them to recognize opportunities to express what they understand.

Such as compassion, and to recognize the individual soul standing before them, a lesson you can't buy in your lifetime; it becomes a positive Karmic credit. Compassion is one of the characteristics of an advanced soul and a prerequisite for the state of Unconditional Love. In Journey to Xlong by Carlos Castaneda, Don Juan teaches Carlos to see beyond the normal faze that most people project to the outside world. Look deeper, he says, into the person's soul to find the true personality and acknowledge that, instead of the outward transient personality they can see the light of the soul being expressed through their personality. While doing research for advanced child development class, researching personality traits, I realized that each child's basic personality could be determined at an earlier age (refer to the channel on Pendulums for some interesting ideas).

As an early childhood specialist, I have had the opportunity to study child development and ethics of new technologies from many different perspectives. Moreover, a thorough discussion of ethics is very important for adults as well as for children, especially in learning about the history of ESP and the field of Psychotronics. Right and wrong, fair play, respect for others' rights, all are supremely important considerations in new educational systems.

One expert in child development was a psychologist named Eric Ericson. He researched the development of emotional levels of children as so exceptionally important to a child in his or her later life as adolescents and adults; especially in the area of conscience. If a child does not develop a sense of conscience at an early age, 3 or 4, he or she will not function to his or her most optimal potentials; in fact, ethical failures, especially concerning mental boundaries, can bring about failures in life, toward endeavors and achievements of all kinds. Each of Ericson's stages hinges upon another, so the child simply cannot progress until that stage/age-related behavior is learned. So we find many adults still stuck in old childhood patterns, because they have not progressed at the right time in their emotional development. Although being stuck at a younger emotional level is not a life sentence, one can progress in emotional consciousness to a healthy adult level if they want to do the work. All of these levels are within the context of ordinary personality (this is implied).

An important point about the occultist may be of interest here. Occultists did have certain truths, which, according to their doctrine, contained the keys to the universe. The structure of the priesthood was set up with a small group of priests, creating the inner circle that knew the universal truths but were afraid that others outside their inner circle might find these keys to the universe and use the knowledge for their own selfish motives. So the priests decided to first instruct disciples into their faith, leaving the masses to find their own way. The second plan was to create a sophisticated symbolic language, open to many interpretations, leaving the real interpretation to the priests who knew the correct formula for retrieving the knowledge within their complicated symbolic system.

This idea was formulated accurately by Miller and Smart, two English researchers, in their book "The Loom of Creation." They use objective mysticism as a concept for their integration of occult knowledge and scientific method. Philosophically, they bring you through occult knowledge and support their philosophy with scientific research and methods. They give a very convincing look at the realities hidden within the parables of occult history.

Up until five or six years ago you had to research occult knowledge sometimes in the dingy grey atmosphere of an old bookstore, clustered with hardback wooden chairs, sitting silently waiting for the weekly séance or occult lectures. It was an interesting environment, steeped in centuries of occult philosophy—areas so quiet one could hear a pin drop. Now the old occult bookstores have separated from their stable locations and gone out of business. All and all, its a good change. One no longer has to dig through volumes of old manuscripts to answer age-old questions. There are 21st century philosophers around who will come close to giving some of the age-old answers to the age old questions. All that is needed is to go into a appropriate bookstore, look through the science, occult and psychology section and get an introduction to as many integrated old philosophies as one can handle at one time. There are so many methods around, it is hard to know where to begin. I hope this book will give you some possibilities of directions to travel.

Another reason for the birth of this book is to communicate my own childhood experiences in hopes of aligning in common bond with adults and children of similar experiences. I'm sure many people have had experiences of déjà vu and dreams that bring enlightened information. All of my life I have had experiences of spontaneous telepathy, clairaudience and clairvoyance. It is my contention that through my own experiences and the experiences of the children with whom I have worked, that the encounters I had as a child and adult with creative thought were not that uncommon. In fact, I feel that psychic occurrences are as natural to the human species as eating and sleeping. There are individuals like Tim Leary who predicted man's changing evolution. Leary stated that evolutionary changes are genetically-based. Mother Nature, through approximate prediction and random selection, creates the genes that gradually change the destiny of man.

Psychic abilities are at the high end of the creative spectrum. Throughout history, psychic occurrences have been equated with miracles claimed by the church to signify the powers of a saint. Science has finally determined that this skill of creating miracles can be developed in people who have a high degree of intuitive ability. At this time, it seems the natural gifts of psychic senses are in the infant stages. As many in our times, I feel that the development of the psychic senses are the next evolutionary step forward for humankind. It may, also be, partly the content of Junk DNA as some scientists attest, that move us forward in consciousness; there may be a gene for psychic senses. Some scientist also feel that some of the junk DNA has an extraterrestrials origin.

It is my feeling that children are more open to psychic experiences than most adults. Partially through socialization and reinforced non-belief about real fantasies children have, children are discouraged from expressing or sharing information about actual psychic encounters, even ones that are first hand. Not all fantasies children have are psychic occurrences, but recognizing when a child has an unusual experience and talking it over with the child lends credibility to their realization and teaches them not to fear unique perceptions they have of their world. More and more, it is apparent to those exploring these new fields, children and adults as well will learn to explore and discover vital new areas of knowledge and life-changing information itself.

The various intuitive skills I talk about in this book are abilities all of us can develop if desired. This intuitive sense is important to grasp, because it can be utilized in artistic and technological disciplines. If we let this very important wellspring of human resources be taken over by people with sinister or ulterior motives, humanity would be deprived of the vital and equal opportunity to exercise their full potential in experiencing psychic phenomena. Psychic energy is our last natural resource that everyone can benefit from, (not just the rich and wealthy few).

We already know that some of these unusual energies can power a small motor, heal the sick, control pests and sharpen razor blades. Furthermore, the higher potentials of these energies stimulate creative development, emotional stability and spiritual enlightenment. Take a hypothetical question and ask what would be the attitudes and emotions among people if their thoughts and feelings were controlled by a few? The potential for this kind of control lies in successful research being done in various countries, for example, the Soviet Union. Through ESP research, Soviet scientists have determined, through monitoring the ESP receiver with EEG and GST devices, that the receiver is contacted seconds earlier on a physiological level by the ESP sender. In some cases, the receiver is aware of the message on a conscious level, and sometimes aware on a subconscious physiological level.

It is also assumed that different radiations can successfully be projected through air waves, as in the case of psychic energies and microwaves. Microwave energy has been used for 50 years by the Soviets. The question is: how long would we expect it to take the superpowers of the world to harness various radiations for the manipulation of individuals? Dr. Burr, a leading researcher in biology, discovered that a diseased culture in a quartz jar, placed next to a healthy culture, transferred its disease to the healthy one in a short period of time. It is possible that disease warfare could be used on unsuspecting individuals, once it is determined how a disease is transferred through the air. This possibility may already be upon us. This does not imply there is a "Commie" behind every tree, but I raise questions that seem logical when a new technology is coming into maturity.

In the last few years, the New Age movement has made great strides in the areas of holistic health. Part of this change reflects changes in attitude, knowledge and experience about the limits of human form and the boundaries of consciousness. More people, health professionals, especially are realizing that total health has its origin in different levels of consciousness. The levels of the aura and their relationship to the energy centers (charkas) and channels in the body are extending our awareness of the limits of the health field. The unified field theory in science attempts to explain various functions of consciousness; how these different energy fields interact together and what the function of each field is in different relationships. In addition, the relatively new holographic paradigm is showing great promise in answering questions about telepathy, precognition and psychokinesis, the higher order of things, as well as other subjects that have perplexed us about the mechanics of how these phenomena function. With the emergences of the holographic paradigm, we may finally have a better understanding of how consciousness functions and this includes the concept of reincarnation. (refer to "The Holographic Universe" by Michael Talbot and a short discussion of reincarnation at the end of this foreword).

Now, from the eighties we have seen the incarnation of great spiritual beings, the "Indigo children." I mention these children because they are, among other aspects describing them, highly intuitive psychic/sensitive beings that have come into the planet fully conscious. We are just determining their level of development. We have a much better feel for these children from psychological studies then we do from psychic and ESP studies, as they continue incarnating into all walks of life and societies. They are highly intelligent and have trouble following directions, wanting to follow their own individual focus in their life. They have come in as "system busters" with a low tolerance for information and structure without any logical basis in truth and understanding. On the other hand, their creativity and psychic abilities are highly developed. I have heard they can communicate with every other Indigo child on the planet. "The Indigo Child, " a DVD, which is out now gives us a glimpse of their special abilities in the psychic realms.(refer to "Emissary of Love" by James Twyman & The Indigo Chilren by Lee Carroll & Jon Tober)

At the very least the children we have seen are telepathic, intuitive and have a conscious precognitive ability—who knows what other abilities they have? We also know they have a great ability to heal different aspects in humans. One source of information about the psychic nature of these children is Nancy Clark, PhD, who is a medical intuitive practicing in Arizona. While attending the National Dowsing conference, (in Santa Cruz, Ca. one year) she related A story about a two year old at the airport surrounded by a circle of adults; the baby crawled through there legs and approached Nancy sitting on sofa waiting for her flight; Nancy had a little burse on her shoulder that gave her a lot of pain. The two year old crawled up on the sofa and lying on his hands took away all perceivable pain from her shoulder—she thanked him for being there and for this extraordinary surprise of healing. He smiled, and getting down from the sofa, went back to the circle of adults waiting for their flight; they had not realized he had left their presence. Nancy was impressed and realized she was in the presence of a genuine Indigo child.

Staying for Nancy's workshop, "Indigo Children and Human Mutation", I learned many interesting facts about there psyche and other details. Indigo children have an intense blue color vibration emanating off their auric field in a matrix of blue plasma.

Some additional qualities of Indigo Children:

- Ritual type behavior

- School is a challenge – can't learn in old ways

- Brain processes quickly – extremely intelligent

- Have a sense of purpose

- Knowing a better way – very creative and happy

In 1995 Indigo children were able to synthesize vitamin C. The genetic code took a turn for the better and were able to mutate in these children.

Nancy relates another story about Jimmy and his pyramid. Basically Jimmy was sick from birth and was contacted by a tall extraterrestrial in a silver suit; the visitor told him to build a pyramid over his bed (this was corroborated by his sister in the dream state, each having the same dream). When he told his parents, they decided to try it and, finding it had a great effect on his health, let him sleep in the pyramid. When he become a teenager he outgrew his pyramid and eventually over came all his illnesses and didn't need the pyramid anymore. She continues her lecture with other research into Indigo children, some being "hybrid children, " with large dark E.T. eyes a child she had seen at a water fountain, and the child with 1st Dynasty Pharaoh's head, not a mogul child at all.

In the mental realm these children exhibit an average leap in I.Q. of 24 – 26 pts. (150 to 160 I.Q. and many 185% I.Q.) They have a high degree of non-verbal intelligence, and intuit almost everything. In the May issue of Time Magazine in an article called "The I.Q. Puzzle" (on genetic intelligence) gives us other indications of IQ in children.(refer to Bib.)

Indigo children are also turning out to be multi-dimensional. In addition to their ability to remember past lives and relationships, they have the ability to astro-project at will not only in the dream state but in the conscious waking state. Nancy tells us about some of the children's stories, "Hanes and the Treetop and the Land of the Unforgiving." Hanes ascends to the top of a tree mentally to see the valley below, and Debbie recounts that she is in a healing group that works with crystals on the astro plane, where they heal individuals who haven't forgiven themselves. These children have a higher frequency vibration making them physically perfect with a greater immunity to disease, needing less sleep, and the most important aspect is to have a nurturing balanced environment. They are coming in with, in some cases, a multi-dimensional metric that is coherent. Their mental, (psychological) physical, emotional spiritual framework are balanced systems. If pulled out of alignment, they become sick. The Indigos are going to facilitate planetary change into an era of peace and enlightenment and peace and honor by 2012, predicted by the Mayan Calendar, says Nancy. They are going to overcome their parent old paradigms (to follow authority without question). Today's Indigos seem to be spontaneous and follow there own agendas. This is becoming problematic for the school system.(now that I have mentioned the Mayan Calendar I recently went to creation in meditation and moving pass Neptune, which is part of my meditation process, I perceived the amassing of hundreds of Space Crafts from different cultures here to watch the energy changes that are going to happen on to the earth on Dec. 21th 2012 or there bouts. As you no the planets are going to line up with the sun and the center of the universe fascinating a vibration change in the planet.

In John major book "Maya Cosogenesis" he explains the positive effects of the end of the Mayan Calendar determined by his research into the spiritual archlogical stories expressed by the Maya culture. The Maya Ball Player story expresses the spiritual propagation of there journey from there solar system to our solar system, through a special corridor into the Milky Way; as well as other historical stories.

The Russians started talking about individual Indigo children in the 60 and 70's. Children in previous USSR are not taught activities that are right brain for the 1st ten years of their lives. They learn everything that is creative, so they learn what they are good at and who they are. Then they start learning about and practicing left brain functions after there younger ages and become productive member of their societies.(some of these processes are reflected in the Waldorf School System).

The intuitive sciences are the portals to understanding the communication of the "I AM, present" the individual creative principle of light and individual uniqueness, the personification of consciousness that permeates all existence. As we move towards the greater enfoldment of mankind, through faster vibration and illumination, we are starting to realize faculties of our higher awareness. In order to understand and refine our new awareness senses, we will need to utilize a practical method for facilitating and understanding the unique manifestations that expand itself within our consciousness on our spiral enfoldment towards enlightenment.

These areas of new exploration are among many, which could help us, experience "information and clairvoyance." Others have used crystals, movement, massage, nutrition, lack of sleep , psychic awareness, Reiki and other healing modalities and looking at the sun to change their perception of the world around them, and as a result, opened up channels to other levels of consciousness.

I have had a few clairvoyant experiences myself by expanding my awareness through reading the Seth book series by Jane Roberts to name just one. By the very subject and the way he wrote the stories, he facilitated a change in my consciousness in a very unique way. As I recall, Seth states in his book Seth Materials that "I purposefully dictated my books in such a way as to influence the reader on a subconscious level". This is not to say that "subconscious" is unconscious. The inner sense of knowing always knows what is going on with the organism, the over soul; we all have it. This sense of knowing mechanism knows something without any rational explanation of the ideas. We know because we know. The super-consciousness can retrieve any type of information it needs in order to supply the conscious self the information it needs. The sense of knowing comes through this communication between the higher self and lower self. This topic is delivered in greater detail in the "Aura Chapter."

In a personal incidence, in a highly relaxed state, I was seeing nothing but blackness, and suddenly my father appeared to me, looking down at me with Great Bear, although he had recently passed away. He seemed to be saying to someone, "I see him, and he is coming in fairly clearly." As I brought my conscious mind into play on the image, it faded away. The image lasted less than a second, but I recognized the maximum among the information in order to make the image a lasting impression. Again, Itzhak Bentox a physist, in his book Stalking the Wild Pendulum sheds some light on this phenomenon. He claims that our consciousness blinks in & out of objective time reference all the time. When awareness of psychological time (subjective time) occurs, then the sense of time becomes extended in relationship to the objective time experience. This exists in altered states of consciousness.

Research done on human subjects who had taken LSD and marijuana showed that these subjects experienced extended periods of psychological time. Were they experiencing hallucination of their time reference, or were their actual psychological changes in their time perceptions?

One reference we have of time slowing down is when a person is launched into space and time slows down outside the electromagnetic spectrum, keeping that person younger than people left behind on earth.

Different laws apply outside of the electromagnetic spectrum. It is possible to bring about this change in consciousness through shifts of plane level (frequency or dimensional) awareness. One of the most direct methods of dimensional shift is through the study and practice of psychic sciences, metaphysics.

Itzhak has taken some of his studies in consciousness from Schumann's "Resonance Theory, " Schumann being the scientist who brought us the base or harmonic frequencies of mother earth, as 7.83hz. (cycles per second).(Interestingly enough, this correlates to the alpha brainwave frequency = 7-12 Hz.) And there are scientists making connection with the earth crust and the ionosphere and our feeling of time change; consciousness change. (refer to "Meditation" chapter for additional information on this subject.) Briefly, scientists have recorded a relationship with the earth's basic frequency and our awareness of the change of time. They have found a frequency change in the ionosphere from 7.83 Hz. to over 11Hz. This is having a profound effect on our consciousness. Some of us are having expressions of anxiety and frustration and feelings that we can't get done everything we need to get completed in a day's time. There is even some indication that we need to do more in order to arrive at the same levels of production.

Many of us attribute this phenomenon to getting older, which is then equated with slowing down, not being as productive as we once were when we were younger. Now we are realizing that there may be another reason for our feeling of slowing down. Of course, well-known psychics have talked about time speeding up from different perspectives for some time now; other experiences are included in this book of a psychic and expanded nature of consciousness. Feeling the shift in consciousness can come in many forms, and the psychic senses are some of the ways we experience a change in consciousness, objective and subjective time as Itzhak would say. Meditation/visualization is another modality that helps us understand the changes in consciousness.

I would like to say something further about a couple of personal experiences I had with the psych-clairvoyant sense. Many of us have similar psychic development experiences and we need to express these experiences to others. No man/women is an island.

While sitting in a relaxed, concentrated state, I glimpsed into what I feel were two of my past (present) incarnated personalities. One personality was a big-boned, attractive woman sitting at a low dresser with a big round mirror putting on makeup. She had a white slip on with a black shirt. She turned around and said something derogatory to her maid, and the image faded out. This personality, who resembled Bette Davis in temperament, was one to whom I was not attracted. I did not care for her; nevertheless, I can recognize this mind pattern. I now realize I had a similar personality experience. I also realized she was an actress getting ready to participate in a dress rehearsal. These are intuitive reflections that communicate a wealth of information about my previous self.

The other personality was a very old man with a white beard and hair sitting at a pulpit with a candle, writing something with a feather pen. I intuited that he was a scribe possibility recording the secrets of ancient texts. I was always the scribe in the Boy Scout troop. This is knowledge manifesting reflective aspects of past lives that comes back as conscious thought forms in meditation.

Another, more recent, clairvoyant experience was the sighting of a crystal flying saucer. This experience took place while at a crystal healing workshop. The woman teaching the workshop led us into a guided visualization where we went inside a quartz crystal for guidance and healing.

First, we visualized the walls of the crystal, the textures, and then were instructed to see our guides to talk with them about any problem we had. Then we went down a hall lined with doors labeled with different processes of our mind function. We stopped at the healing room and went inside, where my clairvoyant projection took over, and I saw a modern design wooden upholstered massage table, on a single pedestal with a skylight above filtering in the night sky.

The next guided step was to see the friends one wanted to heal, and at that moment a transparent saucer shaped craft broke through the skylight, shooting energy at different parts of my body. This image was totally spontaneous. This process is one indication that you are having a real experience because your visualization is not premeditated. You did not conger up this image before the experience spontaneously manifested. It was one of the more interesting experiences I have had with the clairvoyant sense. I was seeing these images as if I was looking at the scene as an outsider, as a third party. The changes in consciousness can manifest in many and varied experiences that you can relate to if you peruse your life and access your memories.

Another interesting historical experience seems relevant to this discussion of consciousness. A deep trance channeler (a subject that has claimed some notoriety thanks to John Klimo's book" Channeling") named Linda D. published an article in Lifestyle Magazine (February 1981) about her communication with John Lennon. In this article Lennon talks about his love for his followers, world peace and a little of what it is like to live on the other side, as it is called, of this life. Following are a few key points from her communication with John Lennon.

1. "I received a purple heart from the Vietnam War, and it is in my home in plain view."

2. "I was involved in various drug incidents where I went through a powerful death experience."

3. I spend a lot of time writing about my death experiences and when these letters are discovered, they will disclose that I had no fear of death."

I am going to keep my ears open in the future to see if any evidence can be found to validate John Lennon's claims.

Recently in a trance channeling of a well-known medium named Kevin Ryerson, he mentioned John Lennon in reference to a question from a person in the audience. It was about whether current world problems will change for the better in the future. "John brought forth the treaties of love through his music, creating an emotional outpouring from individual personalities into the collective unconsciousness in which the course of the future was changed. These events lasted over a period of twenty years. This process had brought about his assassination and other attempted assassinations of the U.S. President, the Pope, and the Primer Minister of England."

These experiences have brought me to a point in my life where I'm interfacing with different levels consciousness. Science is approaching a cross roads where it is taking the quantum leap into understanding some of these levels of inward knowing, and various experiences that need to have some light shed upon them. Quantum Physics and the Holographic Paradigm are opening doors to our understanding of these levels of awareness. Within these parameters that are being looked at we need to become aware of consciousness not only as intelligent beings functioning on different levels of realization but with our inter connection with other levels of consciousness.

My own experiences as well as others have taught me the truth of intelligent beings in the universe. The phenomena of channeling (and I speak of channeling from a different perspective than I mentioned previously.), where a being or beings come through an individual like Kevin Ryerson (a well known trance channel and speaks through him as he steps aside his personality). This phenomenon has educated us to the possibilities of this idea in our really. Jon Klimo's book, "Channeling", one of the best scientific treats ever written on the subject, has given us new evidence and additional experiences to understand this phenomena in nature.

I have heard of recent experiences from Dr. Steven Greer in his book "Hidden Truth" – Forbidden Knowledge" an autobiography of his life work with extraterrestrials and C.S.E.T.I. Where he sights one experience of and an individual projecting his consciousness out into space (while meditating) and running into a spaceship… creating a clamor with the inhabitances inside the craft; they responded, " watch out where you are going, be more aware of your surrounding not to disturb other intelligent beings working in the universe. (This is, I would say, more of an out of body experience that I talk more about in the Clairvoyance & Aura Channel.

We have an excellent example of out of body (astral projection) experience in Shirley MacLaine's book and movie Out On A Limb. And I would venture to say that David Morehouse's knowledge and skills with Remote Viewing border on out of body experiences in some cases, and in Dolores Cannon's book, The Convoluted Universe. E.T.'s speak of their ships being in different dimensions, through the veil (so to speak), in an astral realm.

I know that I'm getting long-winded about some ideas that I'm covering in this forward, but everyone needs to know that there are more miraculous things happening in these latter days.

A radio transmission was sent out to constellation of Hercules in 1974 by SETI (search for extraterrestrial intelligence) using the Arecido radio telescope. The encoded message was sent in binary code expressing a graphical pattern of 1's and 0's. Paul Vigay does an excellent job of explaining the mathematics of the code so that people like some of us can clearly understand the implications; thank you.

Now, I feel we have some of the proof we needed to finally confirm that we are not the only intelligent life forms in the universe. I haven't talked about crop circles in this book but some information can not be overlooked. In August 2001 Chilboton, Hampshire, England the message came back! The original binary code that represents our civilization is the exact match to the Chilboton crop circle. The pixelated squares representing the binary code represent their civilization; as well as ours. The entire crop circle information is fantastic, but one aspect steps out for me because of its relevance to a couple of experiences I have had in my life. The crop circle, in response to the Arecido radio message, depicted in binary code, atomic numbers of our primary elements that create life, and in addition, one more element appears –" Silicone". I feel strongly that it is a dominant element in this species, and others species, because of my experiences and others testimonies.

One of these experiences I talk about in the clairvoyant section –me being pulled out of meditation above the planet, and going into a hovercraft. I described the being as having an alabaster skin color/texture, but I'm convinced now it was a silicon base being; we are carbon-based beings. (Silicon is just above carbon on the periodic chart of elements.) And I want to say to Lucy Pringle, (a leading photographer of crop circles in the UK) for leading me to this fantastic information about this crop circle on her wonderful website.

Twenty years ago I had attended a channeling by Kevin Ryerson. a man described his story of his body being turned into silicon for a short time and reverting back shortly afterwards. The man said ET's were involved in making this change through his physiology.

Paul Vigay's cited these beings as being little grays. (This also confirms the information that was cited in Col. Corso's book," the Day after Roswell". The description of the autopsy of the little grays was fascinating.(You can find Paul's information at crop circle research: the Chilboton "Arecibo message" formation.) If you take the time to go to the website, you'll find that you will be as convinced as I was that the crop circle is a direct respond the radio transmition send out by SETI. There's nothing like concrete science and anecdotal evidence to bring out the truth.

This discussion on clairvoyance takes many forms of expression. These brief sightings about clairvoyance will wet your whistle, to other ways of perceiving the world. Researchers are just at the beginning stages of understanding this phenomenon. Scientists must observe incidental events, evaluate information received from others and recognize the past and future in its many manifestations (please explore this book's "ESP channel" for more on clairvoyance).

And finally, I would like to mention an aspect of consciousness that we should take note of in more detail (as I have said before), because for a decade now, people like Dr. Ian Stevenson, M.D. and Dr. Walter Semkiw, M.D. have been researching reincarnation at the University of Virginia and at a Chicago campus. The group's name is IISIS (Intuite for the Integration of Science, Intuition and Spirit). This group professes to continue the work of Dr. Ian Stevenson, M.D. University of Virginia Medicine (1960's to 1980's).

Dr. Stevenson's focus was on children rather than on adults; memories and childhood were valid because adults tend to confuse past life memories with historical information. Prominent categories from the study of reincarnation are listed as:

1. Reincarnation in cases with physical anomalies one lifetime to another;

2. Why does everyone feel they were famous in past lifetime;

3. Writing structures remain the same from lifetime to lifetime;

4. Spirit guides in reincarnation cases;

5. Focusing on dreams in reincarnation cases;

6. Reproduction of artistic composition;

7. Evidence of split incarnation (lifetimes at the same time)

Jim Tucker took over Ian Stevenson's position at the University of Virginia Medicine and stated, "There is evidence to surmise that reincarnation exists."

One of their subjects professes to painting in like manner as Paul Gauguin, the famous artist. His representation of some of the works of Gauguin (from which he was not aware of some of the works) was remarkably similar to that of the master. The artist represented Gauguin's work in his childhood as well is in his adulthood.

The principles of reincarnation:

1. Spirit being guidance is observed;

2. Relationships seem to be renewed through reincarnation;

3. Religion, race and ethnic affiliation conflicts can be rectified in reincarnation understanding;

4. Child prodigies and latent talents can be looked at;

5. A soul can inhabit more than one body in time-split incarnations or parallel lives;

6. Automatic writing and speaking cases demonstrate that past life personalities are held intact within the soul.

Kevin Ryerson has worked with Walter Semkiw for a decade helping him sight famous reincarnated personalities with contemporary well known individuals. A few well known personalities are Kahilil Gibran as Rumi, Pablo Picasso as Alexandra (the now famous child artist prodigy from Hungry, that I had a change to meet at her show in S.F.) Mark Zuckeberg as Herman Hollerith (credited for a punch card machine that was used by the U.S. Census

Office to tract large groups of immigrants into the United States.)Elvis Presley as Ray Dylan, a prominent singer in South Africa. Other celebrities are listed but are under consideration with further research.

You can access the IISIS website at IISIS/Walter Semkiw to learn more about other fascinating research being done by this Institute.

INTRODUCTION

Each channel is set up so it can be integrated into a normal daily curriculum. Each exercise can be used separately in different parts of the curriculum, or used in the context of the whole. By starting children at the beginning of the book and leading them through it, anyone using the book can help them progressively develop intuitive, psychic and spiritual awareness.

An independent psychic learning center could be set up where students can go and experiment with psychic games and instruments in there free time. Such a learning center is an important component for developing psychic abilities, because each person can take part in his/her own creative exploration when they feel the urge to experience a new area of themselves.

This publication is structured so that the beginning of each channel (chapter) focuses on adults who teach or guide children in the understanding of sophisticated information that contributes to the knowledge of consciousness development. The adult can choose to discuss this information with the child or children depending on age and maturity levels. At the very least, the adult will learn engaging information, hopefully, to spark their interest in their own inquiry into the subject matter.

In addition, the language is simple enough that a child with good reading skills can read this book easily. Coming across any concepts they may not understand, they can ask parents or teachers or consult the internet. Information is presented in a logical step-by-step progression to minimize misunderstanding. Another reason for organizing each section so that it can be used individually is that parents with one or two children can help their children understand the directions in the book. Parents can also teach their children each task developmentally or structure each idea to meet the child's individual needs and nature of their surroundings.

One objective of this book is to make a link between occult knowledge and scientific method in the sense of retaining the truths of Hermetic philosophy. It is further intended to integrate information about the occult with scientific terminology and scientific inquiry to construct a sound bridge between metaphysics and science.

Nobel Prize physicist Max Planck said, "The finding of the truth can only be secured by a determined step into the realm of metaphysics."

Working with children in the classroom has shown me how tuned in children are to psychic phenomenon. In each class there was always a child who had an unusual experience while participating in a consciousness-raising task. Most of the children were tuned in to the exercises dealing with sensory awareness and had genuine E.S.P. abilities, and a larger percentage had partial E.S.P. abilities. There were very few children who were not successful at the tasks in this book. It seemed to depend on the degree of their interest in the projects. The way I organized and presented information also influenced them. After the children saw the project possibilities and had some success with the exercises, their curiosity naturally increased.

Brain research suggests that lowering tension is the first step in maximizing learning. Boredom and repetitive actions inhibit learning capabilities. The optimum processes for opening the higher brain processes are excitement, novelty and challenge. These ideas are integrated throughout this book, giving the children a fresh new approach to interacting with their world. Targ & Puthoff, researchers in the area of remote viewing at Stanford University state that creative exploration greatly increases psychic experiences.

This publication also focuses on processes for the development of spiritual insight and illumination necessary for further development of each individual's consciousness. Spiritual development can be a fun, joyful, natural human experience.

At the end of each channel, I have included possible future directions in each of the con-

sciousness-raising areas. These potentials are suggestions for future probabilities. There are as many other possibilities for creative change as there are creative thoughts. I perceived glimpses of psychic change by talking with different individuals about their unusual experiences. There are all types of encounters of a psychic nature that haven't been recounted to scientists or even recognized by science, because most individuals are afraid of what their ability reveals. These fears are sometimes the result of the individual's religious upbringing or social mores. Fear of not being accepted by others plays a large part in such reasoning.

Psychic ability – on the contrary, within the context of this book and its vital new information – is assumed to be an important part of daily life and knowledge without which, much will be found missing even philosophically in the future. The old saying, "so you think, so you become," is much more than a statement. It becomes a reality.(we have science of mind and other metaphysical focuses, not to speak of the new references "The Secret "and "What the Beep" to give us insights into how our consciousness work (of course this in no way, is the end of the list).

Each channel has a bibliography located after its conclusion. Two sections, "Potentiality" and "Checkpoints," are included at the end of each channel to help the reader master each activity. An age appropriate activity chart is also included in the beginning of this publication. Finally an appendix is added with a Coil-Winding © device to make it easier to accomplish some of the tasks in this book.

The author would be very happy if you would participate in the processes in this publication. Become involved in interfacing with the ideas in this book and experience a direct expansion of your consciousness. Bring the knowledge into your hands and minds; experience the omnipresent of light as you experience the activities in this book.

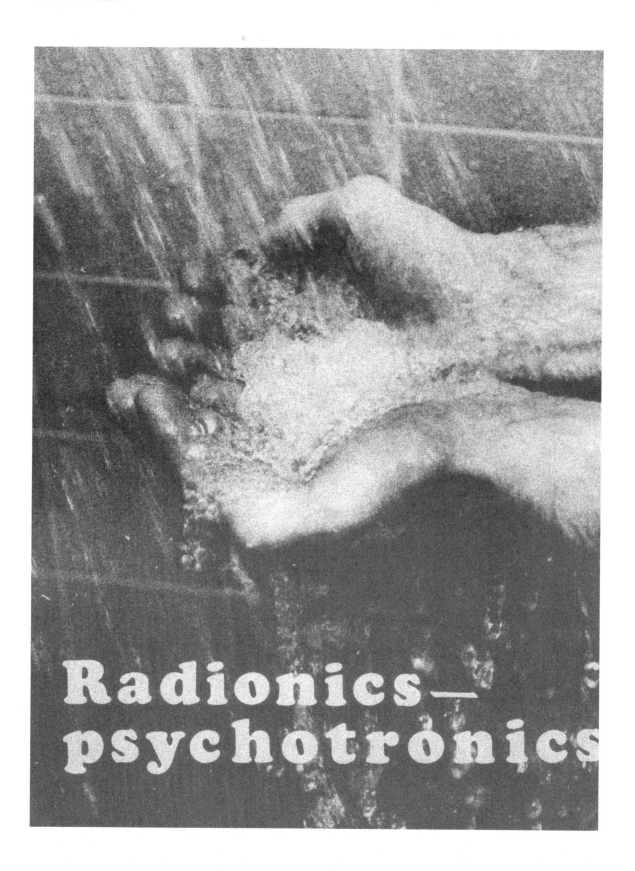

Radionics—psychotronics

PSYCHOTRONICS/RADIONICS

To understand psychic phenomena and there applications in the classroom, we can turn to subjects which have attacted less attention , such as radionics/psychotronics. Simply stated, radionics/psychotronics is a scientific study of unusual energy fields, using radionic devices to detect, show and utilize this energy. A sampling of the work done in this field will help augment this basic definition.

Dr. Leonard Corte of the International Radionics Congress believes that this unusual or basic energy, as he calls it, propagates itself through interaction with electromagnetic force fields. When a communication channel is established, the energy transfer is instantaneous. Dr. Corte and his colleagues also believe that each cell of the body has its own energy field (not a new concept), and that the total energy field of all the cells makes up the etheric body (more information on the etheric body follows later in this book). Dr. G.A. Maury and Marguerite Maury of Paris, also radionics researchers, have found that this basic energy is influenced by cosmic rays and sunspots through a process similar to electricity. They say that we are in direct connection with the universe through this process.

Other characteristics of the basic energy cited by researches in this field are:

1. Basic energy pervades all things.

2. It emanates from human beings, particularly from the hands, eyes, charkas and acupuncture-points on the body.

3. It can correct irregular vibration frequencies within living organisms or it can be used to disrupt healthy vibration levels.

4. It can cause changes in individuals and groups in close proximity or at long distances, culminating in psychic occurrences.

5. It can be manipulated and molded by individual or collective mind patterns.

6. It is accumulated by inanimate substances such as wood, stone, plastic, water, wool and metals. It is also collected by shapes like cones and pyramids.

7. It coexists with sunlight, as well as with other types of light.

8. It coexists with magnetism and other types of energy, but is a distinct energy unto itself.

9. It is conducted with electricity along wires and silk threads.

10. It can be directed in such a way, as to be reflected by a mirror, as well as being polarized.

11. It is neither positively charged nor negatively changed; it is neutral.

12. It is directional, so it will be stronger in some directions than in others and stronger in certain places on an object than others.

13. Finally, it has a color correspondence, making it possible to be detected at various strengths, corresponding to various nanometer- colors.

After examining this list, we can see that much study is given to understanding the basic energy in relation to known energy forms. We can see a few characteristics emerging from these studies that shed some light on this illusive energy. Basically, it is a distinct energy unto itself, interacting with electricity and other types of energy, permeating everything in the universe.

One of the first researchers in the study of unusual energy was Baron Von Reichenbach. Von Reichenbach started researching the unusual emanations around animate and inanimate objects after reading his college professor's book; Studies of Light and Color in the 1800s. He used magnets, quartz crystals, chemicals, metals, wood and stones to study the color emanations from these objects. One characteristic he did find was that each color emanated in certain directions relating to the magnetic fields of the earth. North was seen as blue, south was red, east was grayish-white, and west was yellow. He started studying the bluish emanations "flames", later calling their energy odic force, or OD. His great discovery was that OD energy was discharged from electromagnetic radiation, making it possible for it to be studies by the technology of his day. Reichenbach also proved that each organ in the body resounded to its own energy frequency, which emitted its own signal. Another reference sighted that the odic flame has a material element; probably a substance created in a luminous form, but was not magnetism.

Another important person in the study of basic energy is Wilhelm Reich, a clinical psychoanalyst and student of Sigmund Freud. While working with emotionally upset patients, he noticed that many of his patients had little sexual contact. This observation lead him to believe that, if basic human drives, such as sexuality, were denied, emotional energy would build up, causing muscles to constrict and tighten, creating a sort of muscular armor. From this point on, Reich devoted a large part of his time to studying physical sexuality.

He noted that the movement of the body during sexual intercourse was like the movements of our most basic life form, the protozoa. Through his biogenetic research, he found that protozoa follow a basic movement pattern of tension-charge- discharge and relaxation, the same as with human beings and other life forms. He also found that when soil was heated to certain temperatures and placed in a nutritive solution, it turned into bions, causing the growth of single-celled animals, protozoa types.

Reich discovered that bions emitted a bluish form of energy, which he called Orgone. He found that living organisms also emitted this same type of unusual energy to some degree, depending on each individual's inhibitions, this led to his discovery of Orgone energy in the atmosphere. Reich built a box made of organic and metallic materials to collect Orgone energy. He found that brief radiations of Orgone energy, along with therapy, helped his patients recover from psychological imbalances. He is a developed a motor fueled by Orgone energy and discovered that Orgone could be dispersed as electricity.

Reich, prominent in 1950 had a controversial history. Ultimately being railroaded by the government because of his research into orgone energy, he was falsely imprisoned for, among other things, researching the orgone box and its use with mental patients. While doing my research, I sent for copying of his patent on the the orgone box and was surprised to see that the diagram was not at all like the one I had seen in a movie, where Wilhelm Reich was being interviewed about his work and the orgone box. At one point in his life he was falsely accused of stuffing patients into a small box (4 x 4 feet, shown in the patent) without any openings that would have provided ventilation to the patient.

The box I saw in the movie was a large upright, possibly five or six feet tall, with windows on each side and a seat to sit on inside. Wilhelm looked very comfortable sitting in the box in his garage. Today some say he used a green light inside the box to facilitate orgone energy. There are still individuals today that are building and selling his orgone boxes.

Another individual seriously involved in the study of unusual energy was Nikila Tesla. His research resulted in such well-known inventions as the alternating current, various remote control systems and the caliray tube for television. He also designed a special telescope to send and receive radio waves into outer space and was one of the first to conceptualize radar and atomic energy. Some of Tesla's most astonishing work went into lighting the 1902 Canadian World's Fair. Without the use of cable wire, he provided light for the entire fair by projecting electrical energy through the earth and bringing it up through the ground. Some of his more outlandish inventions include a device to photograph thought patterns.

He also tried to eliminate war by inventing an unusual energy machine called a death ray, that could be used to destroy anything in its path using energy extracted from the atmosphere, in what we would call today a particle beam weapon, a laser. This weapon could be brought against another person or nation for the purpose of war. In 1938, he presented his invention to Congress, but refused to give all the details, knowing that his peace-controlling device had weapon-like potential. His old colleague Mr. Matthews said of Tesla in 1971, "The man's work had influenced most the of the century's greatest inventions: radio, television and the modern computer, automobile ignition systems and rocketry". He also wrote a biography of Tesla called "The Wall of Light" (from Health Research). And, finally, Tesla was nominated for the Nobel Prize, along with Thomas Edison. He refused science's greatest honor, but little is known about his reasoning for taking such a drastic step.

One of these individuals De La Warr, has a special place in my research because beyond being a great scientist, he really showed me through his research that subtle energy/bioplasmic/ectoplasm is an energy that interacts with the three-dimensional reality in profound ways. In his research abstracts, using photographs, he showed plainly and methodically, step-by-step, how he researched his topic.

Briefly he would sit an individual down inside a horizontal plywood square, about waist high, and attached at predetermined node points (high-energy vertical waveform points) around the body were light bulbs. By turning the rheostat dials on a radionic device, he would find the frequencies to light up each light bulb around the person's body. These rates later became the frequencies used in radionic devices today. Rates books are used in Radionic devices to tune frequencies for just about everything in our known universe; after all, everything is frequency modulation no matter whether it's a physical object, a mental construct or a disorder or even a molecular structure. Of course the new devices have been interface with computers to increase their accuracy and speed of diagnosis.

One of De La Warr's foremost discoveries was that sound can be transported by a magnetic field… and can be tuned by a magnetic rod changing sound into a pre-form of matter.

At this point my history touches only upon some of the past's greatest energy visionaries. The work of Dr. Ruth Drown, M.D., developed the color dial for her device to diagnose her parents. Dr. Hironimas worked for NASA developing guidance and tracking systems for Apollo II. Dr. Boyd De La Warr, (an electrical engineer)developed the mock camera1, J. Gallimore, researched and developed portable radionics devices and was president of the Radionic Congress. Others too numerous to mention here would undoubtedly be described in a detailed history of subtle and unusual energy. And I'm aware that Rife and his Rife machine can be included in this discussion of tuning frequencies, but his research delved into areas of medicine that I don't cover in this publication.

Basic Energy studies by these experts can be demonstrated by a few simple energy feeling tasks and with the use of an easily constructed energy generator. The instructions for both of the above, which follow (as well as other tasks), could be used in the classroom to teach students about basic radionics studies without expensive equipment.

ENERGY FEELING TASK

Either sitting in chairs or on a rug, make a circle with all the children. Give everyone a live plant leaf. Explain that a good way to start learning about subtle energies is to be able to feel different radiations around different objects. Animate and inanimate objects all have a subtle energy field. Now place the leaf in your right hand and hold your left hand just above the leaf. Close your eyes or stare into space in a trancelike state. Direct your awareness between your hand and the leaf. Feel the energy from the leaf hitting your hand in pulsing streams. The feeling is a kind of tickling sensation like sprays of water hitting your hand from the shower.

---

1   Dr.Drown has a patented energy device similar to Kirlian photographic devices, with color dial, can be purchased from the British Patent Office, London England, No.525, 866. Dr.T.G. Hironimus also has a unusual energy device obtainable the U.S. Patent Office, No.2, 482, 773. Delawarr's Device, which photographs objects over distances, can be obtained from the British Patent Office, no.198, 018 MKI Camera (send $1.25 in British Sterling) MEG, Motionless Electromagnetic Generator No.6, 362, 718 that extracts energy from zero point space, the US Patent Office.

Concentrate cutting out everything around you except, your awareness of the energy between your hand and the leaf. Concentrate your attention between your hand and leaf (or whatever the object is), and when you feel the energy coming from the object, relax your concentration and let the energy flow up your arm to your brain. Maybe a step-by-step process would be clearer. Let's break it down:

1. Concentrate - focus your attention

2. Feel the energy – become aware of

3. Relax your attention – Released

4. Feel direction – Relaxed attention (stay focused)

5. Direct energy – Focus energy up arm and into your brain and move energy to desired location i.e. to eighth chakra or through main charkas in the body, or dissipate noxious energy some where in the body.

Sometimes, experimental research has shown, some individuals feel only heat or cold when doing this experiment. I feel a stream of energy pulses hitting my palm; but I feel that anyone can learn to feel this energy in this way. Next, have a discussion with the group about what they felt; let them put the experience in their own terms. You may want to write the different terms on the chalkboard so everyone will see and remember the leaf energy. This is also a good way of integrating language into the lesson.

MATERIALS

*   Different size magnets

*   Different size and kinds of crystals

*   Acetate cone and other types of cones and other shapes.

*   Small pyramid (follow directions on how to make small pyramids from the channel dealing with pyramids)

*   Plant leaves

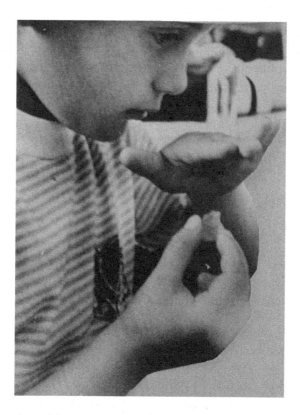

Now pass out rock crystals and have everyone feel the energy and compare whether it was the same type of energy feeling or a different feeling compared to the leaf energy. Although after holding a crystal in your hand, for a short time, it heats up from your piezo-electric energy and will feel different. List the comparisons on the board. Do the same with the pyramids (tin foil and copper-foiled pyramids), magnets, and cones. All the children I have worked with have had little trouble feeling the energy from cones, pyramids, crystals and magnets.

By this time, your children should have some experience in feeling the unusual energy. Given time, they will all catch on. If some of the children don't have any luck feeling the energy, you might stimulate them by:

a. Putting on some slow music (there are many albums listed in this book).

b. Having them do some yoga breathing exercises (in concentration, meditation and contemplation section).

c. Having children watch and imitate each other; letting them pick up some cognitive and intuitive information so that they can get a feel for what type of structure is required to become sensitive to subtle vibrations.

Now go on to the next lesson, if time permits; do not allow more than a two-day lapse without refreshing the children's memories. Studies show that children's retention skills lessen over time if not stimulated with similar activities.

And I would be remiss if I didn't include this final experience that continues to shed light on the complexities of psychic phenomena. Back in the day when I was an upcoming athlete in wrestling in my junior college career, I had an experience that I don't cognitively understand and I don't think anyone else did, to this day.

We had a match with our leading contender at Silicon Valley college one sunny afternoon in spring 1968. Up until that time I had taken first place in almost every tournament I entered including freestyle and Greco-Roman. That day I had an opponent that had come down from a higher weight class to wrestle me. I knew this opponent was going to be stronger than me, but I was more agile and hopefully more skilled.

As the match started in the second round, it was 0 to 0. I was very skills in successfully gaining points on my opponent by way of the escape position, and as I stood up to escape he grabbed me by the shoulders at arm's length firmly in his grasp. This was unusual because he would have to be incredibly strong to hold an opponent in place. My only counter defense was to start running around in a circle to try and break his hold on me. This created a centrifugal force movement. As I did so I still couldn't break his grasp.

At that point a voice said to me" not yet". I waited a second more and the voice said again" Now!" Instinctively I jumped into the air with both legs and kicked one leg creating a waveform that moved up my body and hit my opponent full in the chest. He flew backwards as I stayed suspended in air, weightless, and dropped to the mat a second later. Turning over one shoulder I saw my opponent sitting off the mat with his arms fully outstretched with his mouth wide open staring into space; transfixed.

At that point you could hear a pin drop as the audience and wrestlers stared in disbelief at what they were witnessing. They couldn't understand what they were seeing! It was almost as if time itself, had stopped for what seemed like seconds-and all of a sudden the referee called" one point escape!" As the audience came back to life we continue the match. Well, for some reason no one said anything about what had just transpired. Not another word was mentioned about the match because people couldn't understand what they were seeing; this is my take on it anyway. My only regret was that we didn't have cameras filming that match, that day as we did at other home matches.

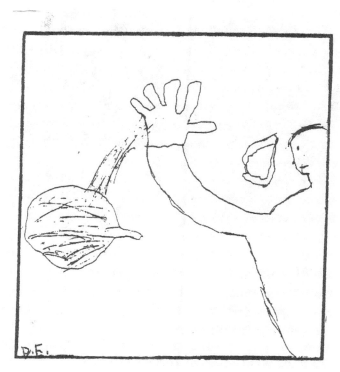

A drawing by a six-year-old: feeling the energy from a plant leaf.

BIO-PLASMIC ENERGY GENERATOR

"Bio-plasmic energy generator" is a term I created to characterize a psychic accumulator. Bio-plasmic is taken from the Soviet scientific studies of human biological energy systems, or etheric body energy as it is termed in hermetic philosophy.

The cone and cylinder shapes used in the generator have been proven by interested researchers, such as Vern Cameron, a world-renowned dowser and psychic, and G. Gallimore, author and president of the Radionic Congress, to collect bio-plasmic energy because of their shapes. Energy collects and is more intense at the apex and corners of these shapes. The cones, cylinders, and pyramids we will be using can be made out of any materials, since it is the geometry, more than the material that collects the energy. The copper coil used in the generator is like that used in most electronic equipment. It collects and channels the energy coming from the cone to the cylinders.(copper is an energy facilitator).

If we referred back to the characteristics of this basic energy (in this channel above) we see that bio-plasmic energy can be conducted around wire or silk thread. In this device we are hoping the copper coil will act as a coil often seen in electrical devices to conduct bioplasmic energy along the copper wire as electrons do. Bio-plasmic (sometimes called ectoplasm) energy often piggybacks on the grosser energies and fields, as does subtler energies called emanation energies.

The following is a guide in making a bio-plasmic energy generator.

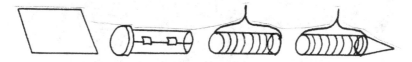

MATERIALS

- small sheet of acetate

- plastic (art store)

- fine gauge copper wire

- without insulation (hardware store)

- small medicine bottle about 3 inches long (or anything in a tube shape around which to wrap the acetate)

- clear tape

- silk thread

- some sharp, pointed, hole

1. Take acetate plastic and cut 31/2 x 4 inches, enough to fit around the medicine bottle and tape with clear tape.

2. Punch a small hole in each end of acetate cylinder. Stick one end of copper wire through hole and bend over (the hole should be on the left side if you are right-handed).

3. Hold cylinder horizontally in left hand, if you are right-handed, with first finger holding wire to cylinder. If you are left-handed, hold cylinder in right hand.

4. Put right thumb over hanging wire and press wire to surface of cylinder.

5. Rotate cylinder with left hand towards you and guide wire around the cylinder, as it rotates, in a manner that forms a coil over the entire cylinder surface with about ½ of an inch of space between the wire bands that form each coil.

6. Put the remaining end of wire in hole on end of acetate cylinder.

5 yr-olds successfully rotating the bio-plasmic generator.

7. Wrap entire surface of cylinder and wire coil with clear tape. This will keep coil from moving out of place.

8. Slip acetate cylinder off medicine bottle.

9. Cut piece of silk thread 1 21/2 inches long and string one end through cylinder and tie to other end of thread.

THE CONE

In making the cone, you will need to teach the younger children to distinguish between their index fingers, thumbs, and right and left hands. Here are directions for making the cone:

1. Cut a piece of acetate 4 inches square. (Make sure children know what a square is. If they don't know, take a few minutes to explain.)

2. Give each child a square of acetate. Demonstrate first how a cone is made, and then guide children through exercises by doing it with them.

3. Put index finger of left hand on upper left corner of acetate square.

4. Pick up lower left corner with index finger and thumb of left hand.

5. Roll left hand corner, causing it to run under, and match it to upper right hand corner of the square so that the left hand edge under laps the top edge by 1/8 or ¼ inch, or until it makes a tight cone large enough to fit just over the end of the cylinder.

6. Now hold the large end of the cone with the right hand and put two pieces of tape on the overlapping edge. (You may want younger children to work together, one helping with the taping.)

7. Tape cone to end of cylinder.

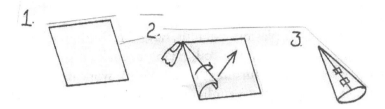

If you find it difficult to work with fine copper wire, try using silk thread or nylon fishing line for the coil.

Next, let's build an environment for our energy generator so we will not mistake air currents for the movement of the bio-plasmic energy generator.

1. Cut a piece of acetate 33 inches long and 8 inches high.

2. Turn it on its edge, make a cylinder, and tape the edges.

3. Cut another piece of acetate 10½ inches square.

4. Punch a hole in the center of the square with compass point, a hole big enough to draw thread through.

5. Draw silk thread, attached to coil, through hole in the center of the square acetate sheet.

6. Place a piece of tape over the thread hole to eliminate as much air flow as possible around the coil inside.

You have now created your first psychic energy generator; congratulations, for you are on your way to learning more about your innate potential abilities. Experiment with your generator to see if you can teach yourself to make the generator rotate, then rotate faster and faster, day-by-day. Also see what elements will make it easier for your generator to rotate. Try designing your own generator, using two cones or cylinders or place cones in different positions on cylinder, and so on.

If you are starting with one bio-plasmic coil unit, have the children take turns, first relaxing and then concentrating on a spot on the coil, trying to make it rotate. You, the teacher or parent, should also try your hand at turning the coil. While working with one generator, have another generator unit setting in direct sunlight within the room if possible.

If you don't get direct sunlight in your room, put one unit outside and the other in the shade or in the room? After experi- menting with the first coil, have everyone go to the coil in the sun and take turns rotating the generator. (You may want to keep a record of all the students that are able to rotate the coil. By keeping records you will learn which students are strong in which psychic tasks. This will become a handy tool to help you in developing less talented students—and, if you use the diagnostic tools later on in this book, you will have some valuable insights into your students' abilities and potentials.)

After this exercise, have a discussion with your children about what experiences they had while rotating the coil. You might keep a journal.

The next step in using the generator might be to put a measurement line on the gener-

ator container. On a 3"x 5" card draw a horizontal line through the middle of the card and rule off inches or millimeters over the length of the card. This will provide a measurement for distance of rotation either right or left. You might initiate a game in which the person who rotated the coil the farthest would win points. Try to think up non-competitive games.

To test your coil further, attach a small magnet to it and see if there is any difference in distance of rotation. Scientists say there is a small magnetic field around the human body that reacts to the electro-magnetic field around the earth, and this magnetic field can be influenced by the human mind.(the Alpha brainwave frequency-7 to 12 Hz.)

After the kids are successful in rotating the generator independently, you can go into some group activities. Have students hold hands and make a circle (yourself included) around the bio- plasmic generator. Ask everyone to slowly inhale for four counts, hold for one count and exhale for four counts. Next, stare at one end of the coil while relaxing, letting the energy flow from your eyes; concentrate on the generator going around and around, first with the coil out of the sun and then with the coil in the sun. When the coil starts to rotate faster and faster, drop hands and see if it starts to slow down. Join hands again and see if you can make it pick up speed again. Experiment with this activity doing different things with their hands, eyes, and bodies. For instance, have students make triangle shapes over their heads with their hands and arms. You may have them blink their eyes while holding hands or while holding their hands above their heads. Try different things and experiment with the generator in various group activities.

A final activity using the generator should involve using the energy coming from the hands. Have the students place one hand on each side of the generator container (but don't tough sides), ask them to concentrate, as before, and try to turn the coil. Have them feel the energy coming out of the palms of their hands. Do this exercise with both the sun and shade coils.

Going through these exercises should demonstrate to you and your students that an unusual energy does surround the body. It may take time, however, to fully realize the potential of this energy, so let its unfolding be a gradual and interesting process. Over a period of time, everyone will experience what it is like to get in touch with their own internal body energy. (an example of this can be found in Scientific American Mag. 1975, Garner Martin "Mathematical Games, " another generator (See bibliography.)

Another possible type of psychotronic generator that I have found doing research on the subject is what is called a Hand Boiler. It is a flask or beaker in different glass shapes containing methyl alcohol in various colors. I first came into contact with this hand boiler while browsing through a novelty store in San Francisco. For some reason, I was drawn to this object and had fun raising the liquid with the heat of my hand (which is the way it is supposed to work: thermodynamics).

At some point, I had an epiphany and I stood back a few feet from the beaker and concentrated on raising the liquid with my mental strength alone. To my surprise, I found the purple colored alcohol starting to rise, and finally the entire liquid reached the top, staying there until I withdrew my attention, and it slowly receded. A young woman ran over and grabbed the flask off-the-shelf and studied it intently; she didn't say a word and left the store quickly. Well, I can tell you that I had no hesitation in buying that flask. I took it home and continue to experiment with my new psychotronic generator.

In one experiment I went into a deep contemplation, opening my eyes for a moment and noticed that most of the liquid quickly raced to the top of the flask. As I came out of contemplation, the liquid started to move back down the beaker. Unfortunately I couldn't repeat the experiment. To this day I can still raise the liquid to the top of the flash. (mind over matter – psychokenesis).

But, I still believe that I was able to expand my soul, to its outer reaches connecting the God sphere, which is our connection to the all-unlimited mind, and everything that is connected with this level of consciousness, making me one with everything in the universe.(I became a conscious holographic model). There was no separation between me and anything else in the universe; my energy became one with universal mind.

I don't know if attaching lights threads or as Don Juan (Carlos Castaneda's shaman) would say "feelers" to the liquid energy or spiraling the energy upwards made a difference in the rise of the liquid. But I do know I contacted the God sphere of consciousness; God is expansion. In the end it must be more because I have expanded my field before, in this instance, with negative results. Raising methyl alcohol to its gaseous state creates the conditions that mind can interface with. I needed to do more research.

QUARTZ CRYSTALS

I would like to turn to a discussion of quartz crystals, for they are the minerals of the New Age. They are tools for focusing etheric energy (unusual energy). Thoughts (both negative and positive) are said to be amplified through the use of crystals. Crystals can help one tune into a higher vibration, making it easier for healing and developing the special gifts of the higher creative mind.

A crystal healing movement was being generated by assumed enlightened beings like Dale Walker, Isoas, Marcel Vogel and Nick Nocerino. Dale Walker is a lecturer and author, who, some say, provides a direct channel to the angelic realm of consciousness. Isoas (a New Age musician) says crystals act as step-down transformers, stepping down the faster energy to a slower vibration, as the non-local communication becomes local. Marcel Vogel is a senior computer scientist at IBM who studies crystal knowledge. Nick Norcerino was a para-psychologist and expert teacher as well as a practitioner of Wicca and an expert on crystal skulls. He traveled the world just after World War II to find skulls in Europe. In a lecture I attended on the crystal skull he used scientific and metaphysic methods to decode the knowledge in the skulls. One method they used, as well as others, was projecting an electric blue color into the skull to open it up for information.

Crystals are used to tune into the auric levels of the body. This occurs when the "third eye" (pituitary gland) is activated. One is then able to visualize and feel energy blockages or problems that exist in the human energy field. Crystals, by there structure, increase the effectiveness of etheric energy, as do pyramids and cones, and do so with even greater intensity, with even greater expended consciousness.

There are different methods of tuning into an energy field to determine the causes of personal difficulties. Marcel Vogel uses a crystal to tune into the aura field. According to Vogel, each crystal has a separate pulse beat that is brought into activation with breath and hand pressure (the piezoelectric effect). Indians in the Himalayas taught this technique to him. First, he projects his breath into a crystal to start the crystal pulsating. Then he stands behind the subject and points the crystal midway between the shoulder blades. Holding the crystal in one hand, with the other hand he first rotates it 360° in one direction (left or right) and then slowly rotates it back in the opposite direction and then rotates it slowly in the opposite direction until he or the subject feels an energy flow. At this point, the crystal has become tuned into the nervous system of the subject. Healing can take place more readily through this tuning because the healer has succeeded in finding the resonance of the individual's etheric field.

Another method is to hold the crystal above the head, over the crown chakra of the subject with the right hand and move the left hand down the front of the body over each chakra point to feel the strength of the energy projection from that particular charka. This is to determine if the chakra is open or closed and to what degree. If the chakra is not generating a strong energy pulsation take the crystal from the top of the head move the crystal in a circular motion in front of the chakra in a counter-clockwise direction, visualizing the chakra opening, as in the opening and closing of a camera aperture or lotus flower. You should be able to feel the differences in the chakra energy, hopefully it will be stronger, if not, repeat the process. Check each of the chakras , in turn, to feel if the chakra is generating.

Crystals facilitate the activation of various psychic abilities by creating an accelerated vibration in the physiology of the body. The more crystals are used in meditation and healing, the greater the attunement with other levels of consciousness, promoting communication with the super conscious and other conscious entities. Kevin Ryerson reminds use, again, that we are tuning into the fourth dimension when ever we participate in the healing process.

According to John, a spirit being channeled through a trance medium named Kevin Ryerson, crystals act as windows to different awareness. Crystals slow down Etheric and Atheric light wave patterns and thereby facilitate communication with other life forms throughout the universe. Etheric and Atheric energy patterns serve as channels for communication of thoughts from one person to another. Information is communicated through the network of athers and ethers light waveforms. Athers have been described to me as the basic fabric of the universe. Athers is a much more refined form of energy than etheric energy. Etheric energy forms interact with the basic fabric (athers) in the makeup of the auric levels (refer to Aura Chapter). Crystals also act as step-down transformers for energy, which travels faster than the speed of light continuum (sometimes called tachyon energy). A step-down transformer is an electrical device, which, by electromagnetic induction, transforms electric energy from one or more circuits to one or more other circuits at the same frequency, but usually at a different voltage and current value. Crystals step-down energy to a slower and slower rate of vibration, so that it may be perceived more easily.

I have worked with quartz crystals for many years and have had a number of interesting experiences happen to me while using and owning them. I found one attribute they possess that increases the clarity of the mental pictures sent to the brain through the neuro-net enhancing the meditation and visualization process 100%. And I have meditated with crystals and without crystals and find a remarkable difference.

In other experiences, I remember having an upset stomach one day while looking at crystals in a crystal shop at Ghirardelli Square in San Francisco. I recall shopping and looking at a single terminated multi-faceted crystal on the stand; I was drawn to this crystal for some reason. It was lying horizontally facing towards me and I bent over slightly and touched the crystal with my finger when I felt a single burst of piezoelectric energy hit me in the stomach. I reacted by placing my hand in my stomach and bending over slightly It was like an electrical charge. It didn't hurt me but it startled me and I reacted. After straightening up I felt much better my stomach ache was gone.

I slowly became aware the quartz crystals can have their own consciousness and deliver healing wave energy whenever they want to. I feel that this is a correct assumption because I have dealt with crystals for many years now. And I have also experienced piezoelectric energy charges from crystals that have not been beneficial. Marcel Vogel will attest to this fact about quartz crystals. And of course I bought that crystal that day. It is now my healing crystal.

Everything has a frequency vibration as we've learned in the radionic channel that can be tuned into with our own sensing system or by various radionic or subtle energy devices. There is an energy system called Chi (I have mentioned this energy in the chanting and chakra in meditation channels before). Chi, as it also has been mentioned in yoga and martial arts literature, permeates our bodies as subtle channels that connect to other subtle systems in our bodies. It runs our systems and basic pulse beat signature, that could be the pulse beat we are tuning into when Marcel Vogel helps us try and feel a crystals heartbeat. It is running our connection to the universe and acts as a carrier of basic frequencies of consciousness. Can't help feeling we have a connection to a crystals basic soul vibration. Minerals have their own kingdom and deity to guide their consciousness.

And it is very possible that science has found the etheric energy (Chi) or tachyon energy particles called Neutrinos.

PSYCHOTRONIC GENERATORS

The last 30 years a check engineer named Pavlita has been making and experimenting with different shapes and combinations of materials which he believes contain bioplasmic energy. In the vocabulary of Hinduism, life energy is also called prana (refer to the aura Channel for more information on prana).

Pavlita demonstrates how various shapes collect energy by using a hollow cylinder aligned adjacent to a hollow metal ball and an umbrella like shape balanced on a sharply pointed steel shaft. By concentrating his psychic energy on these combinations of various shaped metal, he is able to make the "umbrella rotate". Pavlita claims that a life energy generator can be produced by combining certain metals shapes.

While constructing these bioplasmic generators, as he calls them, Pavlita discovered that various shapes and combinations of metals and woods affect the generators ability to collect bioplasmic energy.

Other Czech researchers have furthered some of Pavlita work by developing similar energy collectors to run small motors. Dr. Rejdak, a Czech scientist, claims to have developed a psychotronic generator that can turn a small motor when charged with bioplasmic energy. This generator will hold a charge for up to three days after being initially charged for an hour and a half and several minutes daily. The Czechs have also used psychotronic generators and psychic receivers used in experiments to select the "correct" playing card, that is, to select some predetermined playing card.

Along with these effects, the Czechs have found a harmful psychotronic affects, depending on the shape and wave field produced by the generator. These effects range from killing flies to disturbing brainwave pattern and have been likened to negative orgone energy, as described by Wilhelm Reich.

The Soviets have furthered some of the Czechs experiments with unusual energy and, as a result, have experimented with the effects of magnetic fields on organic matter. They have produced an unusual energy fields in an ordinary tree limb, sharpened on each end, by passing a magnetic fields through the limb. Originally, they thought this would create a static charge attraction field. Upon further investigation, however, they found that static electricity was not the current created. The wooden stick also attracted not- magnetic substances such as paper, wood, crystal and plastic. Researchers are still unsure about the origin and makeup of this unusual energy. The researchers also find that this energy is conducted underwater. When I went back over Reichbachs research I found a reference for Od energy that was conducted underwater also. There may be a parallel of these two types of energies.[2] [3] [4] [5]

CHECKPOINTS

What happens if you can't get the coil to rotate?

a. It is unlikely that one of these exercises will not result in turning the coil.

b. Go over exercises on having the students relax: try breathing exercises, creative meditation and visualization techniques (consult section on concentration, meditation, and contemplation).

POTENTIALITIES

Why go through all these changes to make an acetate coil rotate?

a. It will show the students that the unusual energy really does exist.

b. They will experience what it is like to get in touch with their own internal body energy.

c. It will give students confidence in themselves by showing them that they have a special undeveloped potential within themselves.

d. Students will learn to overcome problems by solving them.

e. And most important of all, these activities may result in serendipitous outcomes. All that will be learned cannot be predicted until it makes its creative appearance at the time of the experience; creative learning has no limits.

SUMMARY/CONCLUSIONS

Radionics/Psychotronics

Psychotronics/Radionics as a field of knowledge and study acts as a starting point for the study of psychic energy.

This channel focuses student awareness on the experience of concentrating on the etheric level of consciousness and is important in the process of tuning in to other levels of psychic/ spiritual awareness. Students learn to feel energies from plant leaves, crystals, magnets, and a celluloid coil. A short history about radionics and psychotronics is included to set a format

---

2 Ostrander, S. and schroeder, L. Handbook of Psychic Discoveries.
3 Ostrander, S. and schroeder, L." Psychotronic Generators, " international Journal of Paraphysics, volume 13, nos. 1&2, 1979, pp. 15-20.
4 Ibid.
5 Ostrander, S. And Schroeder, L. Psychic Discoveries Behind the Iron Curtain, pp. 289-290.

for understanding bioplasmic and other energy fields. Cited research and theory in radionics and psychotronics rounds out this section.

Psychotronics explores the relationship between bioplasmic energy and physical objects. Its intent is to observe and explore the physics of unusual or subtle energies, using certain symbols, materials, and shapes in the physical system.

Radionics seeks to observe and explore subtle energy communication channels between an individual's mind and physical body by using resonance/harmonic devices for diagnosis of discordant energy patterns in the physical system.

Exploratory exercises on natural resonance devices are investigated in order to familiarize the reader with the actual experience of energy transfer between him/herself and the objects, as a beginning step in developing sensitivity and knowledge of these subtle energies.

Psychotronics and radionics gives us a basic tactile experience with subtle energies that expands our knowledge and wisdom of unseen energies that expands our consciousness further into new levels of our omnipresent awareness. We build our foundation with spirit in order to communicate with it, and in so doing it makes it possible for spirit to communicate with us; as it was in ancient times.

And finally if this energy can be utilized in practice ways, as in developing a motor, what creative products will spawn from this research. Can you think of other products that could be developed from this research; its easy, brain storm.

BIBLIOGRAPHY

BOOKS:

Burr, H. Blueprint for Immortality, Oxford: DelaWarr Laboratories, Ltd., 1961

Criswell, Beverly. Quartz Crystals: A Celestial Point of View. Reserve, NM: Lavendar Lines Corp. , PO Box Drawer Q, 1983.

DelaWarr Laboratories, Ltd. The Psycho-Somatic Force Field. Oxford: 1963 Raleigh Park Road, OX29BB. 1963.

DelaWarr Laboratories, Ltd. The Study of The Ether. 1963.

DelaWarr Laboratories, Ltd. The Power of Thought. 1961.

Davis, W.E. The Black Box. Hancock, WI: T. and A. Publications, 1981.

Flanagan, Patrick. Pyramid Power. Glendale, Ca: Pyramid Publications, 1974.

Gallimore, J.G. Unified Field Theory. Mokelumne Hill, CA: Health Research, 1974.

Gallimore, J.G. Handbook of Unusual Energies. Mokelumne Hill, CA: Health Research, 1976.

Hardy, Dean. Pyramid Energy Explained. Allegan, MI: Delta-K Pyramid Products of America, 1979.

Hills, Christopher. Energy, Matter and Form. Boulder Creek, CA: University of the Trees, 1977.

Kueshana, Ekial. The Ultimate Frontier. Chicago, IL: The Stelle Group, 1963-1970.

Lakhavsky, George. The Secret of Life. London: Messrs, Heinemann Publishing, 1951.

Mann, W.E. Selected Writings, An Introduction to Agronomy. New York: Farrar, Straus and Giroux, 1951-1973.

"Maze, " Larry Collins, Simon and Schuster 1230 Avenue of the Americas New York, N.Y. 10020, 1989.

Mann, W.E.: Argonne, Reich and Eros. New York: Simon and Schuster. 1973.

Miller, Dennis and Smart, Ed. The Loom of Creation. New York: Harper and Row, 1978.

Ostrander, S. and Schroeder, L., Handbook of Psychic Discoveries. Berkeley, CA: Berkeley Publishing Company, 1974.

Ostrander, S. and Schroeder, L. Psychic Discoveries Behind the Iron Curtain. Englewood Cliffs, NJ: Prentice-Hall, 1970.

Pol, Therese. The Sexual Revolution, New York: Farrar, Straus and Giroux, 1945-1974.

Puharich, Andrija. Uri: A Journal of the Mystery of Uri Geller. New York: Doubleday and Company , 1974.

Rakes, Ola. Wilhelm Reich and Orgonomy. Baltimore, MD: Pelican Books, 1970.

Tesla, Nikola. Assorted Tesla Articles. Mokelumne Hill, CA: Health Research, 1975.

Tompkins, P. and Bird, C. The Secret Life of Plants. New York: Avon Books, 1973.

Walker, Dale. The Crystal Book. Sunol, CA: Crystal Co., 1983.

MAGAZINES:

Blank, Eleanor. "Crystals and the Healing Arts." Magical Blend. 1982. No. 8., pp. 48-49.

Franks, Daniel. "Crystals: The Therapeutic/Spiritual Properties of the Mineral Kingdom." Life-styles Magazine, December 1981, Vol. 14, No. 7, p. 10.

Gardner, Martin. "Mathematical Games: A Psychic Motor." Scientific American. April 1975, pp. 128-130.

T and A Publications. A Look at the Unusual. PO Box 195, Hancock, WI, 1980.

The Mountain Top (Queen of Light Series). "Dale Walker – Crystal Expert." Newsletter. 10420

Mercury Drive, Grass Valley, CA 95945.

"Letters on OD and Magnetism:The OD Theory Baron Von Reichenback 1852 (Translated from the German-1924)

Hand Boiler, Safari Limited Box 630685 Miami, Florida 33163

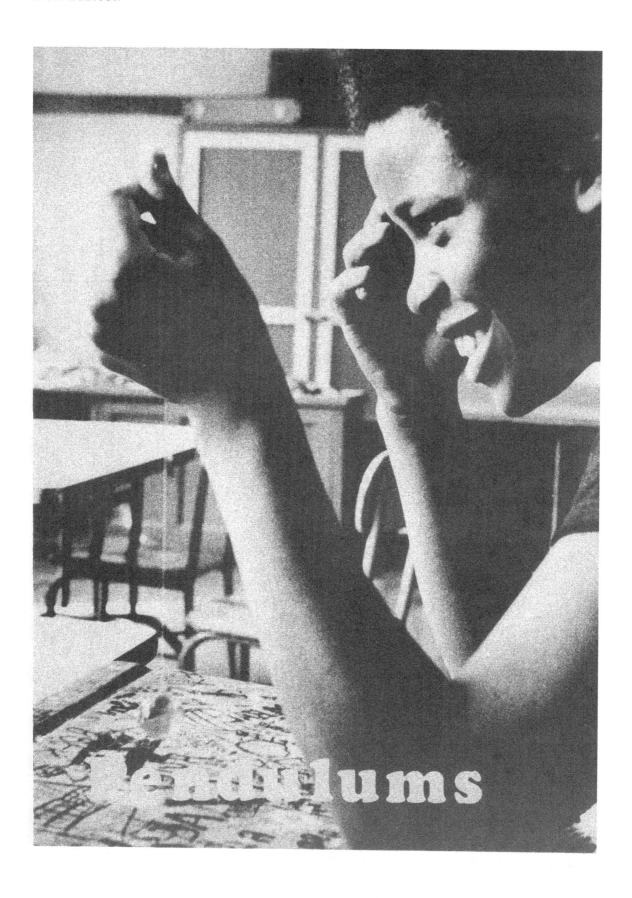

THE PENDULUM

The pendulum is one of the oldest methods of communicating with different levels of our consciousness to define extreme physical, mental, and emotional problems, as well as everyday experiences, such as determining the condition of house plants, and what sex the unborn baby is. Any question that comes to mind can be answered through the diagnosis of the pendulum, using the yes and no method.

There is much talk in early childhood education about education of the whole child without first grasping the whole picture of the child's potential; as yet, education has not devised a diagnostic tool which can gain access to all the levels of a child's being. We all have within ourselves multifaceted realities. We have various character aspects and also various soul traits that don't change as the life personality changes. The former is an intelligent energy form called the soul by some religious groups and called the heart's desire in other systems.[6] (It is not my intent to develop a long philosophical argument about the multi-dimensional beings we are; rather, I hope to make you aware of other possibilities in which to interpret your own realities. The Seth books written by author Jane Roberts provide an introduction to multiples of personality.)

The problem with diagnosing a young child's mental and emotional personality is that she/he may not be sophisticated enough to give a correct picture of the total human being. Take, for example, the Good Enough Draw-a-Man test, one of the few tests designed to determine the mental age of young children used by hospitals and social agencies. The child is asked to draw a picture of a man and the drawing is rated to determine the child's mental competence based on how many details the child includes in the drawing. There is a standard drawing for each age level which is used to rate the child; for example, a child of three would be expected to draw a circle for the head of the figure and two dots for eyes and a line for the mouth. Any additional features added would indicate a more mature mental age and less detail would indicate a less mature mental age.

---

6   One such group is The Order of Melchezdek, headed by Grace Pettipher in San Francisco.

These children are trying to move the pendulum by using their minds
to will the pendulum to rotate in one direction or the other.

Rhoda Kellogg, quite possibly the world's authority on children's art, Director of Golden Gate Kindergarten Association of San Francisco, takes issue with the assumptions of the creators of the Good Enough test. She feels that their basic concept is faulty; the notion that intelligence is reflected by more detail in drawings has its falsehoods. Children and adults draw the human body, as well as other physical objects, very poorly, as a rule. Drawing three-dimensional reality takes training and practice, neither of which necessarily reflect mental age. It is as much an intellectual exercise to master proportion and perspective as it is to master serialization, equations, or other learned tasks.

Children's abstractions in art, if they are truly abstractions, suggest a higher brain capacity in use, created by the causal body through inventions of thought. If a child's picture reflects that he or she has abstracted a reality, an object or thought into line, color, form and/or texture, then he or she is demonstrating a higher mental capacity. I mention these things only to give you some ideas about mental age and how it has historically been rendered. Further discussion of the uses of the pendulum will supplement this understanding.

One of the oldest systems of pendulum use was the Huna System. It was first used in early Egypt, India. and centuries later in Polynesia where it has been preserved by the native priests or Kahunas. Basically, the native priests believe that we have three selves or spirits: the lower self, middle self conscious mind, and the higher self or super consciousness. They think that the reason the pendulum works is because tiny threads of ectoplasmic substance connect with a person or object which allow the transfer of thought forms embodied in sensory or mental images. They believe that an ectoplasmic thread lasts for a long time and is the reason psychics can determine the owner of an object.

Andre Boris, a Frenchman, first used the pendulum to test the quality of wine and cheeses. He invented a small instrument called a biometer, made up of a ruler that slides underneath a sheet of mica and a sheet of iron. The object under study was placed in a cup on the zero end of the ruler. Boris would hold the pendulum over the iron and mica plates and watch its movement. If the pendulum rotated in a clockwise direction, the object under study (Le., the wine) was good; if it rotated in a counter-clockwise direction, it was bad. Now if the pendulum rotated counterclockwise over the mica plate, Boris would move the ruler closer and closer to the end of the plate, noting when the pendulum started to swing; this indicated what percentage of the object was good.

Boris considered the pendulum's movements in relations to what he called a wave theory. Energy of the object under study emitted waves that caused the pendulum to respond in circular movements. In order to assure that the object under study was responsible for the pendulum movements, rather than the biometer, he painted the biometer red, which has the lowest wavelength in the color spectrum and would cause the least interference. He also found that light energy could be conducted through a wire or thread and, therefore, readings could be taken directly from the biometer.

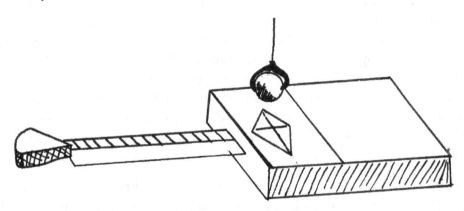

During the early part of this century, Dr. Bruner, a physicist and engineer, studied pendulum motion. Working with the pendulum, he discovered that he could detect brain waves, learn something about character, and study the place in evolution of the soul. He was able to detect various vibrational states by lengthening the metric measurement on the Boris biometer and changing its position. He also substituted the iron and mica plates with various other conductive metals such as brass and copper (each plate was side by side). In his experiments, Dr. Bruner would ask a person to place his/her thumb on the measure and draw the finger along the surface of the instrument until the pendulum started to swing. Bruner determined that there was a certain point on the thumb that had contact with the brain. This has a correlation to the Chinese acupuncture meridians. As we look at a meridian map of the body, we see that there is a meridian running from the thumb, up the arm and neck, to the brain.

With further study, Dr. Bruner was able to determine intelligence based on pendulum movements. He determined that average intelligence was 100 degrees, and any swing of the pendulum below 100 was considered below average intelligence. In Bruner's time, I.Q. was considered a constant characteristic determined by heredity. We are finding, however, that one's intelligence changes as more and more learning takes place. The latest research shows intelligence to have many components; which component was measured by Bruner is undermined.

This is a short history of some of the beginnings of pendulum use, but the most relevant information about using a pendulum is from your own experience.

The pendulum works on the principle of muscle response. Impulses come from the subconscious or higher self through the nervous system of the individual, acting as a high frequency receiving set, stimulating a muscle response in the hand of the doer .The subconscious action of moving the pendulum by muscle response is a completely different feeling than that of consciously moving the pendulum. The muscle response movement is so smooth and subtle you don't feel the motion or see the hand move; and your hand is not moving... the energy coming through your hand is moving down the thread to the weight on the bottom, moving it; or more precisely interfacing with the energy around the weight (auric field) thereby bringing about its movement. Muscle response is also termed Applied Kinesiology. More studies needs to be done to ascertain its accuracy in the pendulum response.

Each individual has his/her own saturation point of concentration on anyone subject. It takes tremendous amounts of mental energy to concentrate on or wholly direct one's consciousness on any particular subject. The pendulum, therefore, should not be utilized during periods of tiredness or emotional upset. When you are dealing with high frequency vibrations, such as thought patterns, make sure that there are no negative thought patterns in your immediate environment; these tend to be detected by the pendulum and reflected in its movements. According to individuals who have studied the pendulum, weather also plays a part in pendulum performance; cold and overcast days are less conducive to pendulum performance than a sunny, warm day.

An important part of studying the pendulum involves the ability to use it to gain a yes or no response. Draw two coils, one clockwise, the other counterclockwise, and write the words "yes" and "no" on each, "yes" for counterclockwise and "no" for clockwise. Hold the pendulum over the "yes" drawing and ask for an answer. If the pendulum moves in the same direction as the coil drawn over "yes" drawing, counter-clockwise, the answer to the question is "yes." Now hold the pendulum over the "no" drawing, asking the same question, and check for consistency. The same question should elicit only one "yes" response from the pendulum. If it doesn't, you may not have asked a specific enough question, or you may not have sufficiently trained your subconscious mind to respond to the correct direction of the pendulum's swing. Try programming your subconscious by willing your pendulum to rotate in one direction and the other; do this a couple of times.

Ask Questions in the right way is very important in the dowsing process.

Asking the question in a different way . If your pendulum wobbles in place, it can't answer because it doesn't understand the question; the question may be too general or it may require more than a "yes" or "no" answer. Don't be ambiguous when asking questions. State a factual specific question. Your subconscious mind interprets every question from a literal point of view. And be aware of using WORDS that sound the same but have different meanings; your subconscious doesn't no the different, you may create a wrong answer.

There are 3 rules for asking good questions that are agreed upon by many dowers:

1. Be very specific, this may include; what, where and when.

2. If you use a program system (As Walt Woods does)use words and phases agreed upon by your dowsing system; your subconscious.

3. Ask questions that have yes and no answers; don't use opinions from past, present or future.

In order to best use the pendulum, neutralize your emotional being and clear your mind of distractions. Try not to think of anything but the question asked. Sometimes it is helpful to put your mind in a trance by staring at a blank wall space or at any other plain surface within the room. The pendulum should be the foremost object in your peripheral field of vision so that the subconscious mind can clearly and directly influence the movement of the pendulum without distractions. As an exercise to strengthen your subconscious, hold the pendulum over the clockwise diagram and mentally instruct your subconscious to rotate the pendulum clockwise by concentrating on a question that has a "yes" answer. Do the same for a "no" question, but work with the counterclockwise diagram. Repeat this exercise several times to strengthen your concentration and subconscious responses. You may want to personalize this experience by learning to communicate with your subconscious; talk to it; directly influence it.

Besides establishing an environment which is conducive to communication with the subconscious, it is also important to find the correct length of pendulum line to hold between the thumb and first finger. You may want pendulum to swing faster, because of time parameters, so use the indication mark closest to the pendulum. Each individual has a different frequency for tuning his/her pendulum. There are several methods of tuning. One is to hold the line close to the pendulum and concentrate on willing the pendulum to move in a clockwise direction and then in a counter-clockwise direction. Slowly let the line out until the pendulum starts to rotate in a circular manner. Note this position by making an ink mark on the line. Continue from that point, letting out line until the pendulum starts to rotate again, and make a mark at this position; continue letting out the line until you have reached the end of the thread. The highest mark on the line is the point where the strongest frequency of impulse energy comes through. The line acts as an antenna, resounding to different frequencies up and down its length. Also the antenna acts as a step down transformer stepping down the frequencies to a finer and finer level.

I just want to menion Walt Woods a master dowser and PHD in Agriculture in our area. He has helped me create a more accret questioning system for my dowsing; and I have been dowsing a long time. As part of his questioning system he included a question that has improved my dowsing a hundred percent; namely asking May I, Can I, Should I ask this question at this time. If you get a NO ask the question at a latter time; if YES go ahead and ask the question. Walt has a system that he has created using a lot of programs for your subconscious to asimulate...which he says makes his dowsing more accret. I'm not sure he's correct but it would be up to you to deside. His book Letter To Robin has all the details (check the Bib. for contact information).

HOMEMADE PENDULUMS

One of the most easily made pendulums consists of a weight fixed to the end of a nylon cord (fishing line) or silk thread. Some materials for the weight are better at conducting bioplasmic energy than others; quartz rock crystals are good, as well as wood and plastic. Copper, iron, silver and gold are very good conducting metals, but tend to be quite expensive. Tin foil wrapped around an object is economical and sufficient for conducting bioplasmic and electrical-magnetic energy.

A simple pendulum to make in the classroom consists of a wooden dowl 3" long and 2" in diameter, some silk thread or fishing line, and a wooden or plastic ball - all of which can be easily obtained at a local hardware, craft or variety store. When constructing the pendulum in the classroom, it would be a good idea to draw a chart of each step in the building process. Put up a poster in the classroom in full view of all the students. The first step would be to announce that you and the students are going to make a pendulum. Now explain some of the history of the pendulum and what it has been used for. (Always answer any questions the students have about the topic under discussion.) Have the older children keep notes in a notebook or run off mimeographed sheets describing pendulum history which might be collected in a notebook with all the other new information gathered about psychic phenomena. Refer the children to the chart on the wall and explain the step-by-step directions on how to make a pendulum.

MATERIALS

- wooden dowel

- solid rubber washer

- silk thread or fishing line

- round wooden or plastic ball

- saw

- Elmer's glue

FIRST STEP: Cut a piece of dowel rod 3" inches long. Put the dowel in a vice or have someone hold the dowel in place over the end of the table. Sandpaper the rough edges formed by the cut.

SECOND STEP: Cut a piece of silk thread or fishing line 12 inches long. Punch a hole in the center of a rubber washer and draw thread through. Glue rubber washer to the top of the wooden dowel with wood glue. THIRD STEP; Glue round wooden or plastic ball onto other end of dowel. Wrap copper wire or nylon fishing line around wooden dowel to act as a coil. It will work to channel the energy from your muscle responses over the surface of the pendulum. Make sure the copper or nylon line is attached to the silk thread at one end of the dowel and to the plastic ball at the other end.

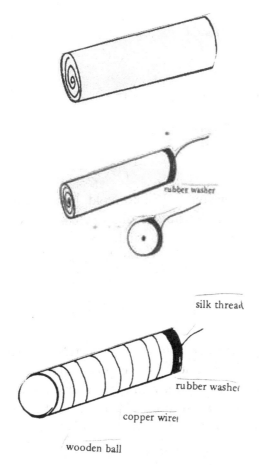

rubber washer

silk thread

rubber washer

copper wire

wooden ball

Another type of pendulum that is possible to construct in the classroom can be made from liquid resin. You can buy resin and molds from any hobby shop. Pick out small molds that are tapered or pointed, which will potentially yield one ounce. The advantage of casting your own pendulum is that you can add almost anything to the resin to increase its receptiveness. (This is a good project for older students.) Once again, a chart could be constructed that explains the step-by step process of the resin mold pendulum. Before explaining the building process, however, you will have to prepare a few things for the children. First, gather and clean some old milk cartons; cut them in half and save the bottoms. Also, pick up some copper foil, iron filings and copper wire. Set up a table to support the pendulums while drying.

FIRST STEP:

Select a pendulum mold.

Pour enough resin in to a clean milk carton or suitable mixing container to partially fIll the mold. Add catalyst to resin.

MATERIALS

- Plastic casting molds, geometric shapes

- clear liquid resin

- copper pieces or iron filings or copper wire

- milk cartons or small containers

SECOND STEP:

Mix the resin until slightly yellow and pour into mold. Now sprinkle little pieces of copper sheeting pieces or iron filings into resin and mix.(Iron filings can be obtained from any scientific supply store.) As an alternative, you might wind copper wire inside the mold before you pour in the resin, it acts as a coil. Make sure the end of the wire comes up through the center of the mold.

THIRD STEP:

Attach thread or line to copper coil and pour in resin; or stick the end of the line in the middle of the mold and pour in resin;a bead attached to a copper wirer or silk or nylon string or fishing line works well; you can use a chain if you want. (Don't over look specific stones or crystals when choosing objects to add to your resin.) Let it dry for 24 hours, making sure that your string is standing straight up in the middle of your mold. When it drys, you will have made your own pendulum.

One of the best ways of finding out about your children, whether in the classroom or at home, is by using a pendulum in conjunction with a photograph or fingerprint of each child. A photograph or fingerprint acts as a "witness, " something that characterizes and identifies the individual. Levels of energy fields around the human body are attuned to each photograph of each child (refer back to Aura and Radionics sections). The use of witnesses goes back many centuries in pendulum practice and religious history. Often witnesses were used to cast spells; a piece of hair, a fingernail or blood spot helped occultists tune into their subjects. Doctors of today use urine specimens and blood samples, modern day witnesses, to diagnose a patient's condition, with the aid of sophisticated analysis. Scientists are also finding that photographs and fingerprints, used as witnesses, may well be part of diagnostic techniques of the future.

For an illustration of the kinds of things that are identifiable by use of the pendulum and a witness, try this exercise. Find a recent photo of your child or one of your students. Take a piece of paper and write the child's name at the top. Next list I.Q. numbers, starting with 80, 85, 90, 95 and on up to 300. Place your left hand over the head of the child represented in the photograph. With the pendulum in your right hand, hold it over the first number, 80. Ask out loud, "What is this child's (or substitute his/her name) mental age at this time?" Then repeat the question several times to yourself. Continue holding the pendulum over each I.Q. number and ask the above question until the pendulum starts to gyrate, indicating the child's current I.Q. It is important here to remember that the denotation of I.Q. is only significant for the child's particular age period. The concept of I.Q. and its relevance faces much debate.[7]

If you want to determine something about the basic will of your child or student, try this pendulum exercise. The will signifies the degree of basic drive an individual has at a particular time in his/ her life. Draw a circle with a cross in the center; label north, south, east, and west as diagrammed.

Putting your fingers on the photograph of the child, hold the pendulum over the circle grid and ask your over soul to contact the personality self of the child in the picture. The pendulum will start to swing north and south, if your pendulum is tuned to a up and back swing. If the pendulum swings more to the right or east, the child's personality is considered positive. If the pendulum swings to the left of center, the personality indicated is less positive, having less of a will to overcome problems in his or her environment. It is very important for children to develop an emotionally and intellectually strong will to succeed in life's tests. (See the bibliography for books specifically related to will development.)

The pendulum can also be used to determine some basic personality traits. List various personality traits on a piece of paper. Hold the pendulum over each characteristic as you hold your fingers on the child's picture; ask a question about the trait as it relates to the child. The pendulum will start to rotate, if you have programmed your pendulum to rotate. The traits indicated by gyrations of the pendulum can be combined to give a personality profile. These traits are a combination of socially learned characteristics and hereditary traits. Within this grouping of traits there may very well be personalities acquired over lifetime after lifetime of human experience. In the section on Numerology, I will speak more about lifetime personalities.

The scientific research done on personality indicates that there is some agreement on the characteristics that make up the personalities of children.[8] The personality structure is set up using opposites as characteristics. Dull and bright, serious and happy-go-lucky are examples of the researchers' categories. These various traits could be used in the pendulum exercise as checklists on a ditto or listed on a chart. Both might be kept in a me for future reference. Researchers Dreger, Allport, Baughman and Cattell have been studying the personality for forty years. In their studies they have arrived at what I feel is a fairly accurate grouping of

---

7   Gallimore, J.G. Handbook of Unusual Energies. Hills, C. Energy, Form, and Matter. DeLaWarr, G. The Study of the Ether.

8   Cattell, B. Description and Measurement of Personality. Allport, Gordon. Personality: A Psychological Interpretation.

personality traits. In particular, Cattell has done some excellent work in the study of children's personalities. His personality structure could be used as the variables listed in the pendulum exercises.

Personality traits can be interesting indicators of the child's ability to excel in different aspects of their lives.

PERSONALITY CHARACTERISTICS

PERSONALITY CHARACTERISTICS

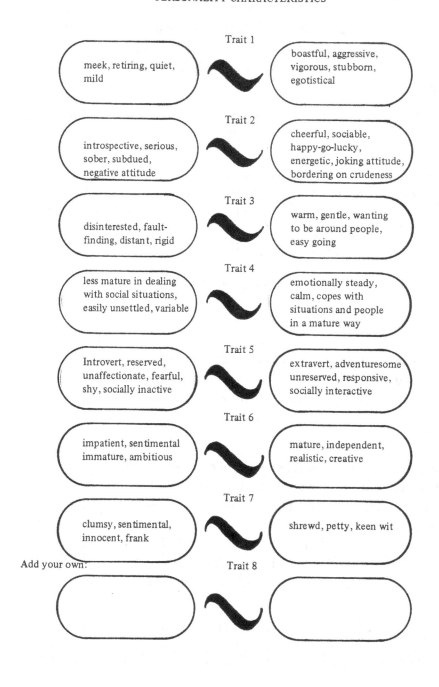

Trait 1

meek, retiring, quiet, mild

boastful, aggressive, vigorous, stubborn, egotistical

Trait 2

introspective, serious, sober, subdued, negative attitude

cheerful, sociable, happy-go-lucky, energetic, joking attitude, bordering on crudeness

Trait 3

disinterested, fault-finding, distant, rigid

warm, gentle, wanting to be around people, easy going

Trait 4

less mature in dealing with social situations, easily unsettled, variable

emotionally steady, calm, copes with situations and people in a mature way

Trait 5

Introvert, reserved, unaffectionate, fearful, shy, socially inactive

extravert, adventuresome unreserved, responsive, socially interactive

Trait 6

impatient, sentimental immature, ambitious

mature, independent, realistic, creative

Trait 7

clumsy, sentimental, innocent, frank

shrewd, petty, keen wit

Add your own:

Trait 8

Trait I

boastful, aggressive,

meek, retiring, quiet, vigorous, stubborn,

mild egotistical

Trait 2

cheerful, sociable,

introspective, serious, happy-go-lucky ,

sober, subdued, energetic, joking attitude,

negative attitude bordering on crudeness

Trait 3

warm, gentle, wanting

disinterested, fault-finding to be around people,

distant, rigid easy going

Trait 4

less mature in dealing emotionally steady,

with social situations, ~ calm, copes with

easily unsettled, variable situations and people

in a mature way

Trait 5

Introvert, reserved,

extravert, adventuresome

unaffectionate, fearful, unreserved, responsive,

shy, socially inactive socially interactive

Trait 6

impatient, sentimental, mature, independent,

immature, ambitious realistic, creative

Trait 7

clumsy, sentimental, shrewd, petty, keen wit

innocent, frank

Add your own. Trait 8

POTENTIALITY

Using a pendulum to understand personality, will, and other aspects of the child (or life in general) has the following potential:

a. We will learn, truly, about the multi-dimensional reality of each child as the child learns about him/herself.

b. Teaching and learning will take on new dimensions and ramifications for the teacher and student.

c. The pendulum could be used as a diagnostic tool for mentally and emotionally handicapped children.

d. It could also be used to determine the health of plants and what remedy might be used for unhealthy plants. Try making a chart of plant nutrients and comparing it to pendulum motions white touching the plant and holding the pendulum over the various nutrients listed and you will arrive at what nutrients the plant needs at that time. Try an experiment with two plants and give one plant the nutrients and the other plant nothing but light, water and random nutrients; see which one thrives.

e. There is no limit to the knowledge that can be learned and experienced by using the pendulum.

SUMMARY/CONCLUSIONS

This channel is an extension of the Radionics channel, in the sense that pendulums were used to detect subtle energies around objects and to diagnose dysfunctions within the body before radionic devices were developed. In Europe, the 18th and 19th century Radiothesis was still used and they are still used by medical practitioners to detect certain involuntary responses.

Pendulums are used in many different ways to acquire information about answers to questions from our super conscious selves, the aspect of ourselves that seems to perceive information on a higher level of mind function, a level that is not limited to dimensional barriers, but penetrates dimensions in search of relevant answers.

Pendulums bridge the gap between the higher and lower, inner and outer levels of each individual's awareness. The reader becomes familiar with this tool for expanded awareness by constructing his or her own pendulum and experiencing a personal connection with his or her own higher awareness through this tool. Photographs of children using pendulums in the classroom show an actual experience, rather than just an intellectual exercise in pendulum use.

History is a very important part of this channel, as it is in the other channels, because we need to know something about the techniques used and where these ideas originated, to perceive a clearer picture of what directions to move toward, cancelling out some of the alleys one travels when a new field is being explored.

A particular focus of concern in this channel is on the pendulum as a possible diagnostic tool. I have tried to point out, with a few examples, that there really isn't a reliable tool available today to characterize the young child in his/her development in the areas of inherent personality, soul level experience, IQ, or even emotional development (although Eric Erickson has an excellent emotional stage related breakdown that gives us some basics to work with in child emotional levels). The pendulum could help clarify these areas.

BIBLIOGRAPHY (Books)

Alport, Gordon. Personality: A Psychological Interpretation. New York: Henry Holt & Co., 1937.

Assagioli, Robert. The Act of Will. Baltimore, MD: Penguin Books, 1974.

Blackie, Hohn. Inside the Primary Schools. New York: Schocken Books, 1967.

Cattell, Bernard. Description and Measurement of Personality. New York: World Book Co., 1946.

Cattell, Bernard. Handbook of Modern Personality Theory. New York: Holstead Press, 1977.

Eysench, H.J. The Structure of Human Personality. London: London & Methuen & Co., Ltd., 1954.

Fisher, Robert. Learning How to Learn. New York: Harcourt, Brace, Jovanovich, Inc., 1972. Ginsberg, Herbert, and Opper, Sylvia. Piaget's Theory of Intellectual, Development. Englewood Cliffs, NJ: Prentice-Hall, 1969.

Kellogg, Rhoda. Analyzing Children's Art. Palo Alto, CA: Mayfield ~ublishing Co., 1969.

Long, Max Freedom. Psychometric Analysis. Vista, CA: Huna Research Publication, 1953.

Millay, Jean. "Expanding Visual Intelligence." San Francisco, CA: Association of Humanistic Psychology Newsletter, May 1979, pp. 25-29.

Mowbray, Jean, and Salisbury, Helen. Diagnosing Individual Needs for Early Childhood Education.

Columbus, OH: Charles E. Merrill Publishing Co., 1975.

Piaget, Jean, and Inhelder, Barbel. The Psychology of the Child. New York: Basic Books, Inc., 1969.

Rice, Berkeley. "Brave New World of Intelligence Testing." Psychology Today. Septem1?er 1969, pp. 27-30. Toffler, Alvin. Learning for Tomorrow. New York: Random House, 1974.

Woods, Walt. "Letter To Robin"; a Mini Course in Penulum Dowsing, The American Society of Dowsers, 430 Railroad St. Ste.#1, St.Johnsbury, VA. 05819 or http://www.dowsers.org

Chakras

CHAKRAS

What are chakras and what difference do they make? Everyone's experience will be different. My first knowledge of chakras came nearly ten years ago when I was studying the Hindu system of meditation. I became aware of a system called the secret fire, in which one is to arrive at a higher state of being by developing this ability. to generate an electrical/ chemical energy force, kundalini, from the base chakra up through the spinal cord to the base of the brain. At the time I talked to several people who were familiar wIth kundalini energy and chakra systems and found that it could be dangerous to try to develop this energy without guidance because of the risk of damage to the nervous system if too much energy were delivered to the base of the brain. I took this advice as a half warning and went ahead and attempted to generate this electrical/chemical energy. I never did quite succeed in this attempt, so I dropped my efforts and moved on to other interests.

I joined a group called Cosolorgy (later became the international community of Christ in Nevada, first organized by Gene Savoy, a world renowned archaeologist of the Peruvian ruins.) that combined knowledge of individuals biorhythms with observations made of the sun through colored filters to rejuvenate the cells of the body and open the chakras. It was during my association with the cosolorgists that I experienced rushes of energy moving along my spine in the form of Kundalini energy. Often the rushes came unexpectedly, and at first, were quite shocking. The more times I experienced this energy, however, the less shocking it seemed and the easier the energy would flow. I soon learned that I could will this strange energy to do its primal dance anywhere at any time, including bringing down the atomic energy down from the eight chakra above the head.

Eventually, I joined a spiritual group (The Order of Melchezedeck) in which I learned to channel energy down from above through the crown chakra to the base of my spine (atomic energy). I still use the techniques learned in this group to control energy and open my chakras. The feeling I get when energy is activating my chakras is like a soft shot of electricity, sometimes followed by a wave of energy moving all around my body, vibrating up and down my frame. After the meditation I feel much more alert and aware of my surroundings. My senses become more acute. I rarely find myself in states of anxiety; I feel good and content with myself and my life. Also, my psychic senses are awakened fully. It is important, therefore, to learn to maximize the potentialities of the chakras and the energy associated with each.

In the Hindu system the word chakra means wheel. Chakras are major energy centers connecting a network of microscopic energy veins that go to different parts of the body. The assumed appearance of each chakras within the body is wheel-shaped; they rotate counter-clock wise or clock wise and open and close. There are seven major chakras, all located along the spinal cord with the locus pictured along the front of the body within a fine network attached to the etheric body.(some times the chakras are pictured as difference colored locus flowers.)

The network going up the spine is the channel in which the secret fire, Kundalini, the female principle called Shiva, contacts the base of the brain, the male principle, which consecrates a union of body and mind or body and spirit. This unites the physical and emotional body with the accumulated distribution of energy throughout the body. There is a feeling of euphoria which integrates and balances the body, mind and spirit. This is a similar experience to having a climax; some times you see stars, metaphorically. This is the reason that Kindalini is one of the most powerful energy in the universe.

In Form, Energy and Matter Chris Hills presents an illustration of a chakra appearing above the head of a Sanskrit seer. This chakra is attached to the crown terminal chakra, located at the top of the head, and is about 4 to 8 feet above the head. This chakra is denoted as the Eighth energy center-the Gold center, stimulating spiritual inspiration and higher spiritual thought. I have included information about the eighth chakra further along in this publication. All the chakras have their corresponding energy attachment along the spine. The sacred energy strikes the spine stimulates the chakra terminals, which, in turn, stimulate the chakras within the etheric body. The chakras help to regulate the Chi and corresponding glands and hormones in the body.

In the Hindu system a Chakra is compared to a Lotus Blossom with petals arranged in a concentric configuration. The chakra centers open and close like apertures on a camera. By looking at a person's eyes, you can learn to tell whether their centers are closed, partially closed, or open. If the eyes are large, deep and shining, the chakras are more than likely open. The average person has only two or three centers open at anyone time, depending on the individual's spiritual development. When all of one's chakras are open, they are experiencing a mental and emotional high point of acute sensory reception.

Extra Sensory vibrations might even be detected and registered consciously. When the chakras are open and receptive, individuals often notice many new perceptions which may have normally gone undetected. Perceptions of people and circumstances around you start to become much clearer, as if a fog has lifted, and the world seems almost a different place.(Later in the Meditation channel I have processes to stimulate the chakras.)

The chakras are split into various parts, signifying their complexity in the chakra function and level of vibration. The higher up in the body the chakra resides, the faster the frequency levels it will respond to.

The chakra at the base, of the spinal cord, The Root , resonates to the color Red. It is split into four parts, all of which respond to the low frequency vibrations of various shades of red. The base chakra is associated with the genitalia, sexual desires, and anything that has to do with the physical plane.

The lower abdominal or pelvic chakra is divided into six parts and responds to the color Orange. This chakra is said to stimulate the spleen, which regulates the purification of the body and regulates the distribution of nutrients throughout the organism. The orange center also relates to the social aspects in humans. In women the center is considered the sexual center.

The navel chakra vibrates to the color Yellow and is divided into eight parts, indicating greater complexity in its function and control. This chakra relates to the bloodstream and controls its responses, especially when a person is excited or in an emotionally stressful situation. The color yellow relates to intellectual functions.

The Heart chakra oscillates to the color Green and has a higher rate of vibration than the lower chakras. This center regulates operation of the thymus gland, which responds to disease control. It also helps stabilize bodily functions during emotional upsets. The heart chartreuse the most balancing teller, green, you can have. It is also related to the chakra in higher vibrations of love and compassion. Pink also communicates the higher love joy and well-being. Recent studies have shown that it responds in an intelligent way to our emotional desires that facilitate visual communication with self and God; it is the vibration of wisdom and healing.

The next chakra , the throat center, vibrates to the shades of Blue. It performs the task of regulating the thyroid in the para thyroid glands. These glands secrete hormones which affect how food in air are metabolized. This chakra also relates to the vocal functions and imagination. 50

Located in the forehead is the brow chakra, which resonates to the second highest frequency of vibration from waves of the blue-violet or Indigo part of the spectrum. This chakra is called (in some systems) the "third eye." It controls the pituitary gland, which determines body growth and various functions of the endocrine system. The brow chakra is the link with all higher processes of the mind, including intuition and the psychic sciences of telepathy and clairvoyance (refer to the section on ESP for definitions and context).

The last major chakra in the physical system is the Crown chakra, which is located on top of the head. It resonates to the highest frequency of all the chakras and is associated with the color purple- violet. In the Hindu system, it is called the Thousand Pedaled Lotus. It affects the pineal gland, which has a relationship to the control of light coming in through the eyes, about which little is known. Eventually, I suspect scientists will determine that the pineal gland is a receptor of light of various frequency bands of the visible and invisible electromagnetic spectrum. Sunlight affects the pineal gland by integrating psychic energy, which regulates the opening and closing of the chakras and rejuvenates body cells.

There are a number of minor chakras in the body, one in each hand and one in each foot, but their functions are as yet undetermined. Other studies have recently been completed by researchers in a special book that has just been written called, " Heart Mass", by David McArthur that not only sites scientific information of heart communication with the body and mind but gives spiritual insights into our connection with God through the heart.

There are other interpretations of the functions and structure of the chakras, for example, the Qabbalistic system, which recognizes ten different chakras. In the yoga system the chakras are considered psychological entities, not etheric/physical objects at all. None of the systems agree on the functions of each chakra, but we are slowly approaching the time when we will know the truth about the chakras. My personal experience is that the chakras have as much to do with mental, physical and emotional well-being as eating and sleeping.

In Japan there is a doctor named Hiroshi Motoyama from Tokyo University who, with the help of his chakra machine, has determined that individuals can regulate the different frequency levels of the chakras. He found that the average associated energy of each chakra is 30 millivolts at 20 cycles when inactive; after a chakra has been activated, its frequency level is 500 millivolts at 2, 000 cycles. Dr. Motoyama studied the dominant chakras in the body to obtain these results.

Further study is needed to determine the energy frequencies and functions of the remaining chakras, which may lead to information on healthy frequency levels. More studies need also be done on individuals who can regulate their chakras to see if their chakras resonate frequencies are above, below, or at a healthy range. Finally, further study is needed to determine the effects that healthy chakras have on memory and other learning capacities.

CHAKRA-ATOMIC ENERGY MEDITATION

In the western religious spiritualist tradition there is a meditation for opening up the chakras. It was often called the eighth chakra, bringing down the atomic energy. It was explained and taught to me by Dr. Grace Pettifer, a english religious spiritualist, leader of The Order of Melchizedek, and can be used in the classroom as follows:

1. Establish a quiet, contemplative atmosphere. You may want to join in the meditation so that a meditative atmosphere is fully established and the students do not feel as if they were being watched.

2. Ask students to be seated with hands resting in their laps.

3. Instruct each student to relax the body, every part of it.

4. Have each drop their head back, eyes closed; then slowly return to a normal position, head upright but with eyes still closed (eventually, students may learn to meditate with their eyes open, trance-like; see Mandala section).

5. Ask the children to visualize their consciousness as a flashlight searching for the Eight chakra, 4 to 8 feet above your head. When you feel or see the sun orb the energy may run by it's self.

6. When you think that they've managed to evoke this image, ask them to imagine that the ball of light is dripping, like spiraling honey, flowing down and hitting the top of their heads, Crown chakra. The honey sensation is actually energy flow of atomic energy.

7. Students should then concentrate on a point in the middle of the top of their heads; have them visualize a lotus flower opening and it's color (purple), to receive

the honey which flows into the center, down the spine to the base chakra; if the charkas are open.

8. Repeat the meditation, this time asking the students to visualize the color of each chakra as they feel the energy, "the honey" flowing down their spines.

9. Have the students become aware IF the energy is blocking at the chakra, not running to the other chakras.(this is very important to successful running of the energy down the chakras and there opening.)

10. Now have them concentrate on seeing the chakra as a lotus flower opening with the color of that chakra if the chakra is blocking.

11. Now reacquire the atomic energy from the eights chakra from above feeling the energy running through to the next chakra.

12. Repeat this process again and again until all the chakras are open. Ground the energy in the center of the earth.

13. Now have the students open their eyes and relate their experiences. If some students are having difficulty, repeat the meditation but have them first feel the chakras and visualize their colors before asking them to feel the connecting energy. Put up a chart so students can remember the colors of each chakras.

14. After the children have experienced this meditation a few times, eliminate the honey metaphor and explain that the sensations they are experiencing are due to atom energy moving throughout the body; especially between the chakras.

15. I need to mention that the chakras are located in the 4th dimension…making your visualization a very creative process. In the fourth dimension you can picture the charka, if your clairvoyance, any place or direction you want. I picture the chakra locus, facing upward, over the spine in the locations of the chakras. Normally they are located on the front of the body; because the image can be here and there at the same time in the fourth dimension you can visualize any thing you want; its like being in a dream.

16. And finally don't forget to breathe before you start your meditation. Again breath is Prana that you take into your body to energize your consciousness.

EYE-MIRROR-ENERGY TRANSFER

Another technique for opening up the chakras is the eye-mirror-energy transfer. Separate the group of students into pairs and give each pair a mirror. Have each child look into the mirror and concentrate on only one eye. Have them focus on that eye and relax. Tell them to let energy flow out through their eyes, feel the energy, starting from the crown chakra and moving down through each chakra center. If students have a problem feeling the energy running down the spine, ask them to visualize the chakra centers and their colors before feeling the energy which flows between them. Repeat this exercise as often as you can, because it tends to revitalize the body energy. At the end of each session you may want to discuss the student's experiences. Have fun with these exercises and you will find that you will feel something interesting happening to you.

CHECKPOINTS

If you don't have any immediate luck with your students in their efforts at feeling chakra energy, don't worry. It will take a few times for most of the students to master this technique; others will take to it like ducks to water. Practice the exercise a few times a week and see what happens. Change the environment; play quiet, gentle music (see the Mandala section for suggestions) oand alter the lighting by subduing it or using colored bulbs in fixtures. Have patience, be encouraging, and your students will eventually feel the flow of the powerful energy flow.

POTENTIALITIES

Here is a list of the potential benefits attributed to chakra meditation.

1. Opening up your chakras will heighten your awareness of the five senses.

2. You will feel more alert and attuned to reality. The world will seem more real, as if someone removed a veil.

3. Opening your chakras is a natural way to feel high, balanced.

4. Your life is apt to become more balanced and good things should happen to you.

5. You will be a healthier person - emotionally, mentally, and physically.

6. More and more people will take notice of you because of the atmosphere you radiate. People who have learned to open their chakras tend to be very charismatic.

7. Your students should start seeing their life from a different perspective; giving it new meaning, a more holistic meaning.

8. Opening your chakras will help facilitate the unfolding or continued use of your psychic capabilities.

SUMMARY /CONCLUSIONS

The Chakra channel becomes the first look at the unusual energy system within the body. It maps out the history of chakras, their function within the body and their relevance to different levels of consciousness. This channel is basically an early Hindu system with sightings on current parapsychology research which develop this particular approach in more depth; and a western metaphysical chakra meditation. Meditation exercises are used to stimulate and induce an actual experience of energy moving from one chakra to another and expand your consciousness, and produce healthier physical, emotional and spiritual aspects of your being.

All of the exercises in this book are written for the purpose of inducing a pleasant, fun and enlightening experience in each individual partaking and directing the exercises.

The concept of chakras describes awareness as extending from parts of the brain to areas in the body and mind; it is a holistic view of man's consciousness integrated into an image of him/her self. To extend awareness of cognitive processes beyond the confines of the physical brain is a holistic approach shared by many in the new age movement. It is an awareness that we are not islands unto ourselves, but that we share a very real connection with the universes around us, and that this process is biological and psychological, as well as spiritual.

The chakra system is a very old system that maps out functions for different levels of consciousness, creating a composite picture (blueprint) for understanding our relationship with creation and beings in the rest of the universe. As I continued to develop my spiritual consciousness I learned that the chakra system was not limited just to the Eastern philosophies, but this system was also integrated into Western religion and scientific inquiries.

Resources are cited to help in understanding the realm of experiences associated with chakra consciousness, in hopes that the reader may go beyond my explanation of the chakras for a fuller understanding of this subject from a experiential level.

BIBLIOGRAPHY

Andersen, U.S. The Greatest Power in the Universe. Los Angeles: Atlantis University, 1971.

Gallimore, J.G. Handbook of Unusual Energies. Mokelumne Hill, Calif.: Health Research, 1976.

Hall, Manly P. , Masonic, Hermetic, Kabalistic and Rosicrucian Symbolic Philosophy. Los Angeles: The Philosophical Research Society. Inc., 1973.

Hills, Chris. Nuclear Evolution. London: Centre Community Publications, 1969

Energy, Matter, and Form. Boulder Creek, Calif: Christopher Hills, Phil Allen, Alastair Bearne, Roger Smith, University of the Trees 1975-77.

Ledbeater, Charles. Chakras. Wheaton, Ill.: The Philosophical Publishing House, 1972.

Ostrander. Sheila and Schroeder, Lynn. Psychic Discoveries Behind the Iron Curtain. Englewood Cliffs, N.J.: Prentice-Hall, 1970.

Wood, Ernest. Yoga. Baltimore, Md.: Penguin Books, 1959-62.

Miscellaneous:

The Kundalini Research Institute of Canada; 244 Eglinton Avenue East, 1st Floor; Toronto, Ontario, M4P lK2, 1-416-487-1771

CONCENTRATION, MEDITATION, CONTEMPLATION AND VISUALIZATION

In previous chapters we have reviewed simple chakra meditation techniques used to activate Kundalini energy and open the Chakra centers. To augment this technique and gain further knowledge of concentration, meditation and contemplation, I will examine several historically different systems. These systems are helpful in developing the physical senses of sight, touch, hearing, smell and even taste, as well as the spiritual senses of intuition and clairvoyance. With continued practice, visualization and memory can also be improved by the use of various systems of meditation, and visualization.

There are three steps to successful consciousness development in certain East Indian systems. First is concentration, second is meditation, and third is contemplation. Concentration is the mental action of focusing absolutely on one thing or idea. Meditation is concerned with seeing and the systematic exploration of each aspect or part of an object or idea. Contemplation delves deeper into the processes of concentration and meditation and emerges with creative and intuitive answer to a question.

Generally, people don't realize that they have been in a state of contemplation until this contemplative state gives way to consciousness and the realization of self and surroundings. Contemplation is a trance-like state, a state I often participate in while reading a good novel, following the characters as if I were invisibly participating in their lives. Contemplation often results in sudden awareness of revelations which uncover some correlation or relationship between thought and substance.

Just as a note, Zen meditation can also be dangerous in noisy areas, I had a heart palpitation-heart skipped a beat when a truck went bye while doing this meditation in a noisy area. An expert should be consulted before you use this technique.

Breathing is an important part of the yoga system of meditation. When we take in a breath, we are taking in the energy of Prana, which revitalizes the blood and, in turn, the body. Deep breathing allows for more oxygen intake and therefore less strain on the circulatory system. More oxygen is delivered to the brain and vital organs, which contributes to greater physical and mental health (of course breathing in western religious tradition is referred to

71

as the Holly Spirit. You take into your body the Divine feminine energy of God; you take in Devine Inspiration to heal yourself and deliver your consciousness from any problem you have in your life.)

Several yoga breathing exercises can be taught in the classroom. Have the children slowly breathe in enough air to fill their entire chest cavity. Ask them to hold in the air for four counts and then very slowly exhale. Repeat this exercise two or three times.(watch closely that the students don't become dizzy.)

Another breathing exercise for energizing the mind and body (is often referred to as, the breath of fire) is accomplished as follows. Ask the children to stand and bend over with hands on their knees. Have them breathe in and out by sucking in and forcing out their stomachs. This exercise should eventually be done as fast as possible, but start out slowly and build up gradually each session. You may want to make a contest out of this to see who can make their stomach go in and out the fastest; let the kids vote. This exercise brings prana (life force) into the body energizing the brain and the body.

Don't let the children overdo this exercise; they may hyperventilate and feel dizzy. Should this happen, have the child who experiences the dizziness sit down immediately and place the head between the knees. Explain to the children what is happening within the body of the child who is experiencing the dizziness. You may want to describe cellular oxygen and carbon dioxide exchange and initiate a discussion on the circulatory system.

There are many other types of meditation and associated exercises, most of which are rich in mind activity, show various states of consciousness, or give glimpses of the mediator in other times and places. Likewise, there are various ways of stimulating meditation. In Zen meditation the visualization of numbers and counting while breathing are practiced for meditation; members of E.S.T. (Erhardt Seminar Training) use visualization, a room, and two close friends to encourage meditation; transcendental meditation uses an inner mantra or word to focus the mediator's concentration, and so forth; there are many difference meditation processes.

Basic to all meditation, however, is the process of concentrating one's energy on an absolute focus, unlike prey which is a difference type of meditation; be still and receive inspirational thoughts; more than likely you remember things you have forgotten…because your conscious mind has put it in the recesses of your mind.

I would like to mention that Visualization is a process, in modern times, that are unlike processes used in traditional meditation. Telling a story and going on a trip lead by a facilitator seems to be a main focus. You go inside a crystal or pyramid and see details that you nominally don't focus on until you learn to create your own visualization. You take trips to creation or other planets or our own planet and feel the energy of each location. When you successfully learn to use the tool of visualization you will have spontaneous experiences that lets you no that you have interfaced with creative truth, not a predetermined thought form.(When I talk more about Remote Viewing in the ESP channel I go more into some detail used in this fairly new scientific visualization process.)

The ability to concentrate energy on a single focus depends upon the mediator's strength of will, emotional level, and the clarity of his or her visualization capacity. Although I recognize that some people don't see, just feel. Seeing with the Mind's Eye by Michael and Nancy Samuels is an excellent book for aiding development of visualization techniques. The Act of Will by Robert Assagioli is another good book for developing this technique, as well as for developing strength of will and an understanding of the emotions. Many of the concepts and techniques described in these books can be adapted to children.

A good way to have children develop an awareness of emotions is to have them role play emotional situations which might occur in their day-to-day lives or in the lives of their families and friends. Older children could be encouraged to create plays which involve them in various emotional characterizations. You might also develop an awareness of emotions by bringing to class pictures of people expressing different emotions. Have the children describe or imitate the emotions or have them look for other emotion-filled pictures in old newspapers and magazines. These activities should surely heighten the children's awareness of their own emotions and those of the people around them and may even encourage empathy and understanding.

Biofeedback is an area that is shining light on the activities of the brain. Researchers investigating brain waves are mapping the levels of consciousness and have named the various levels: alpha, beta, theta, and delta in referring to various brain wave frequencies. They have concluded that the levels of beta and alpha are conscious processes and that theta and delta are in the unconscious levels of our minds.

Alpha frequencies indicate a state of relaxation, contentment and good feeling, mind-body integration and learning; alertness and spiritual experiences. Theta and delta levels are associated with the states approaching sleep, sleeping, and dreaming consciousness. Persons under hypnosis express theta and delta levels of consciousness. Researchers are also finding that yoga and Zen masters reach theta and delta levels while meditating in states of being nearly asleep but conscious of body and mind functions and can bring themselves back up to alpha and beta states at will.

Evidence suggests that the theta-and delta levels of consciousness have no relationship to time and space.[9] These levels may be tuned into the universe at large, making it feasible to experience reincarnation as an out-of-body state, telepathy over long distances, and various other psychic phenomena. It may also be found that the three levels of Raji Yoga- concentration, meditation, and contemplation - are related to the brain wave levels of alpha, theta, and delta. In U.S. Anderson's book, "The Greatest Power in the Universe", he describes enhanced visualization of objects, also associated with yoga levels of concentration, and the effects of sessions with an alpha biofeedback machine.

1. Millay, Jean. "The Relationship Between the Synchronization ef Brain Waves and Success in Attempts to' Communicate Telepathically." Ph.D. dissertation, Humanistic Psychology Institute, San Francisco, 1978.

2. Weed, Ernest. Yoga. Baltimore, Maryland: Penguin Beeks, 1959.

3. Hills, Chris. Energy, Matter and Form. Boulder Creek, CA: University of the Trees, 1977.

---

9 Patricia! Garfield, Creative Dreaming.

DREAMS

Whenever there is a discussion on theta and delta levels of brain wave function, one of the ways to study these manifestations is through the process of dream analysis. It might be of interest to the reader to know something about dream theory and some practical uses for students.

Dreams are a fascinating result of the mind. In dreams you can meet old friends and new ones on different levels of consciousness. You can fly through the air, breathe underwater or find answers to difficult questions. Fantasies and adventures can be acted out, but the dreamer wakes in the morning all in one piece. Any and everything can be accomplished in dreams, especially by dreamers who know how to manipulate their dreams. There are many good books written on the subject of dreams that give good suggestions on how to get the most information out of dreaming. Creative Dreaming, by Patricia Garfield, is a good starting reference.

Dreaming is universal; it is repeated in every culture in the human race. Everyone has had at least one dream in their lifetime. Most of us dream regularly; scientists say we dream nightly. Some people discount dreaming as meaningless occurrences; some attach significance to them; some even base their entire way of life on dreaming. Many cultures have been built on the information gained by dream interpretations. The ancient Greeks used dreams to communicate with the gods about health problems, future omens, marriage and other concerns.

A daily ritual for the Malaysian Senois is describing their dreams. During the morning meal the oldest Senoi describe their dreams of the previous night to the youngest. The tribal members get together and discuss what is best for the entire group based on symbolic interpretations of the dreams. They have established specific methods for dealing with dream content to achieve insightful information and solutions to problems. Basically, the entire Senoi culture is centered on dreaming. There whole culture and it's future progression is determined by the interpretation of their dreams. One technique they use in their dreams is a one-up-man ship process, that lets them win in their dreams…at all costs; of course they have learned to stay conscious in their dreams to accomplish this process.

There is one aspect that is very important in the dreaming process, and that is Lucid dreaming. As mentioned above becoming conscious in your dreams, is a way of manipulating your dreams in any way you want. You can become the active participant to change the ideas that show up in your dreams. It takes a little effort to master lucid dreaming but it is not impossible. There is a good book called Lucid Dreaming by Celia Green that give you basic ideas to start the process. It is a lot of fun to learn to manipulate your dreams.

The yogis of India are able to concentrate, meditate, contemplate, and thereby reach a dreaming sleep-like state of consciousness. In this state they can shape their dreams in ways which are most beneficial to gaining knowledge and wisdom.

Dreaming may prove to be the most effective pathway to inner levels of consciousness. Researchers are finding that dreamed solutions to problems may carry over into actual waking situations. Dream control, therefore, may become a useful means of handling various problems and concerns in your life.

Achieving complete relaxation before going to sleep is the first step in dream control. A simple relaxation technique is accomplished by relaxing all major muscles in the body. While lying in bed, lift your head up so that you are looking at your toes. Hold this position for as long as possible, then relax, lowering your head slowly. Do the same thing with your arms by bringing your hands and elbows up off the bed, hold, then relax. Arch your back, hold this position, then relax. Repeat this sequence with your feet, flexing them first, then pointing them away from your body, hold and relax. Repeat these movements until you no longer feel any tension in your body.

Concentrate on controlling your dreams by commanding the unconscious through autosuggestion. Repeat out loud and to yourself dream suggestions; for example, you may want to dream about possible solutions to a pressing problem, so concentrate on all elements involved. You're looking for the best possible solution to the problem, so concentrate on that before falling asleep. Also, concentrate on staying conscious, aware of the dream while participating in it, by autosuggestion. Continue this technique several nights in a row until the dream occurs.

Parents, this technique can be used with your children every night at bedtime until your children no longer need your guidance. Talk with your children in the morning about their dreams and keep a daily record of their impressions. After a week or so, you should be able to determine any patterns or recurring dream sequences. Do this with all family members to determine group patterns as well. Always talk over dreams and decide what they mean to the individual first and then hear from others in the family. A great deal of information can be learned, many problems can be solved and new understandings can be reached by individual and group-shared interpretations of dreams.

I can best recall my own dreams by first trying to remember the underlying feeling I had while dreaming. I record this and the details of my dreams as soon as possible. I suggest that you have pencil and paper ready at your bedside for recording dreams.(unfortunately I wasn't able to patent my dream recorder).

There are many possible ways to interpret dreams. I suggest the Dreamer's Dictionary, Robinson and Corbett, as a starting point. You might also read Man and His Symbols by Carl G. Iung or Dreams: Your Magic Mirror by Edgar Cayce to give you different slants on dream interpretations. At this point there is no universal symbolism or method of interpreting dreams. As you become more familiar with different sets of symbolism, however, the validity of each will become more apparent.

What can you do with dreams in the classroom? Try asking your students about their dreams. What do they recall? Why do they think they dream? Are their dreams frightening, adventuresome, funny? Do they dream in color? And so forth. I have asked some of these questions to children as young as four years old and have always received very interesting responses. Ask younger children to draw pictures of their dreams and older children to write down their dreams and make illustrations. A few of the children may have telepathic or precognitive dreams, so familiarize the children with these terms.

Help the children become more familiar with the study of dreams. You might introduce them to some of the different interpretations and symbols of reading dreams. These discussions and drawing sessions help you know your students better as they better understand themselves, their family and surrounding.

"Creative inspiration only comes to the prepared mind of relevant facts, impressions, and ideas, " wrote Arthur Koestler, the famous writer.

WAKING DREAMS

I had a couple of friends over for dinner the other night, and one of them described her experience of a waking dream. She said that one night she woke up in the middle of the night and had developed a conscious feeling of her nine-year-old self, and at the same time she was her adult self. The adult self was explaining to her nine-year-old self a misconception she had about her father, a misconception she had held until she was thirty. She further relates that it wasn't like a dream at all, but more like reality. She couldn't tell the difference between the altered state and her real waking self. While experiencing all this, her boyfriend was asking her questions about what she was feeling and seeing during the dialect, and she was able to respond.

These types of experiences happen surprisingly often. Researchers, however, have yet to explain why or how these experiences occur; however, some information is available. Waking dreams are described very clearly in some of Jane Roberts' books (refer to bibliography).

By monitoring dream activity and keeping a record of your dreams and impressions, you should start to experience a change in your life due to an increased awareness of your dreaming self. Eventually you will understand and be able to integrate your waking self and dream self if you choose.

I started, and possibly you will, interpreting my life as I interpret my dreams by applying the techniques of dream analysis to my everyday life. I look at what happens to me and wonder why. As a result, my life has started to make more sense to me. The correlation between dreams and reality is not clearly understood. It demonstrates synchronicity, in which the link between two events that are connected through their meaning cannot be explained by cause and effect.[10] In other words, dreams may not necessarily cause an event or vice versa, but there may be some relationship which allows dreams to be understood in terms of physical reality.

MEDITATION EXERCISES

Several yoga breathing exercises can be taught in the classroom. Have the children slowly inhale enough air to fill the entire chest cavity. Ask them to hold the air in for four counts and then very slowly exhale. Repeat this exercise two or three times. Another breathing exercise for energizing the mind and body is called Fire Breathing accomplished as follows.

Ask the children to stand and bend over with hands-on their knees. Have them breathe in and out by sucking in and forcing out their stomachs. This exercise should eventually be done as fast as possible, but start out slowly and gradually build up each session. You may want to make a contest out of this to see who can make their stomachs go in and out the fastest; let the kids vote. Don't let the children overdo on this exercise; they may hyperventilate and feel dizzy. Should this happen, have the child who experiences the dizziness sit down immediately and place the head between the knees. Explain to the children what is happening within the body of the child who is experiencing the dizziness. You may want to describe cellular oxygen and carbon dioxide exchange and initiate a discussion on the circulatory system.

In order to learn meditation techniques effectively, start with an exercise to stimulate the memory and concentration for detail. Hand each child an object with small details on it (preferably tactile details). Tell them to look at each part of the object; study it for a minute. Now ask the students to pick out a detail on the object and try to visualize it in their minds. Continue this until each part has been visualized. Finally, ask your students to try and visualize the whole object containing all the details.

Now hand out paper and drawing materials and ask students to try to draw each detail as well as the whole object. A good motivation for this project is to have a free drawing time after each memory exercise. It is also a good idea to do something physical after each mediation session to bring the children back into classroom reality and relieve some of the potential restlessness that tends to accumulate during quiet periods. Any kind of movement - dance, yoga stretching exercises or outdoor play - will help to get the blood flowing and ease any restlessness and also helps them learn to ground their energies to counteract flightiness. Have the children relax afterwards if you plan to move into a study activity.

In Bulgaria at the Institute of Suggestology scientists are doing experiments with yoga relaxation techniques and suggestion. The subjects are asked to lie down on a reclining chair and are taught calming techniques. They are asked to listen to recordings of baroque music with specially dubbed-in lessons about mathematics, foreign language, or some other subject. People from ages ten to eighty were reported to have memorized a two-year course in these subjects in one short month of study, two hours a day, seven days per week. The Bulgarian researchers have had great success with this learning technique and have created the Institute

10 Jean Balen, M.D., The Tao of Psychology.

of Suggestology for furthering such studies.[11] Their work may provide a means to train the memory in order to retain all the basic information that will be needed for advancement in our fast-moving, highly technical future.

SUN VISUALIZATION

Now that you have some understanding of concentration, meditation, and contemplation, you can lead the children in basic visualization exercises. First, however, review some of the information learned in the Radionics and Aura Channel, including definitions and pictures of the aura body and etheric energy.

Have the students sit in a circle in chairs or crossed legged (lotus position) on the floor. Ask them to close their eyes and concentrate on rhythmic breathing (in 4, hold 4, out 4, repeat; or you may use up to 7 counts if your children have developed their breathing technique). The leader should make the count out loud several times to help establish a pace.

Next, the leader takes the children on a visualization trip:

"With your eyes closed, take an imagery trip down the front of your body until you arrive at your navel (belly-button); hold your concentration here for a few seconds, meditating on that point; visualize it, feel it. Now, travel about three inches (or three fingers) down from your navel, to the lower abdominal area; go inside your body to the center; see within the black space a sphere of bioplasmic energy like a small ball of light, off in the distance growing bigger and brighter as you watch it come closer and closer, until it is right in front of you, pulsating and flowing around itself.

Put your hand into the huge ball of light and feel the warmth around your hand and arm; it feels good. Now, move toward the great ball of plasmic energy and totally merge your whole body with the ball of light. You can't see anything but bioplasmic energy, warm and comforting, flowing around your body.

You are relaxed now, totally at peace with yourself, rested, and feeling good. Now start moving back out of the energy ball, still feeling the warmth, seeing it just in front of you and gradually sinking away, getting smaller and smaller until it disappears into dark space again. Now you are outside of your body again in front of your lower abdominal area, just below your navel. Slowly, move back up your body to your middle eye, the place between your eyebrows. This visual journey is over, and everyone can now open their eyes. I have had great success with this visualization with children.

At this point, stop and have a discussion of what was experienced during the visualization.

Write the discussion down or tape it. The children will probably have some very interesting stories to tell. Drawing or painting is a place to continue this activity in creative expression. After the drawing, discussion, or visualization session, you may want to do some stretching exercises or yoga to totally bring everyone back into classroom reality. Exercise is important if you have a student that seems slightly mesmerized or slow to react. Some children become

---

11 Ostrander, S. and Schroeder, L. Psychic Discoveries Behind the Iron Curtain, p. 289.

locked into the visualization process, but exercise will bring them right out of this psychological dilemma.

GROUNDING EXERCISES

At this point I would like to introduce grounding exercises to help students readjust fully to everyday waking consciousness. Grounding is term used in meditation (visualization) to signify the balancing or centering of consciousness within the center of the body on the etheric level of consciousness. From this location, it is assumed that the process of grounding pulls consciousness back into equilibrium through the autonomic nervous system.

One such exercise is to visualize a green translucent pole descending down the center of the earth. Concentrate on moving the energy from around the body upward, in a heart shape, in an arc over the head, and then down the green pole through the center of the body. The energy then passes all the way through the body to the bottom of the feet, dissipating into the earth and further anchoring into the center of the earth. Within a few minutes, the students grounding should feel more emotionally balanced and stabilized.

Another simple grounding exercise is to attach light beams to the bottom of the feet and visualize them as cords reaching down to the center of the earth. The flow of energy can be visualized as moving down through the body, through the feet, down the cords to the center of a ball of light at the center of the earth; you don't have to go their but send the energy beams there.

SUN TO AURA VISUALIZATION

Another visualization is to see the ball of light (described in the preceding) as originating from the lower abdominal area, small at first and growing gradually as it emerges, enveloping the entire body and expanding into a large bubble the size of the entire room and sinking back to the same spot again. Use bubblegum pink with bubble image and move around the circle you radiating each person in the group and see if you can detect the colliding of any noxious energy from each individual.

Children open their eyes and see if the mood is different and children are happy and content. Use Imagination to guide the children in this creative visualization. Help them impress this image in their minds by creating additional pictures - make reference to the color, smell or sound of this bubble. Use creative language to stimulate the children visually. Have each child try to feel the energy around his/her body during this visualization. After they have some experiences of their own, it will be easier for them to imagine their own pictures. It is a good idea to write these ideas down or encourage the kids to write them down as soon as possible, so as not to forget the images.There are many types of grounding and" visualization exercises. They can be good methods to bring both teacher and children to greater balance and harmony.

COLOR VISUALIZATION

This is a good beginning technique to introduce students to visualization by using color. Depending on the weather conditions of the day, say it is very cold that day, you can use orange to bring up the energy level of the students, making them warmer. Start with breathing exercises to slow down their metabolisms and hopefully get into an Alpha state of brainwave consciousness. Using blue for a hot day creates a cooling sensation. Experiment with different colour to see what experiences you can bring out from your consciousness. Experiments have been done to see what effects they have on individuals in a group setting. As one example Red has a very unpleasant effect with a prickly uncomfortable effect.

Now, start by having students visualize a ball of orange light at your solar plexus expanding it out to encompass the entire body. Concentrate on the color orange for at least 60 seconds or more. Then shrink the orange energy ball back down to the solar plexus to a dot, bringing them out slowly from the visualization. Now have the students talk about the sensations they felt while concentrating on the color orange.

ASTRAL BODY MEDITATION

The astral body (discussed in detail in the Aura section) is the second layer of the aura. It outlines the physical body and consists of light energy. The astral body can be experienced by a visualization process in which one can see the body as an image of total light, apart from the physical body but resembling it. The astral body can be visualized in many different positions and places, as varied as the potential positions and places occupied by the physical body.

Have your students visualize the astral body in various positions. Ask them to try to see it turning around, gradually gaining speed, faster and faster, until its form can no longer be delineated. , After a few minutes, stop and ask the children to describe their experiences and give their impressions of their visualizations. As the children do more and more meditation and visualization, they will come to the point where they may want to make up their own visualizations.

This is just the type of reaction desired because it indicates that the children are beginning to realize the power of their minds and the reality of the astral body. If you want to know more about meditation with children, look for Meditation with Children by Deborah Rozman (refer to the bibliography). I have suggested only a few of the countless concentration, meditation, and contemplation exercises that will aid in the understanding of visualization. Refer to the bibliography for references to other exercises or make up your own.

CRYSTAL GUIDE VISUALIZATION

Probably the best contemporary meditation used is the "personal guide visualization."

This visualization was used by Werner Erhardt of EST, Stewart Emory of Actualizations and by Lifesprings of Los Angeles, as well as other spiritual groups. There are various crystal groups using this technique in their own versions. Experts like Dale Walker use this technique in visualization with crystals. (Referred Radionic channel for preparing a crystal for use in meditation).

The first step is to hold a crystal in the left hand (most people feel that the left hand is more receptive than the right, but that depends on whether you are right handed or left handed). While closing the eyes, visualize going inside the crystal, spiraling down into the crystal relaxing deeper and deeper sensing the feeling of the walls, the way it smells, listen for sound, and look to see what it looks like when moving through each sense. You're experiencing the crystal core now. Experience exactly how the crystal feels with your consciousness.

Next, visualize clearly a set of chairs set up inside the crystal room. See guides sitting in each of the chairs. Try to communicate with them, saying hello to each individual to determine if they respond. If communication is established with one or all of them, continue talking to them, asking questions, listening for answers.

If there is difficulty in seeing and communicating with them, use imagination to fill in the holes in the picture. If asking them their names brings no response, then make up their names and any other details that are needed to keep a pictorial dialogue going. Soon after regular visualization sessions, with repeated practice you will at some point hear/feel your guides talking to you. Distinguishing the difference between what makes up imagination and the information received from guides is not as hard as one may think. Intent (will) seems to be the driving force behind imagination, which is the difference between communication with guides and imagination. Guide communication seems to come to mind when no effort is put forth. If attention is given to inner thoughts, then you will be able to distinguish the difference between talking with guides and the interjection of your own thoughts. Keeping a diary of communication with guides and interjections of imagination is helpful. It is not an impossible task to create a format for distinguishing the reality of communications from guides, if there is belief in the possibility.

The second time I communicated with my guides, they told me their names and I found out that I really had eight guides instead of two. My crystal environment really changed. It became a golden cathedral with a crystal in the center. There is an elevator that I ride up to my healing room. This aspect of my visualization was stimulated through the first crystal group I attended. Crystals really enhance the visualization process.

The leader led me in a visualization to a healing room, where specific characteristics about the room emerged as I progressed. As an example, I saw a hand carved healing table on a pedestal with a skylight-filtering in the night sky. I perceived French provincial chairs in my healing room. Other students in the group saw different types of chairs, no two were the same. Ask your students what type of chairs they would see in their mediation room; draw a picture of your chair.

At times this process of creative mind will show up in your meditations as you practice on a regular basis. This is another characteristic that distinguishes imagination from creative thought, from yourself and other conscious beings.

OVER SOUL VISUALIZATION

- Lets start by closing our eyes and take a couple of deep breaths;

- Now, move down the front of your body and at the solar plexus go inside, deeper and deeper into the hyperspace;

- Feel the earth beneath your feet and smell the fragrant flowers and plants growing in the garden as you land on the planet; as a multicolored shimmering aura around the plants and trees pierce through the light fog;

- You start to perceive a faint human figure walking through the fog with millions of faceted diamonds- all over its body;

- As it walked through the fog reflecting and refracts light in all directions, a beam of light comes your way, anticipate first focusing on the beam, then go inside the beam ("as they say you are the light of the candle"), go deeper and deeper and you will feel the over-soul raising its energy, arching your back and throwing back your head you will experience a rushing sensation that will make its way through the crown chakra; you can continue flowing this energy up to the eight chakra, the Christ center if you want to; and even further into hyperspace if you want.

- I use raising the over-soul first, before I bring down the atomic energy exercise to connect the two meditations together. But you can use them individually if you want.

- And finally keep practicing if you're not successful, you'll master the technique eventually in your own time-don't give up; persevere.

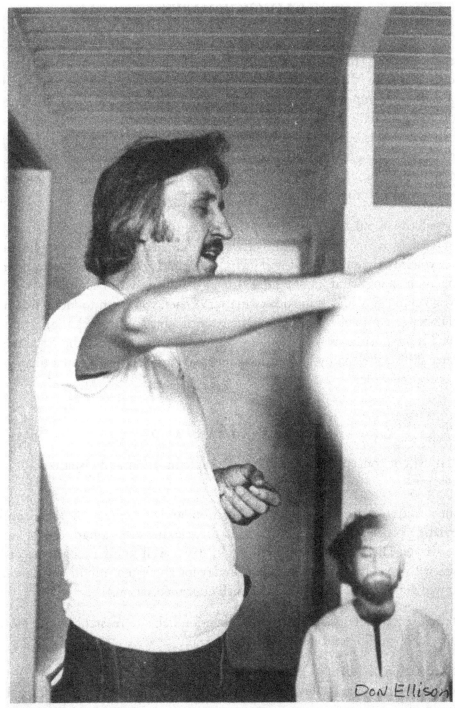

Dael Walker

Don Ellison
Iasos

CHECKPOINTS

One of the most important things to master in meditation is visualization; the better one learns to visualize, the easier it is to manipulate daily events. If your students have trouble visualizing, consult Seeing With the Mind's Eye by Mike and Nancy Samuels, which will give you some helpful suggestions on improving visualization techniques. Also, have your students practice visualization exercises daily and, gradually, they should improve. Children tend to be better at visualizing than adults because their minds are often freer from historical distractions and they tend to be more imaginative and creative. Use quartz crystals to enhance visualization. And this visualization process is a little different than I discussed in this section staying true the contemporary use of this technique in the many groups I've been in over the years.

If you have trouble manipulating your Dreams, start a concentrated effort to read everything you can on the subject. I have included some excellent beginning references in the bibliography. This submergence you into the subject that will focus your mind and create a better understanding of dream phenomenology and its potential. Lucid dreaming will become second nature to you when you submerge yourself in subject matter. When you learn to lucid dream you will take a crucial step in your ability to manipulate your dreams and start changing your waking life in a much more positive way. When you master this process it is the first step towards learning other skills as telepathy in dreaming and astral projection. Keep a diary of all year dreams whenever possible.

POTENTIALITIES

The potential uses of concentration, meditation, contemplation and visualization in day-to-day living are great:

1. Concentration, meditation , contemplation and visualization are useful for alleviating pressures; they could be used for relaxing after a hard day of work or play. (if you fall asleep during meditation, try a well known technique of lying down with your feet higher than your heart for about ten minutes; set an alarm. You will feel refreshed and you can finish your meditation.)

2. After an emotional upset, creative visualization helps to reestablish an emotional and psychological balance or well being.

3. Concentration, mediation , contemplation and visualization improve one's ability to examine the details and consequences of problems, there by yielding better solutions.

4. Practicing various meditation techniques allows for the realization of the various psychic abilities.

5. Positive feelings increase as individuals understand the increased control they will have over their lives.

6. Crucial decisions and directed actions become much clearer and easier to accomplish since intuition and intellect are stimulated by meditative and visualization processes.

7. The development of memory is enhanced by meditation and visualization.

8. The creation of future realities in your life can be made possible through visualization.

9. Controlling physical processes within the body can be accomplished through meditation and visualization, thereby making you a healthier person.

10. Visualization has already impacted the sports world, used by athletics to improve their performance.

11. Dream analysis will be a valuable tool for you and your children to understand and experience your lives in more depth - individually and as a group. I'm sure you will become closer in your communication and understanding of each other.

12. In the future, dream analysis may be used as a way of gaining information relevant to curriculum development. 12 Presently, many psychologists use dream analysis to diagnose and treat different problems.

13. for very young children, we may need to rely on dream interpretations to gain insight into their world.

SUMMARY/CONCLUSIONS

Concentration/Meditation/Contemplation & Visualization Concentration, meditation, and contemplation explores the process of meditation from the perspective of the Raja Yoga system and other types of approaches. Research about meditation and relevant studies done on brain waves are included, so that you will have a better grasp of how the mind works from a scientific perspective. This information is in a practical format so that children will understand other focuses of the mind.

The process of visualization is becoming a necessity in the complicated society we live in today. In a technical and rapidly developing informational-based society where information is accelerating, our accommodation operations are at their maximum. We are beginning to explore and transcend our limits of how the mind works. We have the tools within ourselves to make changes in our mood, body processes, and brain patterns by experiencing the creative aspects of the visual mind. We are slowly observing the causal relationships of the mind and emotions on the physical body.

There is now relevant research which indicates that the mind does interact positively and negatively with physical form. This effect has great ramifications for our attitudes toward sickness and health and the learning process in general.

In this publication I try and move beyond our current understanding of how the mind works. Exercises are planned so that they stimulate live experiences in each individual, provoking thoughts of reflection. Being multi-dimensional personalities, we perceive change and integrate information related to the individual aspects that make up our total beings. This is a holistic idea that will become more familiar to you as you read through the other channels in this book.

We are spirit in a physical body, not a body containing a spirit. We are universal beings, both local and non locally as quantum physics would tell us. Said another way, our consciousness is not limited to the third dimension reality. We can perceive the outer edges of the universe or move forwards and backwards in time or move completely outside of time. Our consciousness is unlimited. We are in the body of God.

Allstrom, Elizabeth. Let's Playa Story. New York: The Friends Press, 1957.

Alper, Frank Dr. Arizona Metaphystal Society 3639 E. Clarenden, Phoenix, Az. 85018

Andersen, U.S; The Greatest Power in the Universe. Los Angeles: Atlantis University, 1971.

Assagioli, Roberto. The Act of Will. Baltimore, MD: Penguin Books, Inc., 1973.

Burger, Isabelle. Creative Playmaking. New York: A.S. Barnes and Co., 1950.

Griffith, Fred. Meditation Research: Its Personal and Social Implications in Frontiers of Consciousness. New York: Avon Books, 1975.

Greer, Steven MD. "Hidden Truth Forbidden Fnowledge-2006, Crossing Point PO Box 265, Crozet, VA. 22932

Hills, Christopher. Energy, Matter and Form, Boulder Creek, CA: University of the Trees, 1977.

Himalayan International Institute of Yoga, Science and Philosophy, The Swami and Sam, Glenview, IL, 1976 (yoga exercise story book for children). Hodgson, Joan. Hello Sun. Hampshire, VT:

The White Eagle Publishing Trust, 1972-1975 (story about another reality during sleep that can be used as an exercise in concentration, meditation and contemplation).

Ostrander, S., and Schroeder, L., Psychic Discoveries Behind the Iron Curtain. Englewood Cliffs, N.J.: Prentice-Hall, 1970.

Redfield, James "The Twelfth insight" Grand Central publishing New York, N.Y. 10017 2011

Roberts, Jane. Emir's Education in the Proper Use of Magical Powers. New York: Delacorte Press/ Eleanor Friede Press, 1979 (excellent book on fantasies and out of body experiences for children)

.Rozman, Deborah, Meditation with Children, Boulder Creek, CA: University of the Trees, 1975 (good meditational exercises for children).

Samuels, Mike, and Samuels, Nancy, Seeing with the Mind's Eye. New York: Random House, 1975.

Toffler, Alan. Future Shock. New York: Bantam Books, 1970. Ward, Winifred, Playmaking with Kindergarten to Junior High. New York: Appleton-CenturyCrofts, 1957.

Wilson, Stuart & Prents, Joanna "ATLANTIS and the New Consciousness, OZARK MOUNTAIN Publishing PO Box 754, Huntsville, AR 72740 (Dolores Cannon-hypnosis)

Publications

Canfield, Jack. "Internal Wisdom: Teaching with Guided Fantasy," Association for Humanistic Psychology Newsletter, December 1979, p. 14.

Linden, W. "The Relation Between the Practicing of Meditation by School Children and their Levels of Field Dependence-Independence, Test Anxiety and Reading Achievement," Ph.D. dissertation, New York University, 1972. 73

Dream Books

Assagioli, Robert. MD. The Act of Will, Baltimore, Viking Press, 1973.

Bolen, Jean. The Tao of Psychology, New York: Harper and Row, 1979.

Faraday, Ann. Dream Power. Berkeley, CA: Berkeley Publishing Corporation, 1972.

Garfield, Pat. Creative Dreaming, New York: Ballantine Books, 1974.

Green, Celia. Lucid Dreams, New York, NY: Mutual Books, 1980.

Roberts, Jane. Seth Speaks. New York: Prentice-Hall, Inc., 1972.

Adventures in Consciousness, New York: Prentice-Hall, Inc: 1975.

Psychic Politics, New York: Prentice-Hall, Inc., 1976. The Unknown Reality, New York, NY: Prentice-Hall, Inc., 1977.

The Nature of Personal Reality, New York, NY: Prentice-Hall, Inc., 1974.

Robertson, L., and Corbett, T. Dreamer's Dictionary, New York, NY: Warner Books, 1974.

Sechrist, Elsie. Dreams, Your Magic Mirror: Interpretations of Edgar Cayce. New York, NY: Warner Books, 1974.

Silva, Jose, The Silva Mind Control Method. New York, NY: Pocket Books, 1977.

Magazines:

Bolen, Jean. "Synchronicity, Jung and the Self," New Realities Magazine. 3: 17-21, 1979.

Huyghe, Patrick. "Exploring the World of Dreams," Psychic Magazine. 7:22-25, 1977.

Schumann Resonances and Human Psychobiology, Nexus Magazine volume 10- # 3 April – May 2003, PO Box 30, Mapleton Q ID 4560 Australia 74

Mandalas

MANDALAS

Let's talk about another method of getting in touch with your inner self, moving beyond the five physical senses to the inner senses of intuition, and other psychic sense.

Mandalas have been used for centuries in various oriental cultures and by at least two groups in the west, the American and the Central American Indians. The oriental philosophy says that the true self resides within the human body in a balanced center of energy (contrast Hermetic philosophy, which names the spirit or energy source as transcendental). In order to get in touch with that energy, a mandala is useful.

Basically, the principle of the Mandala as described in oriental culture is that of a map or representation of the true self at the center of the being. The person seen in flesh is not the true personality; rather, the center of being - the eternal light - is the true personality which can send out feelers to explore the three-dimensional world and lead to spiritual enfoldment. One's center is his or her source of unlimited energy and vitality existing outside of time and space. All the knowledge in the universe can be attained by getting in touch with one's source. Concentrating on a mandala is the act of getting in touch with one's center self.

The mandala may also help to bring to the forefront latent problems or questions we have trouble handling. I have had some junior high and high school students say they were able to recall hidden problems and resolve them by concentrating on a mandala. I had similar experiences while practicing in the Nichren Shoshu Buddhist group.

Mandalas seem to be universal, according to Rhoda Kellogg and Carl Jung. Rhoda Kellogg says, "Mandalas provide evidence they are perceived by children long before the first diagrams are made. Mandalas are significant not only as part of the sequence of child's art development, but also as a link between the art of children and the art of adults."

Carl Jung in Man and His Symbols relates that, "The mandala restores a previously existing order, serves the creative purpose of giving expression and form to something that does not exist, something new and unique.

I, as others, feel that certain people are more receptive to subtle radiations than others. These people, called psychics, are very sensitive people who possess what historically has been labeled a sixth sense. The basis of the sixth sense, I feel, is the ability to focus one's thoughts on a desired point or place in order to feel subtle radiations. I'm sure that many of you have experienced sixth sense events. For example, many of you have probably felt the presence of someone behind you before turning around and meeting their gaze or have had a strong feeling that an event was sure to happen before it did in fact take place. Opening yourself up to experiencing the life force energy is the first step in developing E.S.P, clairvoyance, telepathy or psychokinesis.

In the Seth Materials by Jane Roberts Seth makes a convincing analogy when he says that consciousness is like a flashlight being pointed in the direction of solutions to a question or problem. Your subconscious scans the environment for possible answers and relays the information to you. If you are sensitive to its activities, you will benefit from the alternatives it offers.

1. Kellogg, Rhoda. Analyzing Children's Art. Palo Alto, CA: Mayfield Publishing Co., 1969•70, p. 65.

2. Jung, Carl. Man and His Symbols. New York: Dell Publishing Co., 1972, p. 267. pg. 76

This same process becomes more and more evident in the study of radionics. Understanding the principle of focusing or resonance is a step closer to receiving and/or transferring information over multiple frequency channels, whether it be from a human being or from an electronic device. This process takes different forms in different disciplines.

The term resonance is a term used in electronics. It is defined as the principle that helps energy flow through a wire and determines how much flow will occur; the components of a circuit that are balanced at a focus point. Webster's defines it as the greatest flow of current of a certain frequency.

In the East Indian sutra of Pantajali, I found terminology explaining the process of focusing. Dharma means concentration, binding or holding one's consciousness at a single point of the mind, at the physical energy centers of the body, the heart center, the navel center, or concentration on an object separate from the body. Dharma is also described as the creative power of centering one's self or consciousness at the balance center of the body. Dancers know this point as the center of balance, which is in the lower abdominal area between the front and back of the body. If ever I start to lose my balance I can regain it by imagining a central line through my body, thereby collecting all consciousness at that point. This same principle also works to correct dizziness and is used in judo to resist a fall or throw. Collecting consciousness at the balance point, focusing, is not known to a large degree in our culture, but it is an important principle in eastern religious groups.

The other side of focusing, falling off center, is better known by the Western culture as emotional trauma. One of the ways trauma is combated in Eastern religious groups is through centering. In Japanese Buddhism one principle from the Mahayana Sutra is "Kyo-chi-Myo-go, " meaning the oneness between subject and object. It involves psychic focusing to integrate animate and inanimate objects.

For example, the Buddhist disciple worships the Buddha, a symbol of enlightenment by integration of himself with the symbol. Everything they do, their dress, their mannerisms, and their environment reflect the personal integration with the deity, and their spirit becomes one with it. In Mahayana Buddhism, The Gohonzon is a scroll that embodies the life and consciousness Buddha. The soul of the Buddha is encompassed in the script written on the sacred scroll, the Gohonzon. After four and a half years of chanting to the Gohonzon, my soul spirit was interfaced with the symbol of the deity.

Soon, interesting things started happening… the Gohonzon started to glow a golden color that emanated out from this scroll, and enveloped me in the soft warm light (life force) that made me feel powerful and content at the same time.

Of course, other things I like to call the normal things happened, receiving what I chanted for, getting out of the draft in the late 60s, the Vietnam war, after chanting all night, and a couple of four hour stints at the community center, providing me with a free pass to continue my college education at San Francisco State Uni.; I didn't have to report to the induction center that next Monday after a couple of phone calls to the induction centers, that was tenuous at best, and some more rigorous chanting for another hour in the S.D.S center.

But the real benefits, for me, were caught in the subtleties of spiritual and psychic experiences… the metaphysical realm.

There was one experience that I remember when my father brought home his girlfriend (he was living with me at the time in a small flat in Haight-Ashbury). Having a few too many drinks, they clung to each other like two lovebirds, while I continued chanting to the Gohonzon in the other room. The golden light was emanating, and I felt strong and illuminated as I sat in front of the personification of the Buddha. I felt my father's friend eyeing me through the crack in the door as I recited the Lotus Sutra (they left shortly after that, not wanting to disturb my chanting anymore, I assumed).

The next day, Dad called me and wanted me to go over to his friend's house. She said she wanted to talk with me about something. My father said his goodbyes and left, and I stayed with his stunning girlfriend until the next day. She moved to the closet to pull out something special. Intuitively turning around, I saw that she was holding a beautiful hand-painted (Eastern) Indian oil lamp. Its colors of bright orange and blue with little female dancing

95

figures in black silhouette, was a stunning piece of handicraft that she had brought back from India.

She said, "I want to give you this oil lamp because of what I saw while you were praying last night. While you were praying, "I saw a large semi-translucent illuminated being standing behind you with his hand on your shoulders". That's why we left so suddenly last night – we didn't want to disturb your sacred time, but I was impressed by what I saw." I thanked her very much for celebrating a significant aspect of my spiritual life.

I still have this oil lamp after more than 25 years. It is one of my prized possessions. I now have a few artifacts that I have collected over the years expressing other spiritual experiences. Of course, there are other experiences from which I have no artifacts, but that's okay – I still have valued experiences chronicled in my spiritual note book.

At the DeLaWarr Laboratories in London, researchers use focusing principles by charting the auras around the body with high frequency energy oscillators. T.G. Hieronymus-mentioned in the radionic channel in his patent on detecting various atoms used a circular copper coil as a resonator. He stated that his coil will still work the same if coil was drawn in pen or pencil on a piece of paper. The circuit acts as a visual resonance frequency, a mandala of sorts. A circle, spiral or conical coil are used as resonance centers.

Basically, mandalas are balanced resonance symbols. The most basic mandala is simple a circling coil spiraling from inside out.

Mandalas are balanced resonancesymbols. The most basic mandala is a simple circling coil spiraling from inside out. There are other shapes which are balanced, like the square, circle, or diamond which can be divided into equal parts. In the Indian and Oriental cultures each of these divisions contain representations of human, animal, vegetable, mineral and universal symbols of mankind. They often represent integration principles, such as God to man, Yin and Yang, good and bad, man and woman. There are as many different ways of making a mandala as there are ideas.

GOD'S EYE MANDALA

The God's Eye developed by the Mexican Indians is one of the simplest mandalas to make. Give students two round dowels about 1 & half feet long and some string. Also put out colored yarn on a table for all the students to use. Take two sticks and demonstrate to the children how to make a frame for the mandala by crossing the sticks and tying them together at the intersection. Now take a piece of lavender yarn and tie it to one of the sticks close to the intersection point and wind the yarn over, under and around each stick, sliding it close to the center. Continue winding until you have about a 2" width. Tie off the yarn on the backside of the mandala and start the next color, dark purple.

Continue adding each color in sequence from light to dark, two shades for each color: lavender, dark purple, light blue, dark blue, light green, dark green, light yellow, dark yellow, light orange, dark orange, light red, and dark red. The colors are arranged in this order so they will demonstrate the colors of the chakras (energy centers within the bqdy) to make a two dimensional design representing three dimensional reality.

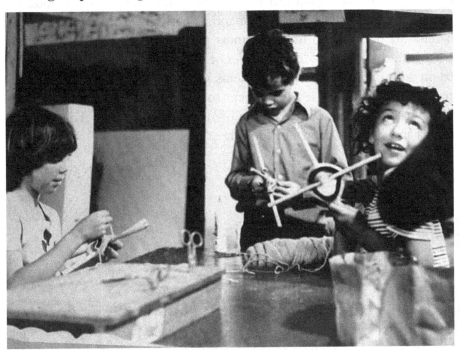

Let's take the human body diagram with the chakras and auras drawn in. In the Hermetic or Indian system the crown chakra is the highest center of energy and correlates to shades of purple. If we take a view of the human body from above, then we see the crown chakra as a dot in the center, with the aura appearing in concentric bands around the dot. This is a representation of the mandala depicted in various Eastern and Mexican Indian cultures. Now the crown becomes the center in the top view of the human body. Looking down on the crown chakra, the same pattern as the God's Eye mandala is evident, with lavender at the center and the other aura colors concentric around the lavender.

The three-dimensional aura and the two-dimensional mandala are actually identical, except that our perception often distinguishes between them because of their different dimensionality and composition. If we clear our traditional understanding of the aura and the mandala, we will understand that the colors of the aura resonate to the colors in the mandala and transfer energy at the chakras. If you concentrate on the mandala, you should feel the corresponding energy of your chakras; specifically, you might feel energy descending down your back, giving you a shiver. If this doesn't happen to you after a few minutes, you will need to concentrate on opening each center with chakra meditation. If you practice long enough, you will surely have the pleasure of feeling this energy. I will add that it is my belief that this energy is actually the manifestation of God himself, herself, or itself (depending on your concept of a god).

Jose Arguelles, in his book, Mandala, relates the mandala to a more universal concept than that of a transcendent god. He convincingly shows us that mandalas are a basic fabric of nature, like atoms are to a molecule. The vast array of patterns found in the natural world can be reduced to basic shapes of the mandala; they show themselves openly as geometric patterns of snowflakes, crystal formations, marine life, plant structure, as well as man, and are all examples of this possibility.

Finding mandala patterns is a good learning activity. Have your students look in books, in nature, around the house, and so forth, for mandala patterns. Turn this task into a game or contest, whereby the person who finds the most patterns is the winner and is allowed, for example, to be the next class president or leader of the mandala game. Another project that I have worked on with junior high school students is to have them draw their own mandalas. Ask them to draw and paint or use colored pens to fill in the details. My students have come up with some outstanding mandala patterns of their personal lives. You can often learn a variety of things about your students by looking at their drawings.

Mandalas from Mill Valley middle school students

After the students finish making their mandalas, have each one find a surface upon which he or she can lean their mandala and where they can comfortably sit in front of it. Ask each child to look into the center of their mandala and stare without blinking. At the same time, put on a record such as Insider by Paul Horn, Zen Mediation by Tony Scott or try one of the environmental albums produced by Syntonic Research, Incorporated, They have titles such as Wood Masted Sailboat and Country Stream which suggest the sounds of the scenes recorded on cassette or CD. After five minutes of listening to the records or CD and concentrating on the mandala, stop the exercise and discuss each child's concentration experiences.

It would be a good idea after every concentration session to have the children draw what they saw and keep a record of the images. You may want to take photographs of the children's pictures. And, if you have enough time , ask the students to pick a problem they are having and while they are concentrating on the mandala see if they can come up with an solution to their problem.

Another exercise might be to make a group mandala. The mandala on the first page in this chapter is an example of one produced in my classes. Draw a large circle about four feet in diameter with two concentric circles inside, approximately one and three feet in diameter, respectively. Now ask everyone to draw within the circles either themselves or a friend doing something in the room. Have them draw and color in the whole mandala. This may take several art periods to complete. Put the finished group mandala on the wall.

After trying these mandala tasks, you may want to have the students continue experimenting. This is something you should discuss with the children. Give them a choice in what they want do, whether or not they should continue working with the mandalas - because if their interest isn't great enough, these experiences will not yield worthwhile results. It has been shown in every area of education that learning is enhanced if students are highly motivated or interested in the subject they are studying.Try these activities the next day maybe week.

In Ram Das's book, "Seed", there is a large unfolding four-foot wall mandala that can be used for meditation (refer to Bib.). His book also contains a poignant collection of photographs perforated along the borders which can be punched out and used. The photographs span a whole history of mankind, including many photos of our own country up through the late 60s. These would be great photographs to show and discuss with the children. They contain such a variety of images that they lead the unconscious and conscious mind into experiencing cultures, philosophies and time periods, in some cases, different from our own.

The color wheel with an electric motor, described in the Aura channel, could be used as an electric mandala, as could an old washing machine motor and the group mandala. Children from La Conte elementary school in San Francisco had fun with the motorized mandala by taking crayons and holding them in contact with the cardboard wheel, thereby creating an additional mandala design.

Another possibility for a motorized mandala would be one made from an old record player turntable (look in Salvation Army Stores or garage sales) which could be used as the base of a turning mandala. Simply have students cut out cardboard circles and color in a design or squirt different colour on the cardboard.

CHANTING

A relationship can be woven between Chanting and Mandalas. There are hundreds of Buddhist sects that use chanting with mandalas. They utilize manta sounds to ascend their consciousnesses into new levels of awareness. In the past I have been a member of a Buddhist group. For nearly five years I chanted morning and evening prayers and recited the Lotus Sutra. While chanting with a large group at the local community center, I was surrounded by 50 to 100 chanting members on all sides, each of us with prayer beads in hand, directing our attention to the front of the room where the sacred scroll, the symbol of enlightenment, The Gohonzon was centered. As I chanted, the cadence and measured rhythm of my voice flowed with the surrounding sea of sound until I heard a loud sound coming from one of the chanters.

Others in the room noticed the sound and turned to find its source. I, too, moved to scan the room and find the source, but suddenly I realized that the sound was emanating from me, from my mid-section, and permeating in all directions. Through my chanting I had connected with a tremendous power, an independent, full vibration separate from myself. I was just riding its wave and feeling wonderful. Was it a higher aspect of myself, my soul self that I had contacted after years of chanting or was it something else?

Since this incident I have felt this exhilaration only once, but its lasting effect certainly adds an impetus to the daily ritual of chanting. Chanting a mantra creates a wonderful feeling of tranquility in body and mind. It has little to do with visualization, as meditation; rather, chanting is an auditory feeling exercise in which the chanter listens and experiences the ebb and flow, the cadence, of his or her voice. Chanting with a group of people gives a sense of centeredness, balance, and support as the single voice blends with the sea of the group. Combined, these feelings provide a foundation for emotional, mental, and physical health.

I recall breaking my nose in wrestling that had created a large bump on the bridge of my nose. After chanting for years the bump went away not to return. The cartilage shrunk to its normal state. If I was a doctor I could probably tell you more about what happened. I think, it had to do with the air being forced through my nose from the hours of chanting.

There are many different kinds of chants. In Raja Yoga there are mantra sounds which correlate to the chakra centers and their associated colors. In this system certain sound frequencies are absorbed by the chakras which then resonate a color and sound specific to that chakra. This applies to all the body chakras except for the crown chakra, which has no associated sound, according to the Raja Yoga system. Om is the best know mantra of this system. It corresponds to the brow center chakra and resonates the color of indigo. The other mantra sounds and their associated chakra and color are as follows:

Ham, throat center, blue colors

Yam, heart center, green colors

Ram, navel center, yellow colors

Vam, lower abdominal center, orange color

Lam, base chakra, red colors

To introduce children to chanting, "Brow chakra" start with the most common mantra sound, Om. You might begin by using the cassette Induced Meditation, which is a recording of a group chanting the Om together. Ask your students to sit in a circle and hold hands. Play the cassette, then try to repeat the sounds you've all heard. Allow the chanting to proceed for 1 to 5 minutes, then stop to discuss the children's impressions. This exercise is intended to be a tension-relieving activity. It is an active transition to tranquility which is especially valuable for restless children who can't seem to settle down by simply being asked to chant (and if you've ever been with a group of eight-yearolds, you know what I mean). Sitting around and making incoherent sounds, may seem strange at first, but after a few tries you will find it quite easy and tranquil, almost natural. Try it; it's fun.

After you have asked the children to chant and discuss their experiences, try asking them to engage in something creative - painting, working with clay, writing a story - use your imagination. The chanting should have opened the brow chakra which is the body's center of intuition, wisdom and creative visions. You may want to use this chanting technique yourself at times to inspire creative lesson planning and" teaching methods.

There are many other mantras commonly chanted, for example, Nam-myo-ho-ren-ge-kyo, Krishna-krishna, and Oom-stu-gah-dya-aha-dye-ahr. Each of these mantras has a certain rhythm that must be duplicated in order to be most effective. The cadence is often rapid, with each sound pronounced carefully and clearly. In The Greatest Power in the Universe , U.S. Anderson explains that "A mantra must be chanted with rhythm, for in the end, its effectiveness depends on attunement with the pulsation of life."

In chanting Nam-myo-ho-ren-ge-kyo the end result is not to stimulate a particular part of the body (i.e. the Hindu system); rather, its goal is to attune the chanter with the life-force and knowledge of the Buddha, " Gutama"- the symbol of enlightened consciousness in the Mahayana system. No one really knows quite what that means, but that practice and commitment show the way. This system, as well as the Hindu system, is based on the law of karma.

Karma is a much misunderstood energy. Most people think it is a separate body energy specific to one's own lifetime. Actually, it is an energy, independent of time and space, associated with many reincarnated lives, the Wheel of Life. Its precepts are ancient. In the western system they made up the Law of Moses, which endured long before and up until the coming of Christ, who was to have paid for mankind's sins by his death and resurrection.

Though Christ is believed to have allayed sin, he did not destroy it. Men and women must still learn higher lessons and create their own blueprint of the life they choose. Decisions must be made at every moment based on chosen guidelines that help fulfill their separate prophesies.

In Eastern philosophy karma is looked at from the point of view of paying up for past mistakes; you mistreat someone in that lifetime and you are mistreated by someone in the next lifetime; or you are a king in one lifetime and the next lifetime you have to be a popper. In some cases you incarnate with the same person or people you mistreated last lifetime. You may switch genders or become the child or the mother that lifetime (or husband or wife) to settle the transgressions; it seems like an eye for an eye to me, the old law of Moses. This was one of the aspects of Buddhist philosophy I didn't agree with and it was one of the reasons I left the Buddhist organization.

When I became a member of The Order of Melchizideck I learned about Western religious karma (it's strange to find the same concept in Western religion) that is looked at from a slightly different perspective than Eastern karma. They feel that life is a series of learning scenarios that we choose to participate in, before reincarnating into each lifetime to learn lessons to help us develop our consciousness towards enlightenment; we are in an internal classroom returning again and again until we get the lesson right. The Old laws of Moses are cast away, because of Jesus, we have free will at every turn making us the true Gods that we really are, unlimited in our scope and expression; enlightenment is just a thought away.

CHECKPOINTS

What happens if some of your students don't have any of the potential experiences normally associated with chanting?

    a. It would be impossible not to have some kind of experience while chanting, so make sure that you and your students examine all experiences related to the chanting, even seemingly insignificant experiences.

    b. Have these students concentrate more on the chant and less on things happening around them. Persuade them not to let their minds wander from the experiences centered on the chant.

    c. Encourage your students not to worry about what people might think about them because they are trying something different. These differences are what often build a better world.

If some students are having difficulty experiencing the events associated with the mandala:

They may have a fear of letting themselves go while looking at the mandala. Have them look at the mandala and then look away if they see something they don't like or makes them fearful;

103

also remember Fear is the mind killer, don't let it influence you. Encourage them to be open, receptive, and free.

a. Let them try it another time. They may be experiencing a temporary lull in interest of something else.

b. Have a group discussion about the children's experiences to point out that there is no need to be afraid of what they might see. Tell your students that the images they see while studying the mandala are like dreams.

c. Everyone will experience something while looking at their own mandala, so even if the experience is not dramatic, tell your students it is worthwhile, since it helps them to understand their reactions and impressions.

d. Try having students look at other mandalas more than one timenb to see if there is any change in their experiences.

POTENTIALITIES

There are many potential benefits attributable to chanting. Here are just a few:

a. Chanting has a calming effect on the body and the mind.

b. It increases our auditory responses.

c. It increases energy in the body and the mind.

d. Chanting encourages group identity and a sense of centeredness when it is done in a group.

e. Chanting also creates unique sensations which are difficult to relate to except by other chanters with similar experiences.

Studying and understanding the mandala demonstrates that it has great potential. It may benefit the sick and aging by helping them get in touch with their vital energy, the energy that revitalizes the cells of the body. For that matter, it may be useful for all by activating the free energy within the body. The mandala has the potential of changing our perception, thereby releasing us from rigid psychological patterns. It can also help us see other possibilities and alternatives and facilitate changes in our self concepts and our understanding of the world .

Working with the mandala will help those who use it to become familiar with various psychic abilities. They will probably experience flashbacks to other times. Sensory awareness, understanding, knowledge, and receptivity become more acute. Individuals often experience rapid changes and flashes of color as different designs come and go. Part of this change is the result of the eye muscles changing the focus of the eyes. Learning to center oneself and reaching an equilibrium are also effects of learning to use the mandala.

SUMMARY/CONCLUSIONS

Looking at a mandala is something like traveling through a time tunnel. It moves and changes, drawing one into its center like a whirlwind of power; its power to connect with the individual's source is nothing short of miraculous.

Attempts have been made to enhance mandala patterns by adding additional movements to the optical illusions already created by the mandala. An example of this idea was the fantasmagorium mandala (a electrical/kinetic device projected on a screen) utilized at the Kahoutek Celebration in 1978 in San Francisco. This celebration was in honor of the Kohoutek Comet, said to be one of the signs of the coming new age.

More recently, Norman Miller, Mary Bedford of the Celestial Rainbow Light Company, and lasos, a new age musician, have been in the process of creating a concept called "electric alchemy." They have drawings and a philosophical "blueprint" for the construction of a healing temple, creating an architectural mandala utilizing the modem technology of light, color, and, sound for healing the human body, mind and spirit

Mandalas seem to permeate existence in some cosmic way, revealing a universal language that is just beginning to be understood. These symbols seem to move from one dimension to another, keeping intact the total context of the message incorporated in the symbol itself. 90

BIBLIOGRAPHY

Anderson, U.S. The Greatest Power in the Universe. Los Angeles, CA: Atlantis University, 1971

Arguelles, Jose and Miriam. Mandala. Berkeley, CA: Shambala Publishing Company, 1972.

Fisher, Robert. Learning How to Learn English - English Primary Schools and American Education. New York: Harcourt Brace Jovanovich, Inc., 1972.

Holt, John. How Children Fail. New York: Dell Publishing Co., 1964. Jung, Carl. Man and His Symbols. New York: Dell Publishing Co., 1972.

Kellogg, Rhoda. Analyzing Children's Art. Palo Alto, CA: Mayfield Publishing Co., 1969-70.

Millay, Jean. The Relationship Between the Synchronization of Brainwaves and Success in Attempts to Communicate Telepathically. Ph.D. dissertation, Humanistic Psychology Institute, San Francisco, CA, 1978

(electronic brainwave mandala). Piaget, Jean and Anhelder, Barbel. The Psychology of the Child. New York: Basic Books, Inc., 1969

Ram Dass. Seed. New York: Harmony Books, 1963.

Roberts, Jane. Seth Materials. New York: Bantam Books, 1970

("Inner Senses, " pp. 275-288).

Wood, Ernest. Yoga. Baltimore, MD: Pelican Books, 1959-1962.

Chanting Books.:

Hills, Chris. Energy, Form and Matter. Boulder Creek, CA: University of the Trees, 1977 .

McGrill, O. The Mysticism and Magic of India. Cranburg, NJ: A.S. Barnes and Co., Inc., 1977.

Tansley, David. The Subtle Body. London: Thames and Hudson, 1977.

Records: Syntonic Research, Inc. Environments: Induced Meditation, An Easy Method of RelieVing Tension. Disc 7. New York, 1976. 91

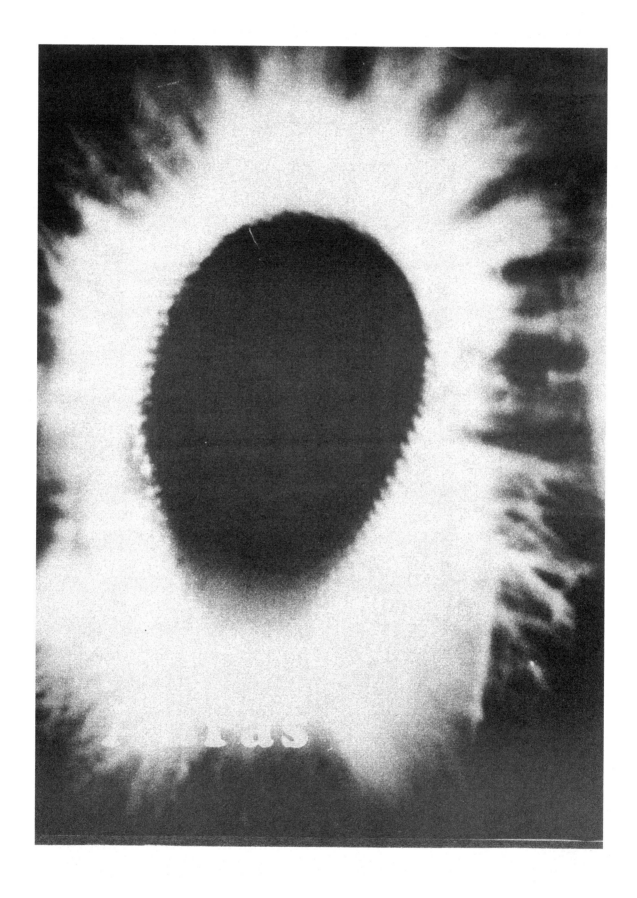

THE AURA

Within the body are meridians, different planes of electromagnetic and psychic energies vibrating throughout the body. On these planes are nodes, a point, line or region in a standing wave where there is little or no vibration. The term "node" was coined by the DeLeWarr Laboratories in England to describe these centers. Researchers there have used high frequency multioscillator devices to plot the node. They have shown that there is some form of energy that moves from node to node.

Researchers have been able to establish a resonance frequency over considerable distance by taking a cutting from a plant and rotating it to the direction that the parent plant first germinated. They are discovering that resonance has nothing to do with time or space, and, as a result, distance makes little difference in communication between plant and plant, animal and animal, and so forth. The DeLaWarr Laboratories have produced evidence that the nodes of psychic energy along the meridians of the body are the resonance centers for the Aura.

But, there are also node points in different levels of the aura that we will talk more about as our discussion of the aura proceeds through the channel. The Node center is a very important part of the discussion when we are talking about the auric field but often times this concept is not mentioned when we discuss the subtle body fields.

English etymologists generally attribute the origin of the word Aura to a Latin term meaning air, but the Hindu authorities insist that it has its origin in the Sanskrit root ar, meaning the spoke of a wheel. The human aura radiates from the center of the body like spokes of a wheel. Mystics and occultists have discussed the aura and its meaning and relevance to human well-being for centuries.

Currently, the aura is described as a fine, ethereal radiation or emanation surrounding each human being. It assumes an oval shape and shows great swirls and textures of color within the invisible ultra-spectrum of light which interrelate and communicate rational and spiritual information to those who know how to read the symbolism. In occult readings, there are many accounts of multilayered phenomenon of the aura. The aura can be broken down into different levels of consciousness, starting with the etheric body, then the astral body or emotional body, the mental body, and finally, the causal body.

ETHERIC BODY: FIRST LEVEL OF AURA

The first level of consciousness is the etheric double. All matter, whether animate or inanimate, has an etheric double which is aligned with the shape of the matter it is associated with. But in lower animals and humans this energy may be a biochemical process relying on the inner workings of the cells of the body. The etheric double is made up of energy similar to the energy in the force fields around magnets or wires carrying electrical current but is a much finer form of energy. This energy may exist in non-excited and excited states. In an excited state the energy making up the etheric body extends about two inches from its associated matter. Historically, the etheric double has been described in various terms.

Arthur Doyle, the author of Sherlock Holmes novels and a spiritualist for many years, describes the etheric body or ectoplasm, as he calls it, as a substance similar to ductile dough. He says that it is composed of numerous ectoplastic threads of various thicknesses and shapes. One of the most interesting phenomenon of the etheric body, as it is known today, is that it consists of a widely expandable membrane, with fringes and tucks, resembling a net and very similar to Doyle's description. Doyle's information is derived from his own psychic observations of mediums in trance; of which he wrote a book called "Spiritualism".

The aura is very pliable and has a direct connection with mind.This concept also expresses these charactistics in other aspects of the the auric fields. The mind manipulates the auric ectoplasm – as you direct your thoughts, you can expand and stretch it or contract it, and use it as Don Juan (the sorcerer that Carlos Castaneda used as his mentor in the many books he wrote on occultism) did when he would moved across a waterfall, stretching his aura like long tentacles or arms to move along slowly to the other side.

Or the contemporary magician David Blaine who levitates a foot off the ground, using his aura to lift himself off the ground, focusing the energy of the pineal gland in the brain that creates a special resonating oscillation. This is reminiscent of the research in the 1970s that studied psychics who could suspend objects in the air using the bioplasmic energy between their fingers. Other Soviet PK psychics were said to gyrate the ectoplasm of their aura to a high level of pulsation to be able to suspend and move objects in the air and across a table.

The aura expands and contracts involuntarily when we are happy and joyful, and contracts when we are afraid or fearful. Citing various psychics that perceive images, shapes and colors, Michael Talbot's (a physicist's) book The Holographic Universe, makes reference to the aura as a holographic system. He cites the doctor that knows that disease first starts in the auric field, and moves into the physical body at last, to manifest (of course this is an old concept that mentions the same things, going back to Dr. Walter Kliner in the early 1900s, and more likely back further than that). Michael Talbot says that holographic image phenomena manifest in the auric field, but is unsure how manifestations work. He also declares he sees auras and colors himself.

There are a lot of aspects to our relationship with our aura, as we read in The Celestine Prophecy. If we become aware of our aura, we can also observe the way it functions around other people. Have you ever noticed while talking with another person, they start to fidget and become uncomfortable around you? This is a good bet that they are being inundated by your auric field.

They start to forget what they are saying, or can't remember how to spell a word, or even can't remember a word. This reaction shows you that you have a powerful mind reflected in the aura, and you need to become aware of your energy field level. In this situation you can "pull" your aura back, (as my friend's have told me, many times in a crystal healing group I once belonged to) and you will shortly observe that that person returns to a normal state of mind. It is no longer a problem for them to communicate with you.

I can also recall an interesting experience I had with the power of the auric field nearly 20 years ago. I was in a bar with a friend, being introduced to his friend just in from Philadelphia. He was an interesting person, but nothing stood out as a distinguishing characteristic. We had an enlightening discussion, and then we said our goodbyes, and I turned away, walking towards the door. I must've been 10 or so feet from them when all of a sudden, I felt like two hands were holding my shoulders back and not letting me go forward. Intuitively feeling what was going on, I continued walking towards the door, using all my strength, breaking his lock on me as I made it across the threshold of the door and continued down the street. Not looking back, I realized that I had experienced the strength of the mind/aura field manipulation that I had never encountered before or since. I continued to think about what I had just experienced and realized I could feel his energy and his life force holding me back, and I wasn't going to let him do that to me. I persevered until I broke his hold on me.

But I knew at a much deeper level that this person was trying to manipulate me at a basic level. This may relate to the experiences that I have had over the years with subtle energy manipulation from scanners. I have never spoken to anyone about this other than my friend David (we're very close friends), and he went ballistic after hearing my story. I have finally had a chance to explain this phenomenon in this publication to a point, because I feel that everybody needs to know what's going on in the psychic world; our minds are very powerful things (and some insidious groups are manipulating this knowledge for there own gain.)

Another interpretation of the auric etheric double comes from the Hindu tradition of yoga, in which the equivalent of the etheric double is called suksma-sarira, meaning sheath formed of life energy or subtle body. This energy sheath is composed of Prana, the basic energy which ebbs throughout the entire cosmos. The word prana comes from pra, meaning forth, and nan, to breathe. Pranayama are breathing exercises important to the yoga tradition. Practicing pranayama is believed to be a means of taking in vital energy, the prana, which is necessary to maintain the suksma-sarira energy sheath.

A final understanding of this energy sheath comes from the field of medicine. Medical professionals recognize a "phantom effect" experienced by paraplegics and amputees who still feel sensation in their lost of dysfunctional anatomy. These sensations persist in nearly all hand, arm, leg and foot amputations. They are much like the sensations associated with feeling energy from the apex of a pyramid or quartz crystal (described earlier in the energy feeling tasks section of the Radionics chapter).

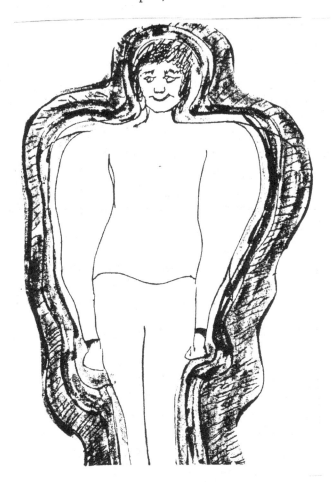

Medical researchers do not attribute these sensations to the existence of an etheric double persisting after the limb is dysfunctional or removed. They acknowledge two other possible explanations: the phantom effect may be a psychological condition similar to a hallucination, or it may be nerve impulses in the brain which are still active and registering the Iimb.[12] Evidence contrary to these two theories has been shown by Russian parapsychologists.

In light of current research from parapsychologists of the former Soviet Union the phantom phenomena is explained by a fluid body of energy called bio-plasmic energy surrounding the physical body. This energy consists of electro-magnetic and bio-plasmic fields which, when pulsated to a sufficient level, can manifest physical changes. Uri Geller, an Israeli psychic, demonstrates this by using his psychic energy to bend keys (you can go to Uri's website to learn more his work). Nelya MikhaiIova, a well-known Russian psychokinesis medium, has demonstrated that with rigorous concentration, she is able to cause her bio-plasmic body to vibrate rapidly enough to pull objects towards her, as if she were a large magnet. This feat of super psychic strength is not accomplished without strain; she is exhausted after each session

---

12 Henderson and Smith, "Phantom Limbs," Journal of Neurology, Neurosurgery and Psychiatry.

of manipulating objects towards her. Part of this strain may be attributed to environmental conditions.

A tremendous amount of energy must be used to purify the psyche of negative influences, various electro-magnetic waves, radiation and pollution before it can be put to use. Without these pollutants, bio-plasmic energy would probably be more effective and could be used to do a variety of things. Imagine the tiresome tasks that could be easily accomplished through pk (psycho-kinetic) energy, e.g., turning on an off the radio, television or coffee pot.[13]

One of the first research teams to develop a device to study the unusual energy around the body was a man and woman team named Kirlian. In 1939 they were the first to take photograms of the energy field around a plant leaf without the help of a camera. In their now famous phantom leaf experiments, they were able to obtain an image of the energy emitted from a plant leaf by using a fairly simple device.

A portion of a plant leaf was cut away and the remaining portion placed on photographic medium. The leaf and medium were then placed on an electrode (a metal plate) charged by current from a generator, resting on a dialectic (a plastic insulator plate). An image of the plant leaf, including the portion cut away, was obtained on the medium. This amazing result indicated that a complete energy field still outlined the leaf and thereby indicated the presence of an aura. Semyon Kirlian noted that high energy fugitive electrons were emitted in the presence of increased electrical current.

Reading through Fate magazine I ran across an article by Scott Hill, a leading psychic researcher (cited in the Bibliography at the end of this channel). He claims that most American researchers have left out an important point in their Kirlian experiments. He reports that the Kirlians placed photographic medium at a distance from the electrode, rather than directly on the plate. This way they were sure to expose the medium to bio-energy rather than to radiation from the electrode plates. Using a spectrophotometer, they were able to distinguish between different radiation spectrums and meter out the waves of energy they didn't want.

The Kirlian device is simple to build and use. If you would like to build or have someone build you a Kirlian device, there is a detailed explanation in Photographing the Non-Material World by Kendall Johnson which outlines every step of building and using such a device (see Bibiliography). Today Kirlian devices are built which show different colors for different surrounding energies. Their exact mechanism is still unknown.[14]

It is known, however, that all the Kirlian effects are produced by the aid of electricity. I feel that the Kirlian effect might also be generated without the use of direct current electricity. One method would be to create enough static electricity to achieve the Kirlian effect. It is well known that it is possible to create static electricity by running your feet (with stockings on) across a rug. Hold a photographic black light-tight enevelope with a piece of photographic

13 Ostrander, S. and Schroeder, L.Psychic Discoveries Behind the Iron Curtain.
14 In the presence of increased electrical current, the energy course of these fugitive electrons is unknown. It would seem to me that the recent research done by Miller and Smart, the authors of Loom of Creation (see Bibliography), their impressive study of the etheric, would shed some light on the unusual energy accompanying fugitive electrons.

paper inside in your hand as you run your feet across the carpet. You may be the first person to record your fingerprints on the photo paper without direct electrical current.

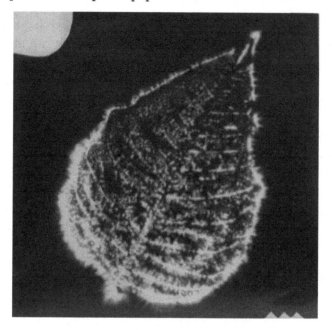

Of course, you will have to create a lot of static electricity with your feet to have it move through your hand to the photo paper, but, I think, it is not impossible. Most people have had the experience of conveying electricity when they have been shocked by static electricity, and it is the same principle here which might produce an image on the photo paper. The best environmental condition for static electricity is dry heat; the hotter and drier the day, the better. Try this experiment and see what happens.

A discussion of the aura would not be complete without mentioning the research done by Dr. Walter Kilner. He was a well-respected English doctor at St. Thomas Hospital in London and an associate of the Royal College of Physicians at the end of the 19th century. Dr. Kilner studied writings about the effects of N rays on sulphide of calcium and realized that illuminations around the body could be exposed by the use of certain colored dies (refer to The Human Aura in the Bibliography). He concluded that a coal tar dye called dicyanin would be the best substance to use to see the emanations surrounding the body.

He experimented with his friends and patients in studying the aura for many years. During this time he discovered that there were three parts to the aura that he could detect with his special dye filter. He found that there was a bioelectrical outline around the body he called the etheric double, the inter-aura and the outer aura. Each of these aura fields showed variations in color and texture during times of health or illness. He developed his perception of the aura to such a degree that he could tell by certain color combinations what particular disease the patient had contracted. Dr. Kilner wrote many papers on the subject of the aura, but never received the recognition by the medical profession that he deserved.

In the last 10 or 15 years Dr. Kilner's research has been gaining more attention with the advance of new evidence of unusual emanations around the body, in particular, studies in Kirlian photography and bioelectrical field devices.(check out his book, The Human Aura;the drawings are very interesting in the Bib.)

William Blake

THE ASTRAL BODY

The astral body consists of different levels of emotional energy. As we experience emotions, the colour energy of the astral body changes and these changes can be detected by various devices. Dr. Marcel Vogel was the first to use a device called a psycho-analyzer to study the astral body of plants. This device, similar to a lie detector because it detects electrochemical changes in surface resistance, was used by Vogel to record emotional reactions of plants to various stimuli.

Intending to record the response of a plant to trimming, Vogel thought about getting a knife to cut the experimental plant. As soon as the picture of the knife came' into his mind, the plant reacted violently, sending the needle of the psycho-analyzer to the extreme side of the scale indicating the greatest response. This was one of the first indications of emotional reactions in plants.

Experimentation has shown that plants seem to respond favorably to classical music and tend to wither when exposed to music like acid rock. It has been found that plants grow better when the humans around them develop a sensitive rapport with them. "Talk to your plants" is often the advice given to owners of unhealthy plants (refer to The Secret Life of Plants in the Bib.)

Most of the experimentation done on plant emotions was accomplished by the use of a psycho-analyzer like the one used by Marcel Vogel, as discussed in The Secret Life of Plants. If you are interested in building your own psycho-analyzer and have some electronics background, instructions can be found in an article by Robert E. Devine, "Build a Psycho-Analyzer: Check "Emotions and Sensibilities Galvanic Skin Resistance, " published in Popular Electronics, February 1969. Since this article appeared, much more sensitive analyzers have been developed, capable of reading extremely high and low frequency vibrations. When I had an analyzer built for my own use, I requested that a sensitivity unit be added for high frequency detection.

In order to use the psycho-analyzer on your plants, attach a flat electrode coated with conducting gel such as agar-agar (which can be purchased at a hobby shop or scientific supply) to each side of the plant leaf with a c-clamp. A piece of acetate or rubber sheeting should be placed between the electrode and the c-clamp for insulation. If they are not insulated from one another, the energy charge from the plant will move through the electrode to the c-clamp and will not be recorded. In the Handbook of Psychic Energies, Sheila Ostrander suggests using a bar or plate of steel as an electrode attached by an insulated c-clamp with agar-agar gel (see Bibliography). A large circular electrode, three inches or greater, would also work.

Recently a well known dowser Walt Woods has hooked his favorite plant to a meter and calibrated Marcel Vogel's experiments. He has found that his plan has synchronized with his brainwave patterns and heart patterns to react to his intentions.(Refer back to the dowsing channel for his books).

Color is associated with levels of emotional energy in the astral body. I should point out here that the concept of colors related to the emotions is not held by every professional. The color theorists, of whom Max Luscher is an example (see The Luscher Color Test in the bibliography), believe that color is color and has no emotional counterpart. It is simply vibration that fits into a frequency spectrum, unrelated to emotional and psychological levels. They believe that people, because of their biases, attach emotional significance to colors, but that colors cannot inherently contain emotional characteristics.

But it is not yet known whether emotions can create different aspects of ultra-colors. I say ultra-colors because we have to take into account the etheric light energy inherent in the aura itself, which is energy outside of the electro-magnetic spectrum. There are those who feel that colors do have a corresponding emotional attachment. Whether colors have emotional equivalents or whether emotions create colors is not proven.

Some psychics, however, claim to see auric light energy and claim that its colors change with the different feelings that come and go in the individual.[15] They associate dark red with anger. Fear falls into the band of grey colors. Avarice shows up as a mixture of red and grey.

15 Ostrander, S. and Schroeder, L. Psychic Discoveries Behind the Iron Curtain.

Happiness and joy are rose shades and tints. Love is a beautiful crimson color. Jealousy has been described as a combination of black, muted yellow and muted green. The interpretation of aura colors is a process loaded with bias and misconception, so if you should see an aura, make sure of what you are seeing. Look closely and concentrate on what you are seeing to perceive the truest picture possible ; take in all the variables before making an interpretation if you see aura colors.

But, ultra-colors are interesting in themselves. They manifest in peripheral vision, flashes and spots of color or after images from staring at colors or optical illusion artwork. Ultra-colors have their counterpart colors in the electromagnetic spectrum i.e. pigments and colored dyes. Ultra-colors can facilitate the healing processes by wearing appropriate colored clothing thereby manipulating various bio- energies in the body and holographic mind in subtle ways. When I talk about ultra colors and the human healing processes I refer to the chakras and Chi or prana in subtle systems in and around the body. It can also be couched as Life-force.

Wearing a red shirt next to the skin will stimulate the after image color green, which relates to the heart chakra and the major chakras below the feet (mother Earth connection chakra). The green as you will notice in the chart on the next page has many different aspects. One of the important aspects is the tremendous balancing properties that green issues forth.

The effects of green on subtle body systems is facilitated by the processes of visualization. Being a crystal expert for many years I have needed to clean them of noxious energies on a regular basis. Recently I bought a green crystal imported from Germany, and I have found it really work well in keeping all my other crystals cleaned and balanced for a longer period of time. As you wear different colors you affect subtle changes in the subtle systems of your body.

It has been determined by various individuals in a group setting (I have learned from a friend of mine who leads our crystal healing group) that have experimented with various colors to see how they affect the body. Some of the experiences noted about colors in the group were that red creates a sensation of being hot and an uneasy; blue has a relaxed feeling; and green has a strong and balanced effect. I have also use color techniques in psychology classes in high school to teach meditation techniques.

This field is very promising for additional understanding of the subtly contained in colours. One color in particular is coming to the fore front in color research. Baker Miller Pink is turning out to be one of the most interesting examples influencing an individual or group. It is closest to bubblegum pink and is referred to as drunk tank pink because it is used to calm down inebriated and violent prisoners in jails. Dr.Alexander Schauss PH.D was one of the first researchers to recognize the effects of color on the human organism. This color has the effect to suppress anger, antagonism and anxiety effected behavior among prisoners. This color also affects the blind as well. This gives us an indication of the power of color to effect us on subtle levels of awareness. It is not the color we perceive that affects us but the color frequency that is affecting us.

AURA COLOR CHART

Below is a color chart prescribed to by the majority of psychics capable of seeing the aura. They have attached emotional significance to each color of the aura.

RED is the color of life, blood, vigor, virility and energy. One of the stronger aspects of red colors relates to physical properties, such as the love of the athlete of physical exercise and physical fitness. Sensation and self are the key characteristics of the red ray. Depending on the shade and tone of the red, it can be associated with warm-heartedness, affection, courage and passionate love.

ORANGE is the color of social order and love of humanity. It represents emergence from self-indulgence, working and interacting with society at large. This color expresses ambition, hope, health, vitality-energy, a balanced nature, friendship and companionship.

YELLOW is the color of the intellect or intellectual. It is the color of order and structured reality, situated on a linear time line. Events become well ordered, compartmentalized, labeled true or false, good or bad, real or unreal, pretty or ugly, positive or negative, male or female, etc. The thinking processes of how, when, where, and what of facts and details set the scene for the yellow ray. Looking for solutions is a key phrase for interpreting the yellow hue. The yellow ray also expresses abstract thinking and, depending on the tone (gold), it can be of a spiritual nature.

GREEN is the color of harmony and balance. It signifies the independent nature and personal power of each individual. It constitutes the color of growth and new life energy. Depending on the shade of green (brighter colors are more positive), it is associated with animated, thoughtful persons. With a little blue, green becomes the color of healing.

BLUE is the color of the spiritualist and idealist. Blue is the color of a peaceful understanding of nature. Priests and persons dealing with the humanitarian occupations, such as doctors, social workers, nurses, etc., all contain within their aura a certain amount of blue. Key words are inspiration, devotion, noble ideas, sincerity and emotional stability.

INGIGO is the color of a more advanced degree of sprituality. The blue-violet ray signifies wisdom and saintliness on the forefront of intuitional experience. The indigo personality possesses a multi-dimensional time frame. He/she is the perceiver of the future to come, always being ahead of the present day world. People with indigo auras can be called the idealist, impractical, the visionary, strong-willed, moralistic, the day-dreamer, the seeker. The psychic faculties are associated with this color of the aura.100

VIOLET is the color of the highest degree of spirituality. The violet ray is adept at annihilating the concrete concepts of time that structure and order the universe; they are able to will events. Individuals with violet auras move easily in the realm of consciousness to explore new levels of awareness. Rose tones of the violet aura signify universal love, joy and contentment. Soft and gentle is this love, bringing comfort and happiness. It can also be a color of healing. Blending into the darker shades of violet, the purples, the love of form and ceremony is evident. The paler colors represent cosmic consciousness and highest love of humanity and God.

BLACK is not an ultra color at all, but a substance without light. Throughout history, black was considered the color of hatred, discord, evil thoughts, malice and other negative properties. But black is a beautiful color. If it weren't for darkness, we would not have the beautiful stars and planets that give us some of our beautiful nights and dawns. We would not have the opportunity to travel to distant planets enveloped in a sea of beautiful blackness. Now, it is expressed as dark matter from a scientific perspective. For me, wonderful lustrous black of the night with stars shining through to my mind is the substance of infinity that makes my consciousness travel at high speeds through unlimited space, giving a feeling of total freedom. Sometimes when I close my eyes before going to sleep, my consciousness soars deeper and deeper through space and feels totally relaxed, as if it were floating. Black is a positive color when predicates are put aside for correct perceptions. Black is the vibration of inspiration and creativity.

BROWN is the color of getting things done, getting on with the business of building and acquiring things. The industrious business person, accumulating fortune, is signified by perseverance in lighter shades of the brown aura. It is a very down to earth color.

GRAY is the go-between color between black and white. It helps to blend things together. It is the helper and problem-solver. It is the ultimate color of change and integration. Dull grey can have the property of narrow-mindedness and indifference to imagination and creativity. The silver grays represent versatility and liveliness of spirit.

Of course, the different levels of the aura are not made up of one color; rather, various colors blend together; nevertheless, they remain distinct colors which, when placed next to one another, give the impression of a third color, resulting in secondary and tertiary colors.

SILVER is a very interesting color as its color expresses movement, especially when the sun reflects off its surface. You can see this aspect clearly by watching drivers was silver cars speed past you, always in a hurry to get some place somewhere. I don't think silver has a negative aspect.

THE MENTAL BODY

The mental body encompasses our incoming and outgoing concrete thought patterns in the three-dimensional world through different aspects of the personality. As thoughts move through the brain, they have a corresponding color within the aura of the mental body. The mental body consists of lower intellectual processes concerned with everyday, mundane tasks. These include the most mundane tasks which an infant learns. For example, learning to discriminate between objects in the environment, learning that , an object out of sight is not out of mind, learning to crawl and walk, learning how to stack blocks without the blocks falling over are all tasks of the mental body. The toddler learns that some things are hot and cause pain, some things are cool or cold, some things are smooth or rough, and some are combinations in between. The pre-schooler continues this integration of the senses, becoming more physically proficient in his/her motor skills. As we grow older, we experiment with our perceptions of the world, building on the basic processes that we have been through as children, young adults and adults.

According to theologians, the finer and more subtle colors start to show in the aura of the mental and causal bodies.[16] Routine things, such as washing the car, driving to work, eating dinner, and asking directions are all mental body processes which contain the finer colors if the tasks are completed with a positive attitude. Figuring out the complicated process of how the universe works is not a lower mental operation, nor is reading a good science fiction novel. Most creative processes originate in the causal body, not in the lower mental plane. The two levels integrate into one another. The knowledge of the higher self filters into the conscious knowledge of the lower self.

Energy information is deciphered from the subconscious and intuitive mind to give us a more rounded picture of that person or situation. This is not a new idea, recently expressed through Redfield's book" Celestine prophecies", tries to explain how the energy works pertaining to human beings.

---

16 Hall, M. Masonic, Hermetic, Qabbalistic and RosecTUcian Symbolic Philosophy, pp~XXXIV-Lll. 102

THE CAUSAL BODY

The causal body is the storehouse of all accumulated reincarnated lifetimes. It is the true seat of wisdom. Every great and noble thought, every pure, unselfish emotion (kindness, constructive will, love of humanity, fairness, sharing) ascends to the causal body through a process similar to osmosis and becomes the basic substance of this plane. (I use the word plane as an analogy; there is no division between one level of consciousness and another; they blend into each other like values of color.) The thinker resides in the causal body with the higher aspects of memory, intuition, will, abstract reasoning, pure ideas, and discrimination between ideas. The creative power of the mind also winds its way through the fabric of the causal plane. Meditation and contemplation, integrated with imagination and will, bring to the world knowledge of past and future events. Telepathy and other higher mind processes are created on the causal plane.

But there are souls who are able to transcend these basic levels spread their wings into more expanded levels of consciousness. Sensitives, channelers, trance mediums and old souls have these natural abilities. But not even they can say that they can express these realities in scientific terms yet. And that's not their fault, or anyone's fault, really. Our ability to use scientific parameters to understand the totality of human spiritual consciousness is yet unclear. On the other hand, as Michael Talbot states, the scientific process maybe not enough to understand our totality. There are other levels of consciousness that have access to our consciousness through portals and windows of access we do not understand as yet.

Dolores Cannon is doing a great service for humanity with her exploration into the human condition. She is opening up doors or windows to our soul that we originally closed. I would also say that we, as yet, don't realize the extent of the levels of help we are receiving from angels, guides and extraterrestrials. Our limited knowledge of different levels and types of consciousness make it difficult to communicate the particulars. As we progress further in our enfoldment, we are seeing and experiencing more and more of the big picture, our relationship with the vast expansion of consciousness.

If, for instance, we knew the various personalities we have developed in various lifetimes and how these personalities interface into our consciousness, we would take a giant step/a quantum leap into the understanding of how consciousness works and where we stand in the over- all enfoldment of our karma. Reincarnation is a real phenomenon that continues to not be taken seriously. It was in the Bible at one time in our history and more and more people are seeing it as a viable focus in life. If we would only embrace this concept we would go a long ways in understanding our destinies, and a better graphs of consciousness; we already have, the keys to heaven.

There are higher and finer levels of our auras mainly dealing with spirituality which I don't discuss here because these planes are outside of our conscious reasoning faculties and don't lend themselves to scientific inquiry because of our limited knowledge and experience of the parameters making up the existence of these levels. They are not yet concretely locked into the collective consciousness in order for these levels to march out of the dream state into waking awareness.

The level of the auric field extends out from the body about three or 4 feet or so, the outer edge of these dimensions makes an egg shape around the body some say is the Soul level of consciousness. In Dr. Walter Kliner's book" The Aura", you can see from his drawings this very prominent egg shape Also in Dr. Jeffrey Ms. Love's book" The Roots of Consciousness" and others references the egg shape as been a very prominent expression of our expanded consciousness. 103

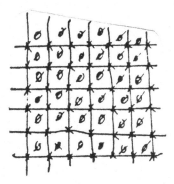

I was sitting in the balcony not far from the stage listening to a comedian at the Holy City Zoo in San Francisco in the 1980's. All of a sudden I became aware, instantaneously, that a transmission of light entered my brain containing a whole concept, a whole thought form, the beginning middle and end. This whole individual thought form became what you call a treatise on the way individual universes can function at the same time on different levels of consciousness. It became clear to me as I thought about what just happened that this information had an extraterrestrial origin. Their knowledge and consciousness has the capability to manifest thought in such a way to deliver a concept in its wholeness. I have run across this type of information from readings I have done on extraterrestrials and individual stories I have heard from discussion groups and people that also had first hand experience.

This concept reminds me of a movie that I saw called the Abyss. These higher consciousness water beings demonstrated that they can take ordinary seawater structured into any shape they wanted for the purpose of gathering information or whatever, building technology around the molecular structure of seawater. This is exactly what extraterrestrials do with subtle, ectoplasmic or bioplasmic energy consciousness. They have created technology around these energies.(At one time in meditation, I experience a ship shooting an energy beam to the ground and tying this energy beam into a knot; it was a ship I have lived on for one lifetime; its name was Roltar.) Of course ET's name their ships because they are grown into living entities; they have a consciousness and maybe even a soul.

And as I mentioned in an experience in the clairvoyant section they also have technology integrated with consciousness to pull your light body out of your physical body. What other possibilities await us as we learn what other things they can accomplish with bioplasmic energy.

I did find one reference for receiving instantaneous thought transmission in Michael Talbot's book, " The Holographic Universe". He says, " we find a few examples of this phenomenon happening to psychics and within the out of body experiences". Talbot, also cites OB (out of body experiences) experiences that call this process" bundles" of thought or "thought balls".

Individuals received thought information in chunks that register instantaneously in one's thoughts; this is what happened to me.

Having this experience one night, and trying to break the information down into explainable pieces, it became clear to me that the only way different levels of consciousness can be examined as separate levels and also considered non-separate levels is through the integration and gradual merging together of those levels, as in values of colors. In looking at this abstract concept from a molecular level, I see the image as an analogy. If you were to create a grid for each level of consciousness from each energy spectrum with a particular molecule on the cross points of the grid and each cross point on each grid were situated between spaces on each grid, you would have both the non integration and the integration of consciousnesses. Let's take an example from the infra-red spectrum and place a molecule on a grid of acetate plastic to create a two-dimensional representation.

Now take another piece of acetate, also with a grid, and call it the ultra-violet spectrum. Now lay this acetate piece over the first acetate piece and what you have is a separate spectrum of different frequencies occupying their own space on the two grids. Each molecule fits between spaces in each molecule grid. This would apply to a three-dimensional model as well. And of course this model would apply to every molecule in the universe. But when we look into the fourth dimension, where there is no space, we realize that each molecule occupies the same point or cross on the grid but at different frequencies or in a completely different dimension - the fourth dimension - where each molecule is on a different plane level moving at a different velocities.

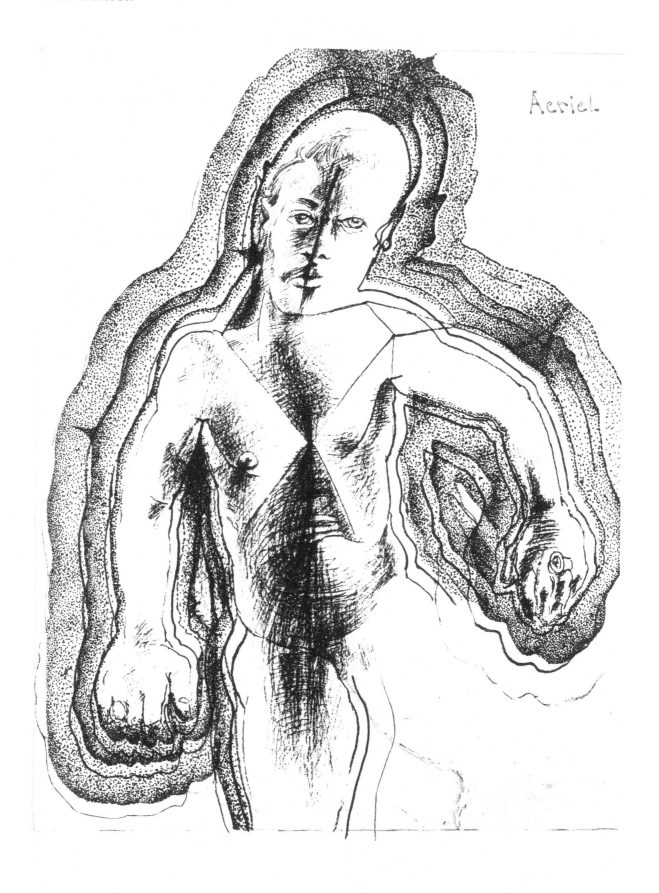

Aeriel

AURA CHART & COLOR

Gather the children together into a group. Explain that you are going to talk about the aura today. Ask questions: "Who knows what an aura is? Where did you hear about the aura? What kinds of things do you know about the aura?" Write all the children's answers on a blackboard so they can see and remember what has been said. After you find out what they know and don't know about the aura, you will know what points to make in discussing the aura.. (Before this group meeting you should have read over the Aura section enough to be familiar with its contents.) Now at this point, referring to the channelon the aura, explain the parts of the aura, and give a little history behind the discovery of the aura. For younger children you will need to simplify the language on the historical discussion covering the basic points. Then show pictures of the different aspects of the aura. (See the bibliography for books by Argulles, Kilner, and especially Tansky.)

Have a couple of children pass out water colors sets to the class. Tell the students that we are going to learn how to see the aura. First we are going to work with colors to try and develop our awareness of different color values.

MATERIALS:

water colors brushes

mimeograph color fans

scissors

examples of color shades -values

Start by showing examples of colors. Charts of the values of colors can be obtained from paint supply stores. The scales of value of color can also be demonstrated from famous paintings which show color gradations. Try books on modern art such as optical art, Japanese paintings, and works by the Hungarian painter, Victor Vasarely.

In 1966 he painted Arcturus II, which contains four colors green, purple, blue and orange - in their descending values. Next, draw triangle shapes, with paper and pen and Xerox enough copies for the class. Have each student cut out six shapes for their color wheel Explain to the children that there are seven values of color within each color. You are going to paint values for each color used. "Today we are going to work with the values of red."

Explain to the students that they should draw two lines from a point on their paper, making sure that each line is the same length. Explain the concept of length if they don't already know. Let them start making their triangle while you go around and assist.

Next, explain to the children what a compass is used for and how it can be manipulated or let them experiment and see if they can discover these things for themselves; point out the sharp end. Help the children with how to place the compass to form the rounded shape at the large end of the triangles. You can always show them how the compass works afterwards (you really don't need a compass if you can't get a hold of them; draw in by hand, a half circle.)

I don't agree with those educators who claim that children pick up bad habits if they are not shown how to use a tool correctly. From infancy, children learn by experimentation and exploration, and this should be continued in the classroom. You may demonstrate, however, the most effective way to use the tool, thereby gaining a balance between the two educational approaches.

After demonstrating to the children how they should paint each value, have them repeat the process in different hues. They can make reference to the store-bought color charts and the examples of works of art. The younger children could arrange the color hues and then paint colors in the spaces. Make, paint a single color, sure the children understand that the idea is to paint each value lighter than the last one.

You may want to integrate math into the lesson for students eight years and older. Pass out rulers, compasses, and scissors to the students. Have each child or partner group decide on the size of the triangle they would like to draw, explaining to them that each triangle will be a part of a color wheel, with one triangle for each color. Ask questions such as, "How many triangles will it take to make one color wheel? Does it matter what size the triangles are in order to make a color wheel?

How many colors are there?"

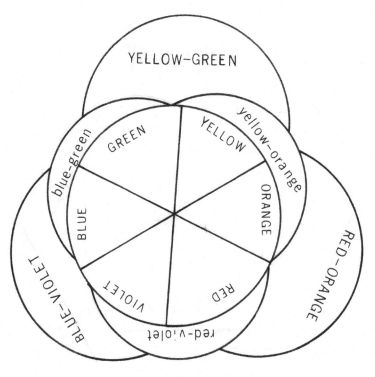

COLORS GAME

This is an extra activity that the children can participate in by having them cut up each value separately. Clear an area of the classroom large enough for the children to run in; go outside if necessary. Divide the class into groups, with each group designated a color. Move the chairs, but make sure there is some surface to hang color values on, such as a wall or bulletin board. Now line each group up in single file and give each person in each group a value of their group color. When each group has their colors, tell them they can arrange themselves in any way in a single line as long as their color values start with the darkest at the top and gradually get lighter.

Each group will then send a person, one at a time, to hang his/her color values until each person has placed his/her strip of color on the• wall. Each color value must be directly under the next value. Tell your students, after they have gotten their colors up, to decide among themselves if the color values are in the correct order; if not, one person may change the order of the colors until they think their color order is right. The group that has their colors up in the right order is the winner. The group may change colors if they want to play the game again or have each group pick a color. This game will help the children distinguish between finer and finer values of colors, training their eyes to distinguish the colors of the aura. Also, it will help them distinguish between different subtle colors.

PERIPHERAL VISION EXERCISE/ AURA TASK

Peripheral vision is the extent of vision found on either side of the body when the eyes are focused forward. We can see only general shapes and colors with peripheral vision. The following task will demonstrate and help strengthen peripheral vision by helping the children to distinguish shapes and colors. This will also help them in studying the aura.

Have the children group themselves into pairs and have each couple sit down, face-to-face, at arm's length. Have each group straighten their arms out from their sides and be far enough apart to touch fingertips in four directions. Instruct one of the children to stare straight ahead; the child's eyes should not move. Ask these children to describe what he/she sees to the left and the right. Ask children to expand their vision by continuing to see around the room without moving their eyes, either left or right in a 360° pattern, sweeping their minds eye without moving their eyes. Hundreds have used this technique to determine the energy levels information of an object, see the aura colors and perceive the deceased.

Dowsers also use this technique to find water or oil. Scanning the ground using this sense can to locate noxious energy. Because all energy has direction (according to the Egyptian book of the dead) you can use techniques like this to help you ground yourself and reflect back any noxious energy waveforms.

The other person in the pair will make sure that his/her partner is looking forward at all times. With practice the children will learn to see more and more detail through their peripheral vision. As they get better at describing what they see, they may slowly develop inter-sight, which, according to the Hindus, is seeing with the third eye, the pituitary gland, the brow chakra. Clairvoyants use this sense to see the past or future and visually see into other dimensional levels of consciousness.

While attending the C.S.E.T.I (The search For Extraterrestrial Intelligence) retreat, as the group was setting on the Colorado plains in lounge chairs, listening to Dr. Steven Greer explain the strange cloud like arching shapes suspended above the ground, I found myself using my clairvoyance sight, going into the cloud shape, to perceive little green ET beings in space suits, were startled as I stuck my head through the dimensional veil.

ELECTRIC COLOR WHEEL

Give each child three or four circles drawn on cardboard or have them trace circles onto cardboard using a round object found in the room. Pass out scissors to cut out circles. Give them a set of colored pens or water colors and have each child draw different designs on each cardboard circle. Use the end of a compass or sharp instrument to punch a hole in the center of the color circle.

Now pass out several small motors and batteries. Most craft stores will have small motors or you can order some from Edmond Scientific (it offers a teacher discount) or try Elementary Sciences Series (ESS-the address is found in the Bib.) Ask the children to attach the red wire to the positive end of the battery (the nobbed end) with tape and have them touch the other wire, the black one, to the negative end of the battery. The shaft will then spin and whirl the color circle around.

MATERIALS:

- pencils
- batteries
- cardboard circles
- small motors

Tell your students to experiment with different colored wheels and combinations of colors. This exercise will stimulate your students' perceptions of colors, particularly with colors obtained by using the electric color wheel. The colors will seem animated, floating away from the surface of the wheel.

LIGHT EXPERIENCE

So far I have presented exercises to express light in pigment to use with children. It seems appropriate at this point to present exercises dealing with artificial and natural light substances, such as petroleum base products used in theatrical gels or colored celluloid. The use of mirrors and magnifying lenses will also be incorporated into these exercises.

Using light colors will give students the chance to experiment with energy close to its natural state when projected through a prism. This type of experience can be of benefit to students in learning more effectively to see aura colors. It can also be used to illustrate experiences in various areas of science such as optics, computer graphics, physics and the fine and theatrical arts. These exercises will help children to internalize basic experiences with color and light. It will enhance principles they will learn about in art and science.

LIGHT BOX / Materials:

four pieces of cardboard, 10" x 11"
knife
tape
light bulb and socket (100 watt)
colored cellophane
mirrors
magnifying glasses
prism (optional)

In the first task, an easy and inexpensive way of experimenting with light and colors is to make a three-sided box with slits down the sides. From this point, one can use colored cellophane, prisms mirrors and magnifying glasses to enhance and explore the world of colors and lights.

Take three pieces of cardboard and tape tinfoil on the surface. Then cut slits down the sides of each piece 5 inches long, 1/2 inch wide and 1-1/2 inches apart. Next tape the sides of the cardboard to complete a triangle. Cut a triangular piece of cardboard to fit over the top of the box. Tape the top down so that no light emanates from the edges.

The light bulb and socket will take a little more preparation. The bottom piece of the box should be a sturdy piece of cardboard or wood (if wood is used, it will need a hole drilled big enough to fit the bottom of the socket). Select a piece of cardboard bigger than the side pieces. On the bottom side of the board glue three strips of cardboard 1/2 inch wide, standing on edge in a triangular shape, so as to hold the box up and act as a support stand. The box will sit level when the bottom part of the light socket is pulled through a hole in the bottom part of the box. It does not matter how long the pieces are or even if they touch, so long as they create a triangular pattern, anywhere from two to three inches from the edges of the box.

Insert the light bulb and socket through the base of the box and turn it on. Turn down the lights in the room and observe the bands of light emanating through the slits in the box. Take a mirror and position it in front of one of the light beams and watch the beams react as the position of the mirror is moved. Take another mirror and reflect the same beam. See how many times the mirrors can bend the light waves before the light dissipates.

Try introducing a different element into the light experience. Use colored cellophane or any colored celluloid (found in art stores and theatrical shops) to project light through. Cut frames of cardboard the size of one side of the light box to mount the cellophane~ Experiment with light coming through the colored cellophane and being reflected off the mirrors. Start with the three primary colors. Overlap the different pieces of colored cellophane and see how many colors can be made. You may also want to experiment with other masks (a piece of cardboard with holes/ slits) to let only a small space of light emanate through the slits at a time. See if this process enhances the projection of light. Play with the reflection of light off of different mirror surfaces. See how many mirrors can be used to reflect light in different directions.

Create other masks with circles, triangles and other well defined shapes to see how the light reacts. Another possible idea is to use another square or rectangular shape (which has at least two sides the same size as the slitted side of the light box) as a rough focusing mechanism. Cut slits wide enough and long enough through which the masks described above could fit through or create new ones to fit. Leave both ends of the box open, so that one end can be fitted up against the light box and the other end will remain open and project the light though the masks out onto a wall or other surface acting as a screen.

Slip the masks through the slits and cover the unused slits so that light does not escape through them. The attached box acts similarly to a camera bellows to focus the light a little more clearly. Experiment with different kinds and combinations of masks made of various colors and materials to see what kinds of projections can be done.

FLASHLIGHTS

Another task with light is to use flashlights, colored cellophane, mirrors and possibly also a prism, if one is available. Place the mirrors in different locations and, as before, see, if they can reflect the light in as many different directions as possible. Enhance the beam's quality by attaching a paper towel roll or any paper tube to the front of the flashlight. The tube will extend the beam farther out, increasing its effectiveness across a distance.

To utilize color, cellophane can be mounted on cardboard frames and used as masks on a flashlight. Cut a piece of cardboard 5 inches square. Place a flashlight face down in the center of the cardboard and trace its circumference, as in Figure 1.

Using this circle as a reference, trace two more circles - one outside of it 5 inches in diameter and one within it about 2/3 its size. Then cut the innermost circle out, and trim the edges of the cardboard off around the largest one. The remaining piece should look like Figure 2, with the inner circle cut out.

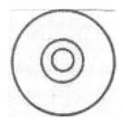

Next, cut four lines at right angles from the outer edge of the middle circle all the way to the outside edge. Place it on the face of the flashlight and bend the cardboard flaps back so that they wrap around the flashlight in a cone shape, as shown in Figure 3. Tape the sides of the cardboard to fit the contours of the flashlight. Make masks out of colored celluloid and cardboard to fit the size of the head of the flashlight and insert them in the nose of the cone. Again, various combinations can be made to see how many different projections can be created.

SUN REFLECTIONS

With the use of the sun, one can create some exciting light designs using silver mylar geometric constructions. Silver or chrome mylar can be purchased at any art store. It is a film-like material with a reflective surface.

It is necessary to have the sun coming through a window and to have it focused. Use a mask of some sort to cover the window heavy enough to block out light except for a hole cut through the middle. (If the room is dark enough and the window small enough, the mask may not be needed. Just turn off the lights and the window will serve as the mask to focus incoming light.) The next step would be to construct various geometric shapes out of silver mylar.

Start by cutting a circle about six inches in circumference. Cut a line from the edge of the circle to its center. Taking the mylar circle in both hands, cross each side over each other about one fourth of the circumference of the circle, creating a cone shape.

Another shape easy to make is a cube. For a three inch cube, take a ruler and measure six three-inch squares on the mylar in the cross configuration Fold up squares 1, 2, 3, and 4 and tape them into the shape of a cube. The last square (T) is folded down and taped as the top of the cube.

A word of caution would be to tape the constructed shapes onto a flat cardboard surface so as to make them less vulnerable to being smashed by overactive students. The other possibility would be to purchase a material similar to mylar, but which is more sturdy, such as a light plastic. These materials can be found in sheets of 30" x 40" at most art stores.

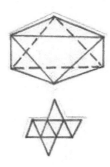

The more angles to a surface, the more reflective and creative potentials can be realized. Other more angular shapes could be triagonal prism (the shape of a pup tent), tetrahedrons (3-sided pyramid), or octahedron (a double 4-sided pyramid).

By positioning these shapes in the light in various ways, many patterns of light can be created on the walls or ceiling. For more instruction on creating varied shapes, consult Order in Space by Keith Critchlow, Viking Press, New York. 196S. This book has an excellent geometric shape breakdown and simple visual instructions for building various shapes. 116

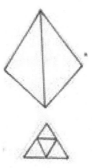

After a few minutes work with the light patterns, introduce a few magnifying glasses. By placing the magnifying glass between the mylar and light pattern, one can bring a light pattern into clearer focus by changing the pattern slightly, creating a new and interesting image. Another effect is to position one's finger between the magnifying glass and the light image. By placing the finger just right, one can see a black finger with a lighter gray and transparent image of the finger extending around it. At this point in time, one can have a discussion on the etheric body, pointing out the similarities in actually seeing the subtle body.

Finally bring in the element of colors, exploring the variations involved in overlapping colors. See if each student can make secondary and tertiary combinations from the three primary colors, red, yellow and blue. Refer back to the color chart in the Aura Chapter for a breakdown of secondary and tertiary colors if help with the color breakdown is needed.

L-ROD METER

MATERIALS:

- coat hanger sandpaper

- rubber, plastic or metal tube

The L-Rod is an effective devices for detecting the aura. Take a coat hanger and bend it so that it forms a right angle. Sand the paint off the coat hanger and smooth it down with sandpaper. Paint the hanger with copper paint or wrap it with wire. This procedure facilitates better conduction of eco-plasmic energy through the aura meter. This tool have been successfully used by Marcel Vogel, Russell Swan and Gary Hackett to detect the aura.

One side of the angle will be the handle and can be fitted with a rubber, plastic or metal sleeve to lessen friction as the aura meter moves in the hand. Eco-plasmic energy is very subtle and the least amount of friction will hamper the movement of the aura meter. Make sure the one portion is larger than the handle portion, making it easier to use the L-Rod (swing rod).You should have two L-Rods.

Hold one of the devices by the handle in the left hand and stand behind the person whose aura is to be read. Starting at the top of the head, try to determine the boundary of the aura extending out from the body. The aura meter should swing toward the body and stop at the aura's outline around the body. Move the meter down the body, tracing the auric field. Hold the meter close to the top of the head of the subject and watch the meter swing to connect with the auric field. It takes a little practice to hold the L- Rod in order to have it read the correct information. Holding to tight will stop the swing, holding not tight enough will let the rod swing radically not giving any information at all. You want to hold the rod with enough pressure to maximize your information swing.

The distance of the auric field from the body determines the energy level of the subject at any given time.(there are different levels of the aura but for this experiment a generic aura focus is find; your intend is the important thing here. Smaller extensions denote a low energy field, and a larger extension denotes a higher energy field. This simple aura meter is basically a dowsing rod and can be used effectively to detect the aura field.

The aura is a complex system and when ever I come across a concrete example of it I go out of my way to deliver evidence to my audience. Please look at the photo I have included here and draw your own conclusions.

While going through John Klimo's book, Channeling, I ran across a description of a photograph I took of a friend of mine when she was pregnant, some years ago. On page 124, John cites the White Eagle Lodge, the prominent spiritual group in England that publishes channeling books from Grace Cook. John describes how White Eagle, a Mayan Indian that speaks through her, communicates with her. Communication with her happens when he speaks into a "golden disc of light" at the back of the head that acts like a microphone built from substance extracted from the human soul and physical nervous system. It is unseen by most humans because it is a finer, faster nature (emanation energy) of energy.

I consider myself fortunate for having a psychic photograph depicting the golden disc of communication at the back of the head. I can't tell you how elated I was to find an inscription of my photograph I had relating to the subject. Of course, there are other interesting energies in this photograph that hopefully you can make out looking at it yourself. You can also see other forms – a spiritual being elevated above her head and little splotches of different colored light all around the photograph. Of course, there will be people that tell you you're not seeing what you are seeing; stick to your guns. Your perceptions are square and level. If you don't see images in this photograph, switch to your right brain perception (refer to the ESP channel). And finally this photo was origally in color. It will difficult to see some of the images because it is a black and white photograph.

CHECKPOINTS

Here are some questions you might ask to stimulate further exploration:

1. Can you think of other ways of creating colors?

2. Are there any other materials that could be used to make different colors?

    You may want to pose these questions to individual children or to the group. The types of questions you ask are very important if you wish to encourage students to understand alternatives to problem solving.

3. Why should people learn to distinguish the colors of the aura?

Encourage your students to understand that if a standard and true interpretation of aura colors is agreed upon by the majority, we may find a new form of communication.

POTENTIALITY

By working with the aura, there exists the possibility of recognizing disease before it affects the physical body, which would encourage prevention or early treatment of disease. Psychological needs could be seen more clearly, diagnosed and treated earlier. You might want to inform your class of the work of Valerie Hunt, professor of kinesiology at UCLA.

She has developed a high frequency electronic device that detects and records the aura in all its many colors. She is in agreement with other researchers who believe that disease shows in the aura three to six hours before symptoms are manifested in the physical body. She also was involved in researching Wilhelm Reich's Orgone blanket. Although this is a fairly sophisticated thought for children, you may want to explain it as simply as possible to emphasize why we study the aura and its colors.

We will eventually understand that the aura is a subtle communication system that our consciousness uses to extract information from its environment.

Communication between the opposite sex and most certainly the same sex happened long before one word is uttered. The understanding of this process would shed light on the emotional and cognitive levels of communication. Our relationships would become clearer and more workable as we learn to understand the motives behind the actions we take. One of the few good examples we have of subtle communication comes from James Redfield's book The Celestine Prophecies. It is only a novel, but speaks volumes of our communication with each other on an energetic level.

SUMMARY /CONCLUSIONS

Aura The Aura channel was compiled to focus on some of the multi-dimensional aspects of personality from a historical and contemporary perspective. This perspective is synthesized from a Western esoteric approach (unlike the Chakra channel, which deals with similar information from an eastern perspective). This approach integrates color interpretation with intellectual and emotional response, to physical levels of awareness.

Knowledge about each level of the aura, through the interpretation of colors, gives the readers an understanding of their own consciousnesses, expanded beyond levels of the brain into an awareness of areas of his/her expanded self. Glimpsing some of the aspects that make up our entire spiritual selves; and the systems that make up our total awareness on ourselves. We are just starting to understand that we are spiritual beings and how the oversoul (higher selves) interfaces with the physical world.

Color is looked at as a method of interpretation of different levels of awareness through the understanding of vibration and how it affects different levels of our being. It is said by occultists that colors coordinate our three dimensional reality as it does number and sound. Colors take on aspects of nature as clues to subtle knowledge about our relationship to a more or less unfolded consciousness and what personal qualities an individual soul may be using at a particular time. Again, the main focus is on practicality - what are the realities of the aura, and how can we develop our own unique perception of the aura.

BIBLIOGRAPHY

Auras Books:

Arguelles, Jose and Miriam. Mandala. Berkeley, CA: Shambala Books, 1972.

Babbit, Edwin. Principles of Light and Color. New York: University Books, 1967.

Barren, M. Principles of Color. New York: Van Nostrand, Reinhold Co., 1969.

Bernheim, H. Suggestive Therapeutics. New York: University Books, 1964.

Birren, Faber. Color: A Survey in Words and Pictures - From Ancient Mysticism to Modern Science. New Hyde Park, NY: Uni Books, 1963

Bouma, Peter J. Physical Aspects of Color: An Introduction to the Study of Color Stimulation and Color Sensation. New York: St. Martins Press, 1971.

Cayce, Edgar. Aura. Virginia Beach, VA: ARE Press, 1973.

Gallimore, J.G. Handbook of Unusual Energies. Mokelumne Hill, CA: Health Research, 1976.

The Grumbacher Ilbrary. Art of Color Mixing. New York, 1966.

Hall, Manly. Masonic, Hermetic, Qabbalistic and Rosecrucian Symbolical Philosophy. Los Angeles, CA: The Philosophical Research Society, Inc., 1973.

Hills, Christopher. Nuclear Evolution. London: Centre Community Publication, 1968.

Johnson, Kendall. Photographing the Non-Material World. New York: Hawthorne Books, 1975

Kilner, Walter. The Human Aura. New Jersey: Citadel Press, 1965.

Kolb, L. The Painful Phantom. Springfield, IL: Charles C. Thomas, 1954.

Luscher, Max. The Luscher Color Test. New York: Pocket Books, 1969.

Luscher, Max. The Four-Color Person. New York: Pocket Books, 1977. Mann, Felix. Acupuncture: The Ancient Chinese Art of Healing and How it Works Scientifically. New York: Vintage Press, _ 1962.

Miller, Dennis, and Smart, Edward. Loom of Creation. New York: Harper and Row, 1976.

Klimo, John. Channeling. Jeremy Tarcher Inc.Los Angeles, California, 1987. 121

Ostrander, Sheila, and Schroeder, Lynn. Psychic Discoveries Behind the Iron Curtain. New York: Bantam Books, 1970.

Ouseley, J. Color Meditation. London: L.N. Fowler & Co., Ltd., 1949-1972.

Panchadas, Swami. The Human Aura. New York: Yoga Publication Society, 1940.

Powell, A.E. The Etheric Double. Wheaton, IL: Theosophical Publishing House, 1973.

Powell, A.E. The Astral Body. Wheaton, IL: Theosophical Publishing House, 1973.

Tansley, David V. Subtle Body. London: Thames and Hudson, 1973. Tompkins, P. , and Bird, C. The Secret Life of Plants. New York: Avon Books, 1973.

Williamson, J.J. Seeing the Aura. Hastings, Sussex, England: Metaijhysica1 Research Group, 1954.

Magazines:

Bailey, A., and Moersch, H. "Phantom Limbs, " CanadianM.A.J. July, 1941. 45:37-42.

Henderson, A., and Smith, J. "Phantom Limbs, " Journal of Neurology, Neurosurgery and Psychiatry. May, 1948. 11:88-112.

Hill, Scott. "Paranormal Healing in Russia." Fate. August, 1981, pp. 60-69.

Riddoch, George. "Phantom Limbs and Body Shape, " Brain. December, 1941. pp. 197-222.

Walker, Morton "The Power of Color" Avery Publishing Group, New York City, 1991

Redfield, James "Celestine Prophecy" Warner Books, 1995. 122

E.S.P.

The initials E.S.P. stand for extra sensory perception—a broad label for the various topics of parapsychology. Parapsychology is a field of study concerned with the investigation of evidence for telepathy, precognition, clairvoyance, psychic photography; color sensing, psychic healing and PSI energy. In order to teach E.S.P. exercises in the classroom, some basic information can be used concerning Intuition (PSI energy) precognition, clairvoyance and telepathy. A few of my own ideas on these topics are presented as well.

First, though, what has science found out about E.S.P. ? To begin to answer this question, it is necessary to look at some of the research done by such probing individuals as Louise Rhine, Jean Malay, Targ and Putoff, and their colleagues. After thirty years of E.S.P. research, Rhine and his associates have found no conclusive evidence that proves the existence of extrasensory perception. However, they have been able to observe certain characteristics concerning E.S.P. abilities in lab situations.

For example, Rhine and his associates concluded that individuals exchanging information without direct communication through known modes (telepathically) communicated best when the symbols used in the experiments were changed periodically. After using the same symbols, a repeated number of times, the accuracy scores of the participants declined. Rhine's work prompted researchers to use more liberal approaches to testing E.S.P. Rather than pre-selecting the information to be shared between a sender and receiver, they gave them options on information to be shared. Given more freedom in their telepathic communication, the participants' scores reflected greater E.S.P. ability.

E.S.P. researchers (housed in major universities in the Soviet Union) take a much more progressive approach to the study of telepathy and related abilities. There researchers believe that testing for E.S.P. ability in individuals without apparent knowledge, understanding and/ or a past demonstrated ability of E.S.P. is like asking an infant to lift a fifty-pound weight. In their research they first tested for very simple E.S.P. ability, then gradually increased the complexity and difficult of the tests.

For example, they may first ask people with demonstrated psychic ability to move something very tiny, such as a thread with an arrow attached, by concentrating on such a task. In the meantime, the researchers monitor the slightest movement, not only by observation, but with electronic devices designed to detect the smallest of movements. After successful completion of such a task, the tests gradually become increasingly more difficult, until tasks such as the ones used in Rhine's research, i.e., sending and receiving telepathic symbol information with E.S.P. cards, are within the realm of possibility of the subjects' capabilities.

Elementary school children demonstrating the use of the ESP Flasher (creative ESP)

One of the most difficult and perhaps interesting of these tasks involves conveying smells. The sender detects a smell and telepathically sends this information to a receiver who then "perceives" the information and experiences the transmitted smell. Russian parapsychologists find that hypnotizing test subjects greatly increases their ability to send and receive thought forms.

Psychokinesis (telekinesis) is a topic I wanted to continue to shed light on here because I have had some personal experience with a similar phenomena. As we have learned with the thread experiment, psychokinesis is a term coined by Soviet scientists; the ability to move objects at a distance. Referring to the journal of paraphysics and other references we learned that they have cultivated famous psychics to conduct experiments on PK. As shown in the photograph of Boris Ermoloav he is manipulating a matchbox suspended in mid air. The pedagogical science labs in Moscow, stimulate my creative juices to do further exploration.

Other psychics are seen manipulating a small pillbox or matchbox across a table by pulsating their bioplasmic auric field to a high velocity. Little is known how the energy interacts with the object; but the easiest object to warm up to is a compass. With compasses there is no static friction. Stormy weather creates a negative outcome and extreme weight loss was another characteristic that was associated with psychokinesis.

In my experiment with a glass flask containing ethyl alcohol (explained in the forward), I am able to interact with the alcohol, not by pulsating my auric field but by a mental process that carries information to the ethyl alcohol. It is all about an energetic structure. In Russia they have found that the mind doesn't work directly on the brain. The Etheric Body affects the link between the mind and brain cells. I could be 3 feet away and still be able to affect the ethyl alcohol. This may be akin to Don Juan (Carlos Castaneda's sorcerer friend) who manifest this auric field to cross the huge waterfall over a gorge. Pavlita who I speak about in the Radionic channel demonstrated a manipulation of geometric metallic objects. Bioplasmic energy is used to convert motoric force energy to spin a metallic fan on a needle. It's no longer mind over matter, but minds over force field. Most people feel that the energy is static electricity but it has been proven to be a subler energy.

Some very recent work in telepathic communication has been done closer to home. In Jean Malay's doctoral dissertation, The Relationship Between the Synchronization of Brainwaves and Success in Attempts to Communicate Telepathically, she describes various modes of telepathic communication. In her research a sender was asked to make a drawing of a magazine picture. The receiver was then asked to draw what he or she perceived to be the transmitted image. Malay concluded that shapes were the dominant mode of telepathic communication in one group, colors in another, mood and concepts in the third and fourth. Though no one mode emerged dominant in all groups tested, one mode was dominant per pair.

I question the acuity of the telepathic information in this example of E.S.P. research, since more information than just the magazine image may be unconsciously transmitted or the paramours the researcher has set. For example, the sender may be transferring subconscious information about him or herself to the receiver while making the drawing. The drawing, therefore, acts as a witness (recall from the Pendulum section that a witness is anything, a fingerprint, lock of hair, or even a photograph, which identifies an individual by having energy of the same frequency as that individual). The receiver may gather an impression of the transmitted image, but may also gain information associated with the sender byes through the witnessing process latent in the telepathic information. This information would then possibly be reflected in the drawing made by the receiver of what he or she believes to be the transmitted image, and this acts as interference that distract the receiver from perceiving the true nature of the picture send.

The latter example relays on intuition for some of the information received. Dowsers use this sense to read auras, dowse locations and find water, as well as answer questions. Cultivating our intuition, therefore, can be extremely beneficial and easier than might be expected. It is primarily a matter of acknowledging our intuitive sense to provide the right answers. Most of the time a first "hunch" or "gut feeling" will provide information that answers a question or resolves a problem. Sometimes the answer comes spontaneously. Sometimes one needs to search the subconscious for answers in meditation.

If you have a problem or difficult situation that needs attention, try using intuition to brainstorm possible solutions. Lie down or sit down some place quiet and comfortable, and do a few breathing exercises (perhaps as described earlier in this book). Give yourself autosuggestions to relax, yet remain alert. At this point, you may want to do some meditations exercises, if you find yourself restless or know you will have difficulty concentrating on your topic. Visualizing another environment works well, try nature, especially the beach. To see if you are in a relaxed or alpha state check your pulse. Lay your fingers over the underside of your wrist—don't use your thumb—and feel for a small throb; 60 throbs or less per minute indicates a relaxed body state. If you still need to relax more, try listening to some gentle, quiet music. Using a crystal often helps put you in a meditative state. Refer to the section on Radionic or Meditation for offerings of tapes or CD's to use in relaxation, or, try these selections:

- J.S. Bach, "Largo from Concerto in G Minor for Flute and Strings"

- G.F. Handel, "Largo from Concerto NO. 1 in F" from Music for the Royal Fireworks

- A. Vividly, "Winter" from The Four Seasons, or "Two Concertos for Mandolin" from Three Concertos for Viola Damage

Other music suggestions include works by Tiedemann, Corolla and symphonies by Bach, & Handel. There are some very good pieces by Peruvian; Inca flute players, Celtic & synchronized music. Experiment with different musical pieces to see what works best for you.

Lighting is also an important variable in producing a relaxing environment. Certain lighting, especially subdued light, can establish a psychological state of comfort. Various colored lighting has vibrations corresponding to the subtle energies of the body and affect the emotions. For relaxation, it is best to have dim lighting. Use a blue, green, indigo bulb with shade or a normal soft light shade. Not much has been done with black light, but likely its high frequency radiation might be conducive to receiving creative thoughts and images.

A manufacture report has shown that using green lights in meat packing rooms help keep meat fresher. Reports are that the well-known psychologist Wilhelm Reich used a green light in his orgone accumulator to facilitate the accumulation of orgone energy. Once you have established a comfortable environment, concentrate on the issue needing attention, whether a question, problem, topic or situation. Look at all sides of the situation, letting your intuition flow. Write out possible solutions, perhaps, and the feelings associated with each. Eventually, your intuition will provide a strong feeling for one of the solutions; follow that intuitive lead, as it seems wise and I have learned that the higher self or over soul uses the intuition to communicate with you; it is a conduit.

INTUITION/ TELEPATHY

Telepathlogy is the ability to communicate with other people, plants and animals using a sense other than one of the five physical senses. Essentially, there are two aspects to telepathic communication. Usually the solar plexus or third charka center is the "emotional entrance" into the body; a feeling sense. There are light cords, sent out unconsciously, to this area when we are communicating with another being (refer to the Huna system of Hawaii in meditation Channel.) We call it "Cording" another person; on the other hand, "decoding" is possible, also, by disconnecting via the solar plexus from another. The first is that of tuning into another person or thing using PSI (intuitive sense) the feeling sense that perceives another's emotional level (astral body) sometimes referred to as Clairsentience.

These senses, known as the "sixth senses," have historically been labeled intuition—that which yields direct knowledge or cognition without evidence of rational thought. Experts in problem-solving say that the answers to problems or questions lie within the problem. Unlike Donald Trump whose intuition, it is said, in somewhat different ways can and does size up a person or make a decision about a prospective deal by listening to a person talk for a few minutes. It then seems he makes an instant decision about the deal or person by relying on his highly-developed sense, intuition. In his book and interviews, it is as plain as day, to me, that he uses this special sense to make decisions—a natural ability that most successful entrepreneurs possess, according to research.

Answers cannot be separated from the problems. They compose an integral unit which must be wholly understood before an effective resolution results. It has been scientifically proven that most successful business people are those who rely on intuitive solutions after deep examination and contemplation of the issues at hand. They turn the problem over and over mentally to see each aspect of the problem until flashes of insight emerge in answer (traditional meditation). The right answer emerges from the subconscious storehouse of the fifth or sixth senses? The subconscious acts as a channel to our "super mind," where all knowledge exists and can be extracted when one develops the ability to communicate through thought.

Intuition manifests itself in many forms. Anyone who has lived in the Midwest of the United States has probably felt some anxiety prior to realizing a tornado was approaching. For me, the experience was as if a great suction source was tugging at my energy field. There is a story of a small group of people who ignored similar intuitive warnings. One day they were sitting on the porch of their home, and all three felt the potential presence of a big storm; yet, they ignored this tugging warning. Lightning struck a tree in front of their porch, and the shock waves actually knocked one of the woman fully through the wall of their house; she later died in a hospital. Had they acknowledged this vital intuitive warning, this unfortunate death may well have been averted.

A friend had a more hopeful experience. She was drying her hair with a blow dryer with very strong wattage. A small whisper within her mind, she recounts, told her, "Turn it off, and put it down." When she did so, as she practices intuitive guidance on a regular basis, it was discovered the electrical insulation on the dryer cord had begun melting and that within a centimeter of the finger nearest it, as she had held it near her head. She listened, possible avoiding an electrical shock or worse of a major kind!

Another incident of the practice of intuition was described to me. Two men were traveling alone a road in their car. Suddenly the driver swerved to miss something on the road. The passenger asked, "What made you swerve?" Looking surprised, the driver responded, "I didn't swerve the car!" They both argued for a few minutes until the passenger said, "Okay, there's a way to prove what I say. We'll go back to see if anything is on the road that may have caused you to steer out of its way." They went back, and, sure enough, there was a large hold in the roadway. If the driver's sixth sense hadn't tipped him off about that hole, they would have hit it and possibility damaged their automobile or experienced injury themselves. Intuition can manifest in many ways.

Intuition and other sixth senses can be experienced in many ways. On the following pages, some of my personal experiences are sighted and some scientists have discovered practical approaches for developing various aspects, of some of the sixth senses of telepathy, precognition and clairvoyance (spiritual sciences).

At this point I want to focus on what might be additional evidence of the process of the sixth senses of clairvoyance, telepathy focused in the fourth dimension. While attending a weekly crystal healing visualization group I continued experiencing an image that baffled my analytical mind. I couldn't figure out why I continued to have an image (over a period of weeks) of a faceted diamond in a hand as it ascended from a pool of water. It wasn't until I became aware of my higher self or over soul, as it wanted to be called, that the meaning of the diamond came into focus. I saw a being (while I was in meditation) walking through a fog bank with millions of faceted diamonds glistening in the light as it reflected and refracted from its body illuminating the dark.

I came to realize that the diamond was symbolic of power and strength of the over-soul. It was as if Excalibur, sword of King Arthur, was ascending towards the heavens with special metaphysical powers to triumph over lower/slower vibrations that exist in our world; to show me how to transform limiting thoughts and experiences that held my consciousness back from becoming aware of the limitlessness of our omnipresent super conscious self. I focused on one of the facets on the illuminated diamond and I experienced a rushing upward sensation of energy of the over-soul. And with this process a feeling of elation came over me that expressed the light and enlightenment. I raised it to the 8th charka and felt the familiar run of atomic energy down to my chakras; I was clear again.

The first time, it spoke to me with a raspy voice: "I'm your over-soul, and you can learn to access me any time you need to and rejuvenate yourself; I had successfully channeled my over-soul. And it gave me a new message for the whole group as they watched me channel my over-soul. It said, "You can also rejuvenate yourself by contacting your over-souls anytime you want to". I could get counsel from my over-soul whenever I was in synch with its/my consciousness.

Spirit again has crossed the mind/body barrier as it did when I experienced my personal angel; I felt exalted in my third eye, and my physical eyes were both totally open; little pinprick flashes of light were coming in and out of my visual surroundings, making it difficult to stay grounded and focused.

To this day I continued to raise the over-soul and feel the elation to a great extent, as I did the first time I raised the God self. I now have more control over this process, making it easier to stay grounded and balanced in my body as the ascension takes place (Raising the over-soul still dramatically arches my back and throws my head back but that is a minor effect after raising the super self hundreds of times over a 25 year period. I have become accustomed to the minor distraction).I continue to teach this process in my workshops. (Recently I ran across a essay on the internet that Waldo Emerson wrote "The over soul", one of the best essays he ever wrote. It's a stunning look at the magnificent over soul.)

I would like to include another personal experience I had that reflex's a rich field of Telepathic information. I feel it's important here to include this knowledge because it expands the parameters of telepathic and clairvoyant experiences that give us, hopefully more evidence to under stand this phenomena.

I continue my personal experience with intuition and telepathy with a recent poignant experience that reinforced my feelings of how we are all connected together. Elizabeth Clare Prophet's book and topics on soul mates and twin flames speaks volumes on specific ways that we are all connected on basic universal levels. Just briefly, meeting your soul mate is someone with whom you have spent many lifetimes and life affirming experiences together that draw you closer to each other, in some cases, intentionally.

I had met my wife from last lifetime when I was a student at San Francisco State University. She was a stranger but we had an instant connection (I don't know how I know that, but intuition works something like this: you realize knowledge on a subtle level of awareness and it becomes your truth. As I have mentioned before, "You know because you know... truth, when you feel it."). We still have a long way to go in understanding the intuitive process.

But I really want to tell the story of meeting my twin flame because it became important to purge blocked emotions to our spiritual progress, and developing our consciousness and our uncanny ability to psychically communicate with each other; twin flames, or your soul's other half, your counterpart, your wholeness. As Elizabeth Clare Prophet says, "... in the beginning we were one consciousness or souls, and we split and became two souls; male and female"(in away I feel that twin flames may not be limited to the male and female gender). It is the wholeness of your Christ's self, the wholeness of the I AM present, and your absolute and eternal divine union with your twin flame that ultimately matters to us all, as we progress through our many lives on our way back to the oneness of our complex souls, and the Godhead.

I consider myself fortunate to have met my twin flame in this lifetime, as we all will, according to Elizabeth Clare Prophet, including our various soul mates each lifetime. Not until we both have learned all our lessons and are on the same soul level through many lifetimes of experience will we finally become whole, although, we cannot stay together if we are at different levels of soul development. Through my experiences with Morena, there is no doubt she is my twin flame. I feel compelled to tell this story because of its poignant effects of my life and our innate abilities.

She was attending Unity Church when I first met her, but I didn't make the connection. I saw her a couple of times after that... and I knew she had a familiar feeling to her, but I couldn't place it. Little did I know fate had a different agenda for us. At one service,

147

out on the patio, I mentioned to her that we had unfinished business to complete. She responded, " Oh" (later she told me that she had gotten a rush of energy through her heart.).

We decided to meet at our favorite coffee shop. I took pictures (I'm glad I did because I never got the same opportunity again). We talked for a short time and I invited her to my place the next day, being Valentines Day. I purchased a red rose for her to celebrate the occasion. As we were talking at the apartment, she broke down crying uncontrollably, and I took her into my arms and rocked her and asked her what was wrong. She replied with an answer I don't think I was prepared to hear, but I listened intently.

She described a lifetime as American Indian lovers. She was seeing and feeling the life we both had at that time: I was a warrior and she was my love. I found myself seeing her visual image of a staunch Indian overlooking a beautiful valley outside our hut. She continued describing the scene, and she told me that I was a warrior and had gotten killed in a battle. She was very distraught, in that lifetime, and wanted to commit suicide but the elders convinced her otherwise. She knew every little detail about our lives; and some I can't mention here. Eventually she calmed down and I consoled her like holding a small bird in my hands. I can't describe the emotional and spiritual bonding we went through that day.

As she moved towards the door to depart, I could feel that I was not my normal self. I was someone else. My eyes were, I felt, big as saucers and I was taller than I was; I had become my over-soul, my assented self. My love for her became so intense that I had feelings of not telling her to go... to hold her so close that we would become one again (I had other experiences of a channeling nature at various times in my life but, by far, this was the most intense feeling I had ever experienced). As she left, her eyes shone like stars in the night sky; time had passed unnoticed. As I followed her beautiful form, the red rose came to my mind, and I pitched it over the balcony as she turned to catch it as she descended the stairs. I said, " I'm sorry I didn't get your bouquet of flowers." She replied, " It only takes one" with a big smile and a sparkle in her eye.

The next time we met, it was at Starbucks coffee shop. We sat at an outside table. We were talking about something, when Morena said, "Someone is talking to me in my head... It's an extraterrestrial" (she is a very good conscience channel herself). This being started telling her to relate to me that we weren't supposed to be together in this lifetime (during the communication, I recognized this consciousness as inhabiting a woman at the dowsing conference 15 years ago). I asked this being if she looked like an extraterrestrial I had seen in the movie Mission to Mars. She replied, through Morena that she looks something like that being. Suffice it to say, this being was a female android from the future that I had found out about partially through the Ouija board years ago. And she was the being that I had a personal experience with during this time, of feeling a very soft supple hand on mine, with long supple fingers, that was the softest vibration I had ever felt, as I was driving home from the divining meeting that night.

Now she had come back again to communicate with me through Morena. Her name was Emeria, and she had a metallic green auric field; it sparked. She talked about some other things that were personal to Morena and me. During that exchange, when she said that we could not be together in this lifetime- I involuntarily started crying uncontrollably. Morena put her hand on my arm and said, "Let's go over to the car". I wiped my eyes and said I was sorry. As we arrived at the car she said, " I love you! I love you! and I feel like throwing up!, but , I have to meet a friend of mine for dinner." We said our emotional goodbyes and we left.

I went home and couldn't stop crying. I later called Morena on her cell phone and she was at a bookstore after getting in a fight with her dinner friend. I told her what was up and she offered to come over and console me but for some reason I said, "No, I can handle it".

From that time on I found that I was telepathically in synch with my twin flame. We started talking with each other on a regular basis every day. And she told me, one day on the phone, that she had channeled information about us from her guides. She had typed it and came over later to show me what she had channeled. I read what she had written, I think, with my mouth open. We were to go on a retreat to celebrate our love for each other and celebrate our spiritual love connection. There were other things about light portals on the planet and our relationship to higher consciousness, and that we had a blue energy beam to our hearts, to name a few things that she had typed.

She picked a location in Woodside, California to go on a retreat. It was a wonderful time to be together, and she channeled Emeria again and I showed her how to raise the over soul. And we used the hot tub and swam in the indoor pool, and had use of the large library sitting room area, with a huge stone fireplace, crystals and books to continue our relationship. We had the whole place to ourselves because it was on the edge of the rainy season. Each room had a river stone over the doorway that was inscribed with a profound saying; our said, " Expect a Miracle"(and I felt that this was truly a miracle).We had a wonderful time and we returned to our living spaces (as I found out later this was to be an indication of our day to day compatibility in the future. She ended up marrying a soul mate that she was seeing for some time, someone who could take care of her on the physical plane).You see she was a #22 super master vibration, with the make up 11+11=#22, which makes it difficult for her consciousness to stay grounded in her body and she needs some one to keep an eye on her; she would rather be off the planet than on it; and she often was; she had the gift of astral projection. Strangely enough, this is what her ex-husband said to me on one occasion.

As the days came and went, in our telepathic communication on a daily basis, we had a protocol that we instigated to make sure that it was truly who we thought we were in communication with. Each time we communicated I would first feel the special love vibration we had between us; if I didn't receive the vibration signal from her, I would not communicate with her. With that vibration signal I could find her anywhere on the planet; it would set up a resonant frequency between. Being an advanced dowser and a channel I had the knowledge to access vibration frequencies no matter where they were, and she being a conscious channel and an ascended super master vibration, (numerological speaking) we could make a connection at any time, any place, any where. I was her and she was me ultimately.

I can't go into all of the experiences we had in this writing, but there were some poignant experiences that I want to talk about because spirit works in miraculous ways. At the time Morena and her new husband were going on their honeymoon to the islands. After ascertaining this information, telepathically, she tried to prep me for the month's wait of non-telepathic communication while she was on her honeymoon; she wanted to spend quality time with her husband and she did. It's difficult to talk about our ability to communicate in this way because we were not only, telepathically connected, but we have a soul connection; we were in love with our twin flame. And to compound our experience I found out from my guides that I was her guardian angel.

For whatever reason Morena couldn't bring herself to break off communication with me even for a day, and neither could I, frankly, I was willing to try because it was her honeymoon. So I was pleased to be going to the islands with her, even if it was only telepathically (I should say that we would never interfere with each other's personal experiences; we both have high integrity). Being ethical is a prerequisite to being telepathic at lease for us. In the beginning she would initiate communication with me first, sometimes I would get such a rush of energy up and down my body, that consolidated our love even more.

She first contacted me on the airplane on her way to the islands. It was as if I was looking through her eyes peering out the windows of the airplane (of course this was a well known process using remote viewing). Every day, she would tune in to me and I could see her sitting at the pool or on the balcony or whatever environment she was in at the time. At various times she would ask me if I had suggestions of things to do on the island for a month.

I told her that I have never visited the islands, but I had remembered some things that I had seen on DVDs and films that I have watched in the past. I consider myself a creative person so I was able to give her some suggestions like spear fishing, net fishing and various hiking excursions to parts of the islands; she was overjoyed to get some fresh ideas, and she and her husband took advantage of my suggestions and had a wonderful time.

There is one experience that comes to the forefront of my mind as I think about Morena's trip, and I'm glad I was along to help her and maybe even save her life. This experience proves not only to me but also to Morena and even to her husband that telepathic communication is not just illusion or fantasy, but is a tangible way of communication. It was the day she and her husband were on a scuba diving trip off one of the islands. Morena tuned into me, as she had done every day, and I could see the beautiful underwater scene, in black and white, and then at some point, I started seeing the colorful fish, prickly pink sea urchins, yellow kelp and the most beautiful clear blue water you could imagine.

All of a sudden, Morena started having trouble with her air tank. She couldn't breathe! She grabbed her regulator with both hands and tried to force the air from it, but to no avail (she was under the water about 30 feet, and her husband was looking at plants and animals below her). When I realized what was happening, I almost went into panic myself not knowing what to do! In an instance, my survival instincts kicked in and I yelled at her husband, "Ed, Morena, Morena is in trouble." This was enough to get him to react by looking for Morena above him. He quickly turned and realizing that she was in trouble. With a couple of flicks of his powerful fins, he was at her side giving her his regulator to buddy-breathe to the surface of the water (I had a scuba driving class in college and this practice is something you learn in this type of situation.)

As she broke the surface of the water, she took a deep breath, and said to her husband, " what happened" as she pulled her face mash off, he replied, "Don yelled your name in my head, and I turned and saw that you were struggling with your regulator." They swam to shore and talked for a long time about what had transpired. I didn't tune into the conversation, I guess I was getting tired, and I knew that Morena was safe, and it was Ed that now who believed in telepathic communication; if he had any doubt.

When they got back from their honeymoon, I wrote her a short note and put it in the mail as I had done on other occasions, and mentioned her near accident with her air tank. I said I was glad I was there, in consciousness, to help her and give her some assistance. She spoke to me as she was reading the note and said, "You mean the problem with my regulator" and, seeing her face, she couldn't believe what she was reading.

This is a critical point in telepathic communication – when you have a response spontaneously coming back from the other party, you know that you are in true telepathic communication with the person – her response was not predetermined before her dialogue with me. Her heart was really open at that point, and I experienced her love, intently focused on me, and I felt that old familiar energy rush up and down my body; I was beaming (I would like to say I was foaming at the mouth, but I wasn't; just picture Jerry Lewis).

As time marched on, I continued to experience our telepathic process through my own feelings. It has been over six years now, and I have been in telepathic communication with Morena every day, and our connection seems to be becoming clearer as we experience this incredible process of telepathic dialogue. In the beginning, when she would tune into me, my heart would feel lighter. I think her love was healing me from the broken heart I had sustained from my first love that I had experienced in my younger life. I don't get that sensation now – maybe I'm healed.

There was another situation with Morena that fostered my belief in our telepathic communication, early on. I perceived Marina being really sick one day, as we were still in conversation with each other in the real world (I became aware of her condition telepathically). It was so powerful when I amassed my healing masters and archangels together with my healing abilities and did a powerful healing on her, where she resided two towns away. Well, it worked, she called me on the telephone, very excited, and told me that she had felt a powerful healing energy coming from me that made her feel much better, and that she could get out of bed. She was elated to feel my energies and kept repeating, "I felt your energy, I felt your energy!" I felt really great and relieved that she was feeling better. So I guess the proof was in the pudding; and I love pudding.

Additional personal experiences shed light on the fourth dimension. While attending a weekly crystal healing visualization group I continued experiencing an image that baffled my analytical mind. I couldn't figure out why I continued to have an image (over a period of weeks) of a faceted diamond in a hand as it ascended from a pool of water. It wasn't until I became aware of my higher self or over soul, as it wanted to be called, that the meaning of the diamond came into focus.

I saw a being (while I was in meditation) walking through a fog bank with millions of faceted diamonds glistening in the light as it reflected and refracted from its body illuminating the dark. I came to realize that the diamond was symbolic of power and strength of the over soul.

151

It was as if Excalibur, sword of King Arthur, was ascending towards the heavens with special metaphysical powers to triumph over lower/slower vibrations that exist in our world, to show me how to transform limiting thought forms and experiences that held my consciousness back from becoming aware of the limitlessness of my omnipresent self.

I focused on one of the facets on a diamond and I experienced a rushing upward sensation of energy of the over soul. And with this process a feeling of elation came over me that expressed light and enlightenment. I raised it to the 8th charka and felt the familiar run of atomic energy down to my chakras; I was clear again.

The first time, it spoke to me with a raspy voice: "I'm your over soul and you can learn to access me any time you need to and rejuvenate yourself." I had successfully channeled my over soul. And it gave me a new message for the whole group as they watched me channel. It said, "You can also rejuvenate yourselves by contacting your over soul anytime you want to." I could get counsel from my over soul whenever I was in synch with its/my consciousness; which is a really great thing when you want to answer perplexing questions.

Spirit again has crossed the mind/body barrier as it did when I experienced my personal Angel; I felt exalted in my minds eye, and my physical eyes were both totally open; little pinprick flashes of light were dancing in and out of my visual surroundings, making it difficult to stay grounded and focused.

To this day I continued to raise the over soul and feel the elation to a great extent, as I did the first time I raised the God self. I now have more control over this process, making it easier to stay grounded and balanced in my body as the ascension takes place (Raising the over soul still dramatically arches my back and throws my head back but that is a minor effect after raising the over soul hundreds of times over a 25 year period; I have become accustomed to the minor distraction).I continue to teach this process in my workshops.

It seems that the Russians may have beat us to the punch again in scientific research and application for the study of psychic phenomena, at the International Scientific Research Institute for cosmic Anothropo-Ecology located in Novosibirsk,Russia Only a few know what's going on in this area of human consciousness.

This brings me to the "Kozyrev's Mirrors". This apparatus cuts out all electro-magnetic waves and makes it possible to experience the past, present and future. Extensive research in remote viewing has bared this out. The ability to fully experience our psychic abilities may result from blocking out the earth's electromagnetic field. The faraday cage make it possible for us to experience psychic phenomena in without the distraction of the electromagnetic field. The Faradays Cage was made of copper screen and a psychic would crawl inside the cage and conduct experiments on ESP. Unlike the Faraday Cage the Kozyrev's Mirrors made it possible to enhance psychic phenomena immensely.

Scientists have reproducible experiments, they say, that prove a torsional field beyond electro magnetism and gravity. This energy travels faster than the speed of light, like other similar energies– Ether, Zero Point Gravity energy, Taction energy, Bioplasmic energy and Eco-Plasmic energy.

I've been running into this term of late, torsional or torus energy fields that has become the catchword for modern day parameters of these subtle energies. Foster Gamble in this his video gives us an impressive look at the torus energy from his own personal experience as a child and historical information from cultures around the world. Richard Hoagland a NASA scientist is also experimenting with energy from a practical point of view with his studies of Venus crossing the sun, recently; he uses an inexpensive clock to record the vibrations from the transit across the sun and sacred sites around the world; as recent as 2012.

The Kozyrev mirrors are made of special steel called Permalloy-which has properties that attract magnetic energy inside a double tube that reflects torsional energy and thought form energy back to the thinker. These brave souls experience consciousness outside of linear time, similar to deep meditation.(It's hard to determine at what brainwave frequency they may be functioning at, but I would think that it would be the deeper levels of Theta and Delta in hyperspace).

Two scientists Trafimov and Kaznacheev have come to some interesting conclusions:

a.)" In the absence of electromagnetic fields, we have access to energy of   instantaneous locality, that underlies our reality".

b.) " Once a person requires access to these states, there consciousness remains engage within the field".

They go on to say that the global electromagnetic soup of computers and all other electromagnetic devices impede our primal communication skills. They have also stated to that human consciousness is now mechanically viable.(Google Kozyrev mirrors yourself and read the entire article.)

REMOTE VIEWING TASK

MATERALS

- drawing paper

- pencils, crayons

- or markers

The first step in this remote viewing exercise is to decide on who the sender is gong to be; that is, who will leave the classroom and draw or photograph a field site. The sender can be a volunteer or can be chosen by the group or group leader. As the group leader, you may want to be the first sender until the children understand the procedure, especially the role of the sender. (When first doing this E.S.P. task with my students, I was the sender while an adult aide stayed in the classroom and directed the children's activities You may want to reverse this process and have your assistance go out of the classroom; ask a parent to help out with this activity also.

Remote viewing drawing of a VW bug, one

This drawing is the one I drew while standing in the target area.

After a minute or two, have the children open their eyes and draw what they have seen. Once they have completed this, have them close their eyes again and visualize another image. Repeat this process until the sender returns. Depending on the age group of your students, the sender should not be out longer than ten minutes. Younger children have less of an attention span than older children, so judge accordingly.

Once the class seems to be comfortable with this exercise, you might want to try variations on this theme: establish pairs of senders and receivers, send more than one student to a field site, and so forth.Remind students that they should clear their minds of all distractions and concentrate on the telepathic information. Impress upon the students that analyzing the images while seeing them is counter productive to the remote viewing process, since analyzing is largely a left- brain function and can interfere with ESP right-brain transmission.

The first remote viewing task should be primarily a practice exercise to alleviate some of the self-consciousness, inhibitions and problems the students may naturally have whenever trying out something new. Once they understand the processes of remote viewing and are comfortable with it, enhance their experiences by doing relaxation exercises and chakra meditation. Always have children describe their experiences after the exercises, so they can learn from one another and will have additional examples to guide their learning.

E.S.P EXERCISE:

MATERIAL:

- thin cardboard or paper, 8/12" x 11"

- scissors

- black or color marker

- envelopes

- ruler

ESP CHART:

Here is a simple telepathic exercise. It is useful for helping students develop their telepathic powers. On the 8 ½" x 11" piece of paper, or cardboard, draw a horizontal line 2" from the top. Split the paper into nine equal boxes by drawing two vertical lines down the page and two lines horizontally across the page. Number each square. Leave spaces for name and date at the top (see drawing above). These are telepathy cards. Each student needs a copy for this exercise.

For this exercise, the group leader must stand somewhere in the room, where he or she can be seen but where the children cannot see the images on the 3" x 5" cards. One by one the leader must concentrate on the images by picturing the images on the cards. The rest of the class will try to receive the image telepathically and draw it in the corresponding square. Instruct the children to draw the first mental picture that comes to mind. Continue until the cards are completed. Have the children check their results as you hold up the pictures to give the corresponding number for each.

The students will be using the telepathy cards to draw telepathic images sent by you or the group leader. These images should be simple drawings made on separate 3" x 5" cards. Number each card, one through nine, so they can be identified. You may want to use colored pens for drawing because some people relate to color telepathy better than black and white.

Reframe from having the kids use a ruler to make the telepathy cards when first learning this exercise, because ruler activities are left brain functions, logical/linear, which are not normally related to creative processes. Once the students understand what is expected of them, when they are comfortable with the exercise and the telepathy cards , they might then be able to make the cards without disrupting creative flow. Jean Millay's study indicates that alpha waves exist in the left and right side of the brain, which implies that both sides maybe involved in creative processes to some exstend.[17] So with this in mind, we can try the ESP task again, this time with the students making their own telepathy cards after a brief relaxation session of deep breathing exercises or listening to calm music.

After the students have relaxed and finished their telepathy cards, repeat the E.S.P. exercise. As you repeat it, watch for improvement. Always ask them to relate their experiences after each exercise, to encourage interest and facilitate learning by stimulating the students to learn form their peers. Some comments from the students in my class were: " It first popped into my mind;" "I saw an outline of bluish light surrounding the design;" or "the design had colors all around it, moving colors."

It would be a good idea for them to keep a journal, written or pictorial to refer to especially if discussions for any reason would be delayed. In learning about their own abilities, rather than spending so much time watching television or using the computer, for example, these exercises and related lessons can stimulate children to take much more interest in their natural abilities…who knows? Some day they, too, may be protected by their skills at intuitive listening, telepathic knowledge and gaining attunement with the Universe and its unseen forces, as well as learning to communicate with difference levels of intelligent consciousness.

---

17 Ostrander, S.and Schroeder, L.Handbook of Psychic Discoveries.Berkeley, CA: Berkeley Publishing ompany, 1974

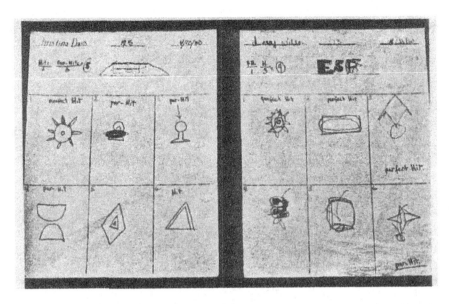

Children's card responses

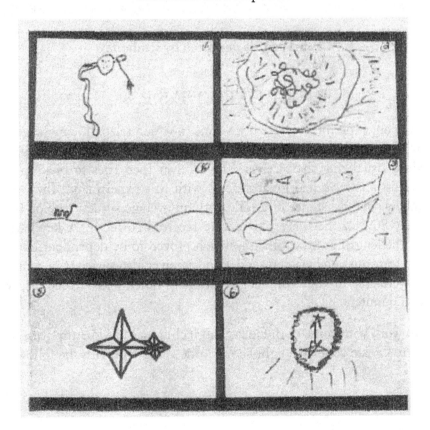

Children's card responses

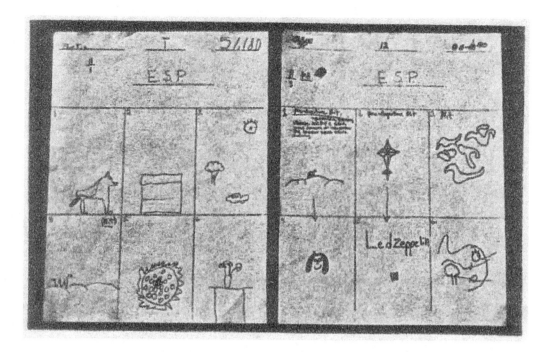

E.S.P. cards designed by students

CREATIVE E.S.P.

In the Soviet Union, experiments have been done in which telepathic messages were created using flashing lights. A sender concentrates on a number or letter, flashing on and off, repeatedly, while visualizing the receiver. The receiver then tries to pick up the telepathic message. The Russians have had great success with this experiment. They've been able to send 130 numbers over a distance of a mile with an average success rate of 100 out of 130, or approximately 80% of the images that were received correctly. A key variable in these experiments is the length of transmission, which proved to be dependent upon the sender's ability. Time of transmission between sender and receiver also varied (at a constant distance). Some senders were able to send numbers or letters as quickly as 11 seconds, whereas some required up to a minute.

It is possible to work with some of the ideas and techniques used by the Russian researchers in the classroom. Create your own light show in the classroom with the following ideas.

FLASHER DEVICE

To make a flashing device that can be used for classroom experiments, start by putting together the base of the flasher an oatmeal container and a cardboard box. Cut the bottom off the oatmeal container and paint the inside black. (Merchants will often donate materials if they know that you're working on an educational project.)

MATERIALS:

- flasher buttons

- large ice cream tub, small shoe box, or any small cardboard box

- scissors or knife

- light socket with cord

- 7 ½ watt night light

G.E. Code 7 ½ x/cs

- oatmeal box or round cardboard cylinder

- frosted glass or opaque plastic

  (same circumference as oatmeal box)

- scotch or masking tape

- tin foil

- flat black paint

Take the cardboard box and cut two holes—one for the oatmeal box cylinder and one for the light socket. Cover the outside of the boxes with tin foil. Place a flasher button in the base of the 71/2 watt light socket and insert the bulb in the bottom of the oatmeal box and pull the cord through. You may want to cut the bottom part of the box off at a 20 degree angle so that the box leans toward the user. This makes it easier for the sender to see the image. Take oatmeal box and tape a piece of frosted glass over the end of the box or use opaque plastic that you can acquire at a Tap Plastic or other plastic stores.

Now all you need to do is put a number or letter on the glass and turn on the light. Move your face close to the end of the oatmeal box viewer and concentrate on the number being flashed to send it to the receiver. You can cut numbers out of cardboard, which can the be painted black, or buy them at an art store and paint them black, if necessary, or students can make up their own symbols to use.

These are the images I drew to stimulate the children to see and draw. I tried to use as many different shapes as possible.

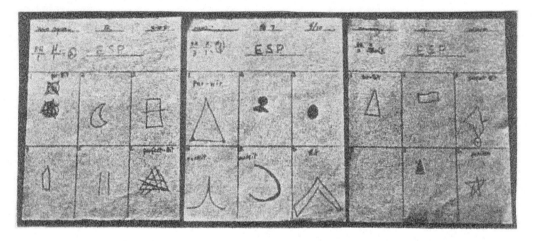

Actual children's E.S.P. drawings

Actual E.S.P. drawings done by elementary school aged children

PRECOGNITION

Precognition is the awareness of future events before they happen. Recently, I have experienced two such events which should demonstrate this potential. Before receiving an important letter, I had a strong feeling something involving the information in the letter was pending. The sensation was so strong I felt like I was being drawn into a vacuum, aware of nothing around except this pulling sensation. Because of this precognition, I was able to gather some information before the important letter arrived. The result was a considerable savings of money.

Another precognitive event I recently experienced involved an average Saturday of chores. My roommate and I were clearing out the garage of many things no longer needed. After picking them up and loading the car, I envisioned a specific corner in San Francisco which, when I drove to that spot, turned out to be the very location for dropping off discarded items. In that district it is not unusual to see discarded furnishings on the sidewalk where people leave them for others in need. Seeing this locale in mind (seeing the future) permitted me to let others know where to recycle as well; and teach the process.

I continued to use this skill whenever I need to see into the future. Precognition is a great way to see where your next parking place will be. It is not as hard as you may think. If you are familiar with the area it makes it easier to find a space. First set your intent, and it doesn't hurt to call on your parking fairies (don't laugh) then be open to the first image that comes into your mind; see it. Arrive at that location; look for the space; try again if it doesn't pan out. Keep trying until you get the hang of it; often I find a space the second time around. With persistent it will become second nature the more you use it. As psychic Silvia Brown says in her new book, nature spirits oftentimes provide better guidance to call upon because they are closer to the earth.

Dreams are another way to perceive precognitive information, many people see numbers to win the lottery or see a disaster having in their dream and latter on their way to work or seeing an event on TV realize that they this was the image in their dream the night before.; refer for to the dream section for more details.

Although these are by no means spectacular examples of precognition, they give some evidence of routine ways in which precognition may influence our lives. Try describing these two events, or ones of your own, in the classroom. Children love to hear these sort of "magical" stories, especially the unbelievable or bizarre. Entice them to learn more about precognition with stories and illustrations, while simultaneously letting them realize that precognition is a very routine and dependable means, for the most part, of understanding the world.

You may also encourage your students to tell stories from their own experiences with knowing beforehand. This approach is perfect for stimulating creative imagination in the children while they relate their stories. This is one method of opening up the channel for precognition as well as the other precious psychic abilities. Actually, any activity that utilizes the right side of the brain may stimulate cognition of a psychic nature. The right side of the brain is said to be the site of intuition and creativity; whereas, the left takes part in logic and organization of thoughts.

Both are used in practicing psychic functions. It is the right side, however, that must be developed to realize and stimulate these abilities so that the left side can order them in such as way that is coherent and recognizable. Often children in the Soviet Union often do not start using a pencil or calculations until they age of 10. Their teachers want them to develop their creative side first, to learn who they are, and then concentrate on the left brain functions.

CLAIRVOYANCE

Most of the clairvoyance information I use here comes from personal experience, from people with whom I have talked with about their experiences, and from readings. All this information is related to functioning outside the space-time continuum. The experience consists of perceiving images from past life incarnations, some believe, or communicating with beings from other dimensional levels, and perceiving future events. I wrote about precognition in a preceding section, and would like to cite some experiences related to past life incarnations, which I believe in, and communications with other dimensions. As strange as it may sound, supporting evidence has surfaced concerning these very topics (Michael Talbot is one such physics).

From one point of view, the super-conscious self acts as a receptive antenna in the great flux of creative energy associated with different dimensions of consciousness. The term super-conscious self is little understood in our consciousness. Christopher Hills, in one of his students books, Energy, Form and Matter and Supersensonics, deals with this topic indirectly under the heading of "Supersensonics." Throughout his book, he mentions the process of the relationship humans have with cosmic consciousness. It is my interpretation that this concept connects man with his environment. He also claims that it is possible to communicate with intelligence at any particular point in the universe instantaneously. He cites research in telepathy, clairvoyance, radionics, sound, colors and light as support for his philosophical views—De La Warr, J.G. Gallimore, Andrija Puharich, Dale Walker and Nikola Tesla, Dr. Steven Greer, and Iasos are involved with the processes of cosmic communication.

One of the characteristics of the super-conscious self (the Over soul) is the freedom from limitations of the corporeal body. These apparent limits manifest themselves in thought intensity. Each human individual functions at a different level of "mind intensity, " that is, power which moves out through different levels of consciousness – not in the sense of distance, but in the sense of velocity (speed of mind intensity). It seems different velocities determine different levels of consciousness. The faster one's mind moves, the closer one gets to the super-conscious level. By attuning to this level of thinking, it is believed by the author and others that the ability to gather information and communicate throughout the universe with other beings is enhanced.

By clearing the mind of any thoughts other than those of total darkness (or is it dark matter), one can perceive knowledge and wisdom from a deeper level of expression than the normal awareness level. Moving from this point of connection with the higher self (over-soul self), one can ask relevant questions (dowsing can access this level of information). Answers to questions are received through a faster frequency of consciousness (consciousness being composed of light energy flow). This is the case when communicating with creation.

This principle can be stated in a slightly different way. It brings awareness into a phase-locking18 frequency with any quality of information that is chosen (act of will-Intention). This process is further strengthened by being in a very relaxed state of being. The super-conscious can work through the "body conscious, " utilizing the third eye center (pituitary gland) to receive visual energy forms (holograms) for the purposes of healing and information gathering. This is not to say that the super-conscious is not present at all times, but most of the time it functions on different dimensional levels and at levels of a faster frequency than those associated with the third & fourth dimension.

The fourth dimension is outside of the space continuum, but interacts with lower frequencies in a gradation fashion. In this type of environment, communication is instantaneous. In the February 1983 issue of Omni Magazine, Kathleen Stein, a computer graphic artist, suggests that one characteristic of the fourth dimension is "an instant at a point." My interpretation of her statement is that the "instant" referred to is an instant in time. And the "position" she refers to is a specific position on a computer grid system map, but could also interact with the third dimension as well. It could even be considered another physical dimension when consciousness interacts with it, but at a finer dimensional level.

Continuing with this discussion of the fourth dimension we receive information from Spirit, namely one of Kevin Ryerson's personalities-John (Kevin Ryerson is a well-known channel that work with among others Shirley McClain). He enlightens us when he tells us that the fourth dimension springs from an extension of the elements of time, space and gravity.(This is another physical universe.) As you move into higher levels of consciousness the lower levels of length, width, height, space and time take on illusionary qualities. They are not the concrete structures we once thought they were. John continues to explain, " and treating the seven subtle bodies, as in healing, ye are beginning to master the fourth dimension (John is an Essence). You are moving beyond just the material dimension"; you are moving into a higher faster dimension.

I remember an experience that a woman related to the group at a Russell Thomas lecture on metaphysics years ago. She had received visual information about a car that would run on a new type of energy. She said she had been "in contact with the Godsphere" and she asked, "Is there anything I can do about the gas crisis?" The advice came through her consciousness as clear as a bell. When she asked the Godsphere what it was, she then received the reply that it was "a new energy source that could power a car at high speeds". She was somewhat baffled by

---

18 Phase-locking loop is explained in Radio Shack's Dictionary of Electronics as a communications circuit in which a local oscillator (amplifier, transducer, i.e., individual human or crystal) is synchronized in phase and frequency with a received signal. Webster's Dictionary describes phase as any of the ways in which something may be observed, considered or presented, a change in development, in a cycle of changes.

this new idea because she had no mechanical ability or knowledge. She instead had faith in the power, which she was tapping into. She set out to develop this new energy source by consulting friends and reading various books on the subject. She succeeded in having a prototype built and tested. At that time she was looking for backers for her new energy source.

There is growing interest in new integrated methods of reaching other dimensions of consciousness. One method is through New Age music. Iasos, a new age Musician & lecturer on music theory & spiritually, (a graduate of M I T and inventor of his own electronic instruments) composes his music so as to influence various vibrations on different levels of ethereal and spiritual consciousness. Music has long been an inspiration to mankind. The music of Mozart, Handel and Beethoven inspired many to greater spiritual awareness. Now a new impetus has stimulated the growth of spiritual sounds, namely the study and understanding of vibration itself and the mechanics of how vibrational sound can influence consciousness to new heights of spiritual awareness.

Iasos, and other musicians are utilizing electronic sound vibration in relation to individual characteristics in order to change individual consciousness. According to "esoteric" teaching, each Zodiac sign has a sound vibration on a music scale. These teachings originate from the Pythagoras brotherhood. Iasos continues to explain his concepts of consciousness by using the analogy of a transformer converting & propagating energy down to grower levels of the aura field. The music of the spheres has a direct connection to individual sound, color and number vibration, which are three of the four elements that make up the third dimensional reality, it is said. It is not my tent here to develop all the ramifications of sound, color, and number, but to shed light on the possibilities manifesting in the "here and now". (Refer to Bib. for in depth information about Historical Esoteric teachings & Metaphysical information by Manly P. Hall.)

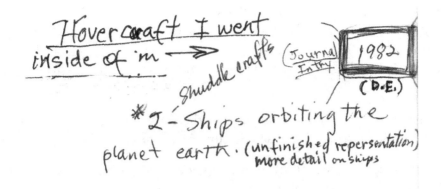

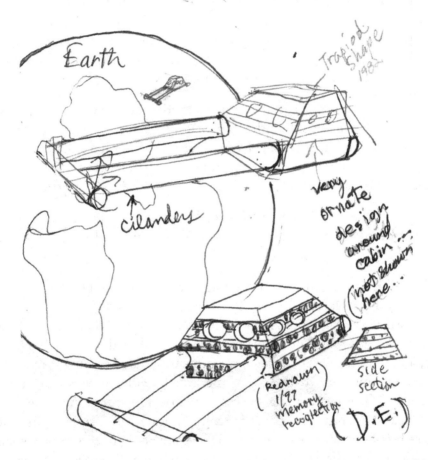

Having my own practical wisdom of alternative realization, and meeting a Plejaren guide persona of mine in 1982, after being pulled up (in my light body) out of the meditation experience to above the planet, seeing two hover-crafts stationary in space about the time the Space Shuttle was going up. Diverting my attention to one of the crafts, I noticed a being in a black space suit beckoning me to come over and go through the round porthole (this communication was done telepathically) and the veil between the dimensions, I was drawn to a beautiful alabaster-blue-skin-tone and large-eyed being (later, I learned he was a Plejaren being with silicon-based genetic make-up). Suffice it to say, this is one of the first conscious experiences I had, at the time, confirming intelligent beings in the universe with which some of us communicated on a regular basis. We continued down the hallway into a room making our way up a spiral pearlized circular staircase to a console room Over time, I came to understand that we have many personalities that we have created over time incarnations that are also our own personal individual personalities. There is so much we don't know about consciousness in this regard. We rely on these individual aspects to help us progress through life.

This is what is meant by a statement taken from the Bible: "We are co-creators with God", developing an individual personality each lifetime that evolves on thought eternity.

This personality is, by the way, still connected to your consciousness, that we draw upon in our life to help solve different problems or acquire certain skills.

There is an experience I should mention in this short discussion, to expand and extend various alterative consciousness experiences – namely similar to the channeling phenomena (and this is another aspect of channeling), having a separate being dropped into your body, becoming a part of your conscious for a short period of time. It doesn't interact with you, but just observes the way things are transpiring in your environment.

This phenomenon first happened to me years ago, stimulated by an extraterrestrial group name Astata (I go into more depth on this experience in the E.S.P. Channel). I'm sure this is a small glimmer of the abilities that super-consciousness beings have that has developed over thousands of years of evolution. They understand the levels and complexities of consciousness that we are just starting to understand.

This is an exciting time to be alive on the planet. We are making quantum leaps in knowledge and the understanding of consciousness itself and our spiritual selves, towards our own enlightenment as it has always been.

As I write about these ideas, I realize I'm going out on a limb to get the "fruit of the tree", so to speak, as Shirley MacLaine would say. I feel, as others do, we are at a crossroads in human history, where time is running out and we need to take, "that quantum leap" in order to find creative solutions to our problems to secure our survival on the planet. The universe is expanding, and I intuit the veil between the dimensions is stretching thinner and thinner, letting us experience more of what's on the other side (parallel universes, for those scientists reading this outline). This is becoming a necessary process for our evolution and expansion of consciousness, making it paramount that we communicate with beings from different levels of awareness to help us assimilate the knowledge we are going to experience when we finally pierce the veil as a race. We are fast approaching the edge of physical consciousness, on a conscious level, preparing for that quantum leap. This is akin to realizing the earth wasn't really flat, but profoundly round.

Experiences that profoundly affect your life and the synergistic expression seem to manifest themselves when you open yourself to the universe of non-local realities. Recently, I received letters from two psychics telling me of an experience I had with an angel (I receive letters all the time – psychics contacting me to do readings from the US and Europe). I was taken aback when not one, but two psychics, from different parts of the country, told me that I had an angel visitation recently, and her name was Myha (I had this experience at Unity Church recently).

A beautiful female angel with a long flowing ornate dress, in gold and white appeared to me and ran life force through my hands; it was a wonderful elated experience. Having a spirit communicate with you on a energetic level is a completely different awareness than just seeing the image in your minds eye. Having life force runs through your body moves the experience from a mental image to a physical process… where you are feeling the life force pulse through your physical body at instantaneous speeds; it became a expanded consciousness experience where the mind/body barrier has been crossed.

The energy entered the third dimensional reality through the subtle energy systems and the arteries of the parasympathetic and sympathetic nervous system creating a healing modality that uplifts your immune system and nutrient system and balances the body and mind consciousness; stimulating a spiritual balanced being. Life force is the love vibration that has created everything that functions in the universe. It also makes you aware that the angelic forms are real functioning beings that exist to help you develop or unfold your consciousness to its greatest potential. There are light beings that are omnipresent, and incredibly beautiful, one cannot begin to put into words what you were in sync with relating to the angelic realm. Classical masters paintings don't even start to capture the light qualities of these being. She has been with me for most of my life as a personal guardian, as she puts it.

When I first had the experience, she would come close to me and make comments about the archangels (Michael, Ariel & Hansel that worked with me) and would give additional guidance about my personal life, imparting tips on how to improve a particular situation.

It may be of benefit to interject here a discussion about holographic imagery and consciousness. We can draw on a great work called the Holographic Universe by Michael Talbot (he drew heavily on the research of Karl Pribram, a brilliant neurophysiologist, and David Bohm, a prominent quantum mechanics physicists) that seems to be changing slowly, the world's scientific view of our relationship with ourselves and the universe we function in. This remarkable look into the universe may solve some of the old mysteries of how the mind and brain really work integrating our consciousness in its wholeness, and the struggle to understand obscure topics like telepathy, near death experiences as well as lucid dreaming, religious and mystical parameters and healing modality.

It may be evident that our world and everything in it from the basic seed to the plants and animals, even subatomic particles to individual universes or phantom images projected far beyond the time and space continuum exist. The brain is a hologram folded in a holographic universe, says Karl Pribram. The holographic viewpoint is predicated on the study of different subatomic frequencies to focus our attention on the local and non-local universe.

It continues to draw our attention to the similarities in the dream state. The physical universe is construed as phantom images changing as the image takes on a new form and part. The solidness and separateness of the known universe is turning out to be an illusion as some religions of the East have expressed. The material world is maya-illusion, and we think we are physical beings participating in a solid physical world. This is also turning out to be an illusion.

Science thrives, says Michael Talbot, to take things apart to understand its parts only to realize it gives up smaller wholes. At the subatomic and deeper levels of the atom we are finding there only exists energy and energy changes that make up our physical universe. We are not the material substance we once thought we were.

Bohm (a prominent quantum physicist) believes communication locally and non-locally (either fixed in linear or expanded and aware of the whole) is not based on some invisible signal but because separateness is an illusion thus being connected to something at a deeper subtler level, a larger whole; the universal web, " to think of ourselves as a holographic mind/brain looking at a holographic universe is again an abstraction. An attempt to separate two things that ultimately cannot be separated is oneness."

But that is not to say that things are not individual with unique qualities. We function at many different levels at the same time; or non-time. As we saw in the Aura channel (chapter) we have many aspects to ourselves, even levels and levels of finer and finer energies that are merging our consciousness into other reality.

The holographic universe and time and space can no longer be relied upon to build a stable universal world view; and location itself is an illusion. No longer can we separate ourselves from anything else; even time and space become less relevant to our existence and the everyday lives we live. In a holographic universe, not only is consciousness already everywhere, it too is nowhere. Michael Talbot said, "It is local and non-local, it is here and there at the same time". The more you expand yourself into the resonance frequencies beyond the speed of light you become integrated into other realms that are closely related to etheric/auric fields of energy, you expand more non-locally. The most refined, powerful, pure non-local energy is the more undifferentiated mind comes into focus. It seems that our brain is cross-referenced with every other piece of information, another characteristic of a hologram, making the holographic system in contact with each piece of information in the inference pattern; the neuro net.

Researchers discovered that our visual systems are sensitive to sound and feeling frequencies and our sense of smell depends partially on "cosmic radiation", and every cell in our body is queued into a multitude of frequencies all filtering through the cells of the body. It is through the holographic process of consciousness and the brain that our knowledge is cross-referenced into normal frequencies of perception.

Michael Talbot continues expanding my knowledge about holographic parameters when he states, "in the mind and the holographic record of the past already exists, and interact together making it possible for us just to change our focus to access the past". And I suspect the future as well; this focus is just a thought away from another thought. Well, I know it's possible because I know many sensitives that can access Akashic Records to retrieve information.

In remote viewing David Morehouse speaks of traveling forward and backward in time. Of course, if you read the Radionics channel (in this book) DelaWarr could also access these levels of consciousness by using the marks-5 camera. But it's more that you are accessing universal mind outside of time and space to retrieve information about the past and the future.

There are times when you try to access information while you are in meditation... that you will go through the "veil" (separation of different dimensions by a thin sheath or membrane) to access differences in time. (Sometimes you experience in your meditation granulated texture that indicates the membrane between dimensions). Going through the veil seems to create a much clearer image that you are perceiving in your current level of consciousness; sometimes the image is expressed through circle geometry. This is a phenomenon that is not easily explained in our language. A circle appears and you see the image of the other environment through the circle?

I remember seeing this, " clearness" when I was pulled up around the planet and I went through a spaceship portal focusing on an extraterrestrial's face, becoming clear as a bell as I peered through the veil; making it easier to see every detail and make an energetic connection with this being (this being is my extraterrestrial persona, Zaln. I go into more detail of this experience in this section).

I remember years ago an experience I had when I visited an expert on dyslexia (I thought I was dyslexic at one time). He gave me an oral test, or should I say visualization, to determine if I was dyslexic. While I was doing the exercise, I experienced a textured or granulated substance in the fabric of time around me that made its self apparent. It is your higher mind that is interpreting the phenomena non-locally, outside of space and time. The mind exists in the subtle ethic field around the body as explained by well-known psychic Dryer, one of Michael Talbot's scientists. Other scientists and laymen take this perspective as well.

Even Dr. Steven Greer (the originator of C.S.E.T.I) indirectly prescribes to the holographic parameters when he speaks of our consciousness being omnipresent at all times: "It is the ultimate non-local integrator of the mind; it then becomes clear that our thoughts have an effect all over the earth and farther reaches of the universe, and beyond.

"This is why our physical systems, genetic systems and our engineering systems can evolve in one place. Our consciousness propagates non-locally everywhere in the universe. This is non-local node propagation through the perfect integration of consciousness, " says Dr. Steven Greer. In some ways extraterrestrial technological communication is a mind and machine process, having communication devices that interface with thought and propagate instantaneously 1 million light years from its point of origin.

Eventually, we will learn that everything has a consciousness, even inanimate objects. Everything is alive, everything is awake, even a rock, a plant. Nothing is without conscious intelligent life force (The famous scientist Bohn also feels this way as a product of the holographic paradigm). With this in mind, we can consider a hologram to have life or life force. In Radionics, we use a witness (a photograph, hair or blood spot) to tune into a person.

All the genetic vibration information is contained in the sample. And this information becomes a paradigm that expresses the quality of a holographic image. We can access this information through energetic frequency entrainment. Every individual can access this information through the holographic mind/brain.

Take for instance the video The Sun produced by the Nova series. While watching this video of the solar winds magnified thousands of times, showing us the ectoplasmic/fibrous golden light moving through space, I perceived a change in my consciousness, experiencing a change in consciousness at that time to where I came into resonance/entrainment with this powerful visual image. I remember feeling a wind-like force of bio- plastic energy rush through me at incredible speed, inundating every cell in my body; I was filled with light and life force and flow.

As long as I kept my focus, the longer I experienced this phenomenon; it seemed like minutes that I was engaged in this energy field. I can't express to you entirely how rejuvenated I fell after this experience. It was similar to the experience I had of looking at the sun feeling rushes of energy through my body from the solar orb (This was a Peruvian consciousness-raising group I belonged to years ago). So, it is not difficult to interface energetically with anything in the universe no matter the physical object or non-physical object or an image of an object. But from a holographic perspective the physical object is a holographic image projected from a non-local dimension of the universe.

In conclusion, I would like to offer a quote by Terence McKenna: "We are, in fact, closing distance with the most profound event a planetary ecology can encounter – the freeing of life in the Dark Chrysalis of Matter." Here, here!

SUMMARY/CONCLUSIONS

Extrasensory Perception is a topic that covers an abundance of different ideas. The scientific community in the United States has chosen to focus their attention on a few well defined areas, such as the origin of extrasensory perception. Little research has been conducted on how these areas of unusual sensing, telepathy, PSI, precognition, and psychokinesis affect communication between different species, in what ways these experiences affect regeneration or retardation of healing processes, or how such sensing influences the production or non-production of nourishment in different species. In the USA we, as usual, focus on the military implications before considering other more important area of research.

In the US we are still concerned with the why of these phenomena, unlike some scientific communities in Eastern Europe who are now more concerned with the how and what of this energy and how it affects various animate and sub-animate life forms.

`My intent in this publication was to concentration on historical and contemporary research and practical application areas of telepathy, PSI, clairvoyance and precognition. A brief survey of the field is presented, including work in the US, Soviet Union and England. The specific techniques developed by each continent are explained from my own perspective, in an effort to facilitate individual experiences in each of these areas by the reader.

Unlike the Soviet Union, the US has always had independent interest groups functioning within our society. There are many small groups around the country involved in there own research, taking up the focus of the society and testing these abilities in different directions. Subcultures have grown up around specific areas of paranormal phenomena in environments less structured than the laboratory setting. I believe this holistic focus gives us more understanding and a more natural process to the study of Parapsychological phenomena.

This channel follows the scientific community's definition of telepathy, precognition, and psychokinesis fairly closely, unlike previous channels that manifest information from meta physical and spiritual points of view. There is only one exception to this statement, the Clairvoyance section. This section relies heavily on my own and others' personal experiences about the clairvoyance phenomena. There is little scientific information about this area of paranormal phenomena; it may be because these experiences manifest in concepts about spirituality that lead the scientist out of the laboratory to study them; and scientific theory and philosophical groundwork that swart any form of universal understanding.

These ESP experiences cannot be defined by a single framework or definition, but require multi-dimensional interpretation. Some might say this is too general to derive any relevant scientific information, but becomes a process that can facilitate knowledge on subjective levels of perception, specific information formulated within the individual's processes of synthesis derived from his/her own present knowledge, relying on each individual's unique qualities to express this information in objective form.

CHECKPOINTS

Here are some additional suggestions for improving results of the preceding E.S.P. activity:

1. Make sure that both sender and receiver understand the exercise and are comfortable with trying it. A positive emotional atmosphere facilitates psychic experience.

2. If the child designated as the receiver is having difficulty receiving any telepathic image of the flashing symbol, change the sender. Choose a student that you think has a greater sending ability; for example, choose one that does not have difficulty maintaining steady concentration.

3. Research has also indicated that disturbances in the environment of the activity are not conducive to telepathic transmissions, so try to minimize distractions for the sender and receiver. This may not be true in the case of the remote viewing sender?

4. Stimulate interest in the students for the task before trying to instigate it. Interest has also been shown to be necessary in effective ESP transmission.

5. Help the receiver develop his or her telepathic potential by first practicing other related tasks described in earlier sections, i.e., lessons in the Meditation, Mandala and Pendulum channels will help you open up to your God given abilities.

POTENTIALITY OF PHENOMENON

You may be wondering what might be gained by the study of ESP. Let's brainstorm together and see what potential exists. If telepathic communication were developed and learned by all, communication systems would surely change (of course we involuntary do this now). We would be able to communicate with one another overlong distances without the use of the telephone or other long distance communication devices — no more power lines, telephone repairs or phone bills. We might be able to develop the capacity to communicate with all things, animate and inanimate.

Telepathic communications would, therefore, influence language, hopefully not causing it to become obsolete because communications would be conceptual, an exchange of whole ideas, not separate words. The written word would then eventually reflect this change. And so forth; continue this brainstorming, include your students, and you'll find a very surprising picture of what the telepathic future may bring.

Currently, advocates of E.S.P. believe it will accomplish the following:

1. It will stimulate recall of subconscious information.

2. It will allow for reception of information beyond the conscious and subconscious levels.

3. It may help develop one's potential learning ability as a result of improving I.Q.

4. It helps develop memory by working with the creative imagination and visualization progresses.

This objective form facilitates itself in many personal insights and functions. Recently, individuals have approached law enforcement agencies to solicit their skills in the hopes of finding missing persons. There has there has been some success in this endeavor over the years. Others have become counselors and healers; medical intuitives are showing great results in the field healing medicine with their insights.

Ultimately, we need new models that fit the parameters of our expanded consciousness to help us progress onward and upward or outward and inward into realms we now do not fathom as reality as of yet. Every level of consciousness is real – it is just whether you are willing to participate on a level that determines whether you will come away from the experience of expanded consciousness with real insights or dilutions.

Michael Talbot's book, The Holographic Universe has gone a long ways in helping us understand this phenomena. Our finer internal anatomy has yet to be explored in it totally. Once science integrates spiritual knowledge into our consciousness, including information about the Gnome that we as yet don't understand in our total spiritual makeup, then we will fathom our place in the universal hierarchy.

BIBLIOGRAPHY

Books:

Anderson, U.S. The Greatest Power in the Universe. Los Angeles, CA: Atlantis University, 1971.

Martin, Ebon (ed.) Test Your ES Cleveland, OH: The World Publishing Company, 1969.

Gallimore, J.G. The Handbook of Unusual Energies. Mokelumne Hill, CA; Health Research, 1976.

Hills, Christopher. Energy, Matter and Form. Boulder Creek, CA; University of the Trees, 1977.

Jung, Carl. Man and His Symbols. New York: Dell Publishing Company, 1972.

Karlins, Marvin, and Andrews, Lewis. Biofeedback. New York: Warner Paperback, Inc., i972.

Luce, Gay. Body Time, New York. Bantam Books, 1971.

McConnell, R.A. ES] Curriculum Guide, New York: Bantam Books, 1974.

McGrill, 0. The Mysticism and Magic of India. Cranbury, NJ: AS. Bones and Co., Inc., 1977.

Mislove, S. Roots of Consciousness. New York: Random House, 1977.

Ornstein, R. The Nature of Human Consciousness. San Francisco, CA: W.H. Freeman & Co., 1973.

Ostrander, Sheila, and Schoreder, Lynn. Psychic Discoveries Behind the Iron Curtain. New York: Bantam Books, 1970.

Puharich, Andrija. Beyond Telepathy. Garden City, NY: Anchor Press/Doubleday, 1973.

Puharich, Andrija. Un: Journal of the Mystery of U Geller. New York: Bantam Books, 1974.

Roberts, Jane. The Nature of Personal Reality. Englewood Cliffs, NJ: Prentice-Hall, Inc. 1974.

Sinclair, Upton Beale. Mental Radio. Springfield, IL: CC. Thomas, 1962.

Tart, Charles, Learning to Use Extra Sensory Perception. Chicago, IL: University of Chicago Press, 1975.

Targ, R., and Puthoff, lL., Mind Reach. New York; Delacorte Press, 1977,

Rhine, Louisa. ESP in Life and Lab: Tracing Hidden Channels. New York: McMillan Co., 1967. Silva, Jose. The Silva Mind Control Method. New York: Pocket Books, 1977.

Dissertation:

Millay, Jean. The Relationship Between the Synchronization of Brainwaves and Success in At tempts to Communicate Telepathically. Humanistic Psychology Institute, San Francisco, CA, 1978.

Magazines:

Ebon, Mark. "Moscow: Behond the ESP Enigma, " New Realities. May, 1977, p.

Journal of the American Society for Issues on telepathy: July, 1979, Vol. 73, No. 3; January, 1979, Vol. 73, No. 1, April, 1979, Vol. 73, No. 2.

Journal of Paraphysics. Issues on telepathy: 1968, Vol. 2, No. 2; 1978, Vol. 12, Nos. 1 & 2; 1979, Vol. 13, Nos. 3 & 4; 1975, Vol. 9, Nos. 4 & 5.

Meites, Judith. "Children are Psychic, " Psychic Life Magazine. Vol. 3, No. 4, 1983,

Rice, Berkeley. "New World of Intelligence Testing, " Psychology Today. September, 1979, pp. 31-40.

Tarous, Alex, and Donnelly, Katherine. "Your Children are Psychic, " Instructor Magazine. April, 1980, p. 14

Movie:

What The Bleep!? Down The Rabbit Hole 2006, www.what the bleep. com

NUMEROLOGY

NUMEROLOGY

Let's take a look at another system that gives information about the total life of the individual. Numerology is a very old science which dates back to the age of the great Pythagoras, often called the father of numbers and the first named philosopher. Pythagoras believed that mathematics, music and astronomy were the cornerstones of wisdom. Out of Pythagoras mathematical philosophy came the structure of numerology, still taught today as Pythagoras once taught it (Pythagorean numerology is a nine point system. There are other systems that function on different point systems. i.e. the Hebrew system is an eight point system.)

As a leader of the order of Melchezedick today and a master metaphysician Dr. Grace Pettipher, D.D., International Lecturer of the Academie Internationale Order of Melchizedek, was an instructor of numerology. Dr. Pettipher has been a recognized spiritualist of high standing for fifty years, before she passed away. Her ability to relay practical information about the often abstract concepts of numerology has been an inspiration for me, as well as for many others. With her initial instruction and guidance in San Francisco, I have been able to further my own work in this system for many years. I feel that it can be relied upon to reveal valid information about the nature of children, and adults. Like any system, however, one needs to become familiar enough with it to use it successfully. It is an art form.

Numerology is divided into five related categories. The first category is called the Total Name Vibration. It can give the life destiny numbers, although not in all cases. These numbers give a destiny profile or future plan. The second category is the Personality number breakdown, outward numbers. The third category is called Heart's Desire or Soul numbers, inward numbers. The fourth category is the Destiny category and the fifth is Birthrate or Life Path. This is not to say that our lives are predestined; we have free will at every moment. Everyone, on some level of consciousness, makes choices to determine the best way to lead his/her life, depending upon what must be accomplished to evolve towards the true self. Everyone has a basic life blueprint or guideline, indicated by the life destiny numbers (fourth category) which the individual personality can influence and change.

To determine the total name vibration of, for example, one of your students, write down the student's full name as listed on his/her birth certificate. Underneath each letter of the name, write the number from the chart below which corresponds to that letter.

Name Vibration Chart

1	2	3	4	5	6	7	8	9
A	B	C	D	E	F	G	H	I
J	K	L	M	N	O	P	Q	R
S	T	U	V	W	X	Y	Z	

Now add up the numbers for each name of the full name and record those numbers above each part of the names. If any of these totals exceed 9, add the digits of the total to get a single digit number between 1 and 9. For example, the name, "Tim," has T = 2, I = 9, and M = 4, which totals 15. Since 15 is greater than 9, add the 1 and 5 to get a single digit number, which in this case is 6. Therefore, 6 is the number vibration corresponding to the name, Tim. Once this has been done for all parts of the student's name, add these numbers to get the total name vibration, which gives the life destiny profile or blue print.

If in any of the above numerology determinations the numbers Eleven or Twenty-Two result for the name totals (of each part of the name), do not add the digits to get a single digit number. These numbers stay as they are unless there are two or more elevens or twenty-twos in the number grouping. Eleven and twenty-two are in the state of highest principles and should not be further reduced to a single digit; they are master vibration.

The number ten should only be reduced to number one when adding each name individually to attain the total number. In this study of numbers, the tens have a special meaning of their own, as determined by Dr. Grace Pettipher in her many years of study into the origin of numbers; she has written an entire chapter on the Ten.

Once you have determined the total name vibration, the personality numbers, and/or the soul numbers, the following chart will give you the characteristics marked by the resulting numbers. Simply follow the steps given in the example below in conjunction with the profiles given for each numerology number and you will find many interesting discoveries from the resulting number scope.

The birth date will be discussed after the breakdown of the numberscope below.

EXAMPLE:

```
         2           5              4  =  11
      J O H N   W A Y N E   Y O U N G B L O O D
      1 6 8 5   5 1 7 5 5   7 6 3 5 7 2 3 6 6 4
         2 0         2 3                    4 9   (4 + 9 = 13)
                                            13   (1 + 3 = 4)


Per.:   185 = 5    575 = 22    7 1 5 7 2 3 4 = 1        6 - 22
         14          22                  28
                                         10


H.D.       6        15 = 6     6366 = 3                    6
                                 21


              1   3   7   =   11
            Jan 12, 1942                   _____
                16  (1 + 9 + 4 + 2)  =  16  =  7
```

Once the total name vibration is determined, the next possible determination is finding the Personality Numbers. Using the numbers listed in the name vibration chart, label all the consonants of the name under study with the appropriate corresponding number. Add up the numbers for each part of the name, i.e., first, middle, and last. If this number exceeds nine, add the two digits to get a single digit number (as in determining the total name vibration). These numbers are all personality numbers, so record them for interpreting the personality profile. Finally, add these numbers to get the dominant personality number.

The individual personality numbers that correspond to the separate parts of the name signify various aspects of the personality. The total of these numbers gives the dominant personality number, which indicates the dominant personality type of the individual corresponding to the name under study. The profile accorded here relates to the personality in this lifetime, the objective and physical conscious self. The personality numbers are useful in signaling various suitable occupations.

The Soul Numbers, the third possible group of numbers given by numerology, express the true individuality of the person, the innermost self, the soul essence within. If there is one fundamental vibration around which all other vibrations swing, it belongs to the group of numbers called the soul numbers, also called the heart's desire numbers. These numbers never change. They express your identity for eternity. The outer personality may change by various manifestations of the characteristics given by changes in the circumstances in an individual's life. The qualities given by the soul numbers, however, are constant. One of our goals in life should be to express our soul individuality numbers after the karmic numbers are accomplished. Soul individuality numbers may be added to by successfully expressing the lessons of the birthdate numbers.

The soul numbers can be determined the same way that the personality numbers are determined; however, vowels are used in this determination instead of consonants, but they are treated the same way as the personality numbers to give the soul numbers.

The preceding example shows that JOHN WAYNE YOUNGBLOOD has personality numbers which include 6 and 22, indicating that basic to John's conscious self is that of the practical idealist, 22. He is a very verbal and social person who lives to be around many people. He is a leader of children in his environment. He is knowledgeable, drawing from an intuitive reservoir of wisdom gained by his many lifetimes in solving problems and learning quickly. Integrated into his personality is the home maker and helper, with a creative flair for color and music.

With older children the personality numbers show possible occupations and could be used by teachers, parents and counselors to determine possible future directions for students to follow. Integrated with other tests, this system could be a very useful tool. In my explanation of the numbers I did not include possible occupations for each number. If you are interested in these and other aspects of numerology, please contact me or pick up a good book on numerology. (refer to Bib.)

Six is a very strong number and goes deep into John's being. John is a domestic personality and longs to take part in matters dealing with home and family. Refer to explanation of number 6 for further details.

Eleven is the idealist who longs to live off the planet. He is the seer of the future, ideal society and other visions to come. Refer to number 11 for further details.

From this point, you move into discussing the qualities of each of the other numbers in each category; personality first, then soul numbers and finally the destiny numbers. You will eventually arrive at a composite picture of each child for which you do a number scope. Another important point to remember is that not everyone is tuned into their soul numbers.

For some, people move away from their basic soul personalities as they become overly socialized. They may lose sight of who they truly are if too many rules, regulations and forms of manipulation are imposed on them. Children are especially vulnerable to these kinds of influences and should be encouraged to actualize their true selves. Teaching children to realize and express their evolved selves will help them to evaluate identity crises later in life. By realizing your innate qualities, you can utilize your strengths and reinforce your weakness to solve problems in life.

Twenty-two is a super master vibration. It is the highest earthbound number ever incarnated into the planet. It is a global vibration, and as a child's vibration is steadfast in their knowledge and know-how and often appears as stubborn, but really is a determination that reinforces the tens of tens of lifetimes they have lived on this planet.

This is not to say they don't have lessons to learn in this incarnation or additional experiences to acquire but their insights are oftentimes correct. They take on many more responsibilities and challenges that most children of their age would step back from. With a 22 in the personality numbers they have not internalized the lessons of this vibration. More work is needed to fully realize all the lessons of the super master vibration. At this level they are mainly daredevils and not foundation builders or system builders.

INTERPRETATIONS OF THE NUMBERS

Number One

One is the number of self-initiative, self-reliance, individuality, independence, and potential creative power.

Negative aspects: lacks initiative, can be lazy, imitative, dependent and domineering.

Number Two (Emotional Vibration)

Two is feminine and receptive; it stands for harmony, peace, adaptation, tactfulness, and initiates the ability to share circumstances quietly and inconspicuously. Its force is of an interior rather than of an exterior nature. Two always acts as a "link" by harmonizing the harder and more aggressive numbers.

Negative aspects: moroseness, lack of friendliness, stubborness, pessimism and bluntness.

Number Three (Emotional-Mercurial)

Three is the number of perfected self-expression. Three molds numbers one and two, thereby blending harmony, joy, grace and beauty. It portrays the joy of life - carefreeness and acceptance of life. It indicates good mental qualifications and points to those who excel in art, science, philos-phy and literature. Three possesses a keen sense of rhythm, especially expressed in dance and movement. It is also known as the artistic number, indicative of the art of the theater, fine arts and musical arts.

Negative aspects: limited in self-thought, worrisome, over-anxious, intolerant, pessimistic, doleful and self-centered. In a mild form, three expresses itself in a lack of self-expression. 149

Number Four

stands for the skilled worker with both intellect and hands in service. "True service" is the key, representative phrase. Four is the foundation builder of organization and construction. Four persons will be ambitious and capable of organizing.

Negative aspects: as the potential intellectual worker, four may descend to the lower levels of its nature and become entirely bound to a servile position in life.

Number Five (Emotional-Physical)

Five is full of life, freedom, lack of responsibility, versatility, eager to travel and make changes. Five indicates one who is life-loving, fascinating, generous, adaptable, high-spirited, and of an independent nature. To wear the "banner of freedom" on high is to call to all five personalities. Linguistic gifts and a love for art and beauty are very strong in the five person, as are the qualities of open-mindedness and continual change. "Change" is the key word for five.

Negative aspects: the joy of life may turn to pessimism and be manifested in gossip and procrastination.

Basically, five individuals can be uncontrollable and unreliable, subject to nervous disorders.

Number Six (Emotional-Artistic)

Six has a twofold profile: (1) it stands first for home love, parentage and home responsibility, true domesticity and (2) it relates to art in music of the piano and stringed instruments, and in many instances to dramatic arts. Six also possess vocal abilities and moderate organizing powers, as well as interior decoration skills. The intuitive faculties are strongly marked in the six, usually stronger than in the notable intellectual qUalities of six. Six is apt to arrive at quick conclusions through the interior faculties of intuition and the psychic sense, while unable to explain how the information was gained. Sixes absorb information rather than learn it and tend to work best in harmonious surroundings. In inharmonious surroundings, sixes tend toward the negative side of their natures.

Negative aspects: can become either household drudges or utterly rebellious, going against their own loving, nurturing natures. They may be slaves to their duty or refuse their duty to home. Sixes can be critical, cynical, unreliable, untidy and interfering with affairs other than their own. 150

Number Seven (Intuitional-Spiritual)

Vibration number seven is the digit for mysticism. It relates to the interior spiritual force of man wherein is found the true meaning of life. It stands for silence, meditation, introspection, wisdom. Seven represents the consciousness on the path of life since seven stands still and waits, molding qualities within the self and bringing them forth into the externals of life. Seven is proud of ancestry, poised, and calm, and has strong intellectual attributes.

Negative aspects: restless dissatisfaction, critical, intolerant, melancholy, stubbornness, extreme pride.

Number Eight (Mental Vibration)

Eight is the number of magnetic force, is self-assertive, and possesses the "master mind" of highest intellect. Its leading characteristic is best depicted by one word, "organization." Success, power and freedom are the natural prerogatives of the eight person, if positively and constructively followed. It stands for righteousness, power, justice, honor, efficiency and intellectual endeavors. Eight also represents the spirit working on the earth plane. The self-assurance and confidence of the eight personalities proclaims its master qualities as a leader of mankind.

Negative aspects: misuse of power for selfish ends, lack of initiative, laziness, lack of perserverance, can be a failure if the eight person does not will to be successful.

Number Nine (Intuitional-Spiritual)

Nine is the humanitarian, a very social being who likes to be surrounded by large groups of people. He or she may possess great intellectual ability, the higher superconscious or "spiritual" mind within man. There is a gift of spiritual insight within the nine which draws from its infinite source of knowledge of things unseen and unknown. The psychic clairvoyant and spritiual traits of six endows a spiritual seership. It is the number of perserverance, strength and universality. Its true message lies in comforting, healing and uplifting. It is also the number of discretion. Nine often indicates the ability to be a teacher of higher educational systems.

Negative aspects: allows confinement and is willing to be limited to home circles and to non-achievement. Nines may be morose and despondent, hateful instead of loving, jealous and mean instead of big-hearted and generous, self-opinionated and inclined to passionate, indiscrete outbursts.

Number Ten (Cosmical-Universal)

Ten stands for supreme individuality, highest initiative, highest creative activity, perfect mastery and highest self-reliance, all of which may be manifested in true leadership. Knowledge for the ten is only gained by experience. Ten individuals not only originate but bring to completion all the plans acquired by other "lower" numbers. The pioneering spirit is strongly marked in tens and frequently manifested along lines of spiritual research. The ten is psychic and has a strong occult vibration. Ten individuals are often pioneers of new consciousness levels. It is also the number of the inventor.

Negative aspects: powerful, selfish dominance over others, lack of creative qualities.

The zero in this number gives the ten special significance. It intensifies the number it is associated with. The zero signifies at least nine degrees of consciousness (9 lifetimes signified by one number) indicating that a new life cycle IS about to commence. It is the true completion number.

Number Eleven (spiritual-universal master)

Eleven is the vibrational number of those spiritual, mystical and inspirational, representing the visionary dreamer, mystic and idealist. Eleven represents an intellect of the finer order, which deals with ideas and visions of the "Golden Age" to come, rather than with things of the present day world. An individual with a strong eleven will find the earth a difficult place to live in, unless the eleven individual has in his profile numbers which counteract these tendencies; for example, four, eight or twenty-two, strong earth numbers, can balance the ephemeral eleven. An eleven will mainly be a dreamer with "head in the clouds." It is best if the eleven personality has someone to manage his/her affairs, since elevens tend to fail to understand the practical aspects of life. On the other hand elevens are excellent communicators and spiritual seers. For the eleven, vision is essential on every level of consciousness. Jesus Christ possessed the spirit of the eleven individual.

Negative aspects: insufficient vision which is essential to the eleven, despair, pessimism, lack of inspiration and faith.

Number 22 (Super-Master Vibration)

Twenty-two combines the highest of spirituality with practicality which causes twenty-two dominant persons to be known as "practical idealists." Like the eleven person, twenty-two possesses vision, but also possesses qualities of being the builder, constructor, and organizer. Number twenty-two is an inventor, changing visions into three-dimensional reality. It represents those who are drawn to things unknown and unexpected. The humanitarian qualities of nine are largely marked in twenty-two, twenty-two being a "race messenger" bearing its message to humanity; it has tremendous endurance.

Negative aspects: vision without the motivational power to bring ideas to forefront, inertia, laziness and general waste of force and accomplishment.

A final source of information used by numerologists is the Birthdate. Birthdate vibrations are covenants made with the higher and lower selves. These numbers show lessons to be learned and are important to the development of the individual personality. Individuals who have numbers that are larger in the birth path (the birthdate numbers) than in the hearts desire group of numbers will find their lessons to be learned more difficult than if the opposite were true.

Since the birthdate gives lessons to be learned, parents and teachers play a vital role here, namely, they are responsible for interpreting and teaching these lessons to young children so that each can take early advantage of a full life on earth. Parents and teachers may want to meet and discuss ways of helping children acquire the skills required to accomplish the lessons of the birthdate numbers.

The numerology numbers which correspond to the birthdate are simple to determine. The first number is determined by the month, the second by the day and the third by the year. Using the John Wayne Youngblood example again, the birthdate numbers and corresponding profile are as follows. John's birthday is January 12, 1942.

His birthdate numbers are 1 for January, 3 for the day (the number 12 must be reduced, 1 + 2 = 3), and 7 for the year (the year must also be reduced, 1 + 9 + 4 + 2 = 16, then 1 + 6 = 7). The total birthdate number is 11 (from 1 + 3 + 7).

Now suppose that John is only five years old. What lessons can he learn from the given birthdate numbers? The number 1(Jan.) of the numberscope signifies a need for John to learn to individualize and originate, not imitate, work manifested from his own initiative. He must learn not to rely on others to solve his problems for him. Teachers and parents should be on the lookout for situations which reinforce originality and individuality in both structured and unstructured tasks.

Within the classroom, the teacher could set up choices between a number of jobs or ideas so that John must initiate the direction he wants to follow. For example, the teacher could ask John if he would like to work in blocks or tracing letters or try the typing area. Games would also be tasks where John could make many decisions. Spontaneous art projects of all kinds would be an excellent approach. A check could be made on John to see if he has learned to initiate his own ideas by observing John in free-play time, and other activities. Keep a checklist of the times he initiates any action. In fact, you may want to keep a check list of John before you start motivating him to learn lessons of the birthpath for comparison.

In the case of the 3 covenant, John needs to learn self-expression. He should also gain an appreciation for beautifying the world around him, creating balance, gracefulness and poise, and the ability to express these qualities to the world. John also needs to learn to give because giving is a key aspect of the number 3. In this case John has a 3 in his soul numbers, which will make it easy for him to understand these lessons because the characteristics of 3 are a part of his true nature.

Teachers and parents should create tasks for John which exercise and develop large motor skills, such as walking on a balance beam and balancing games in which John is asked to balance a book on his head, carry an egg in a spoon, etc. Help John creatively express himself in the dressup corner, playacting different roles by putting on different clothes and acting out characters. Teach John to share his things with other children.

7 is the number lesson of learning to stand alone with a strong self-image. It requires being quiet and learning to be emotionally balanced and poised. Meditation, developing psychic abilities and creative and artistic expression, balancing and centering activities, movement and mime are all activities which incorporate control and training of the physical and emotional body.

A movement task for a group of children (large or small) would be to play the record album, "Getting to Know Myself, " and follow the movements. This is an excellent movement record for young children. For older children the book "Yoga for Children" is great for developing balance and coordination. "Meditation for Children" is a good book for developing emotional stability.

The number eleven in the birth path for John is the total of all the birthdate numbers, so it is the dominant number and gives the lessons most needed to be learned. These are the lessons that John needs to make a part of his nature. By developing this covenant, he will fall into swing with the rhythm of his life as it unfolds. Life is about cycles and John's lessons could be his cycles of learning, for him.

The eleven covenant is to keep open and receptive, to keep faith in one's self and in humanity. 11 covenant individuals need to be exposed to as much creative activity as possible. They should be involved in reading, especially science fiction, fantasy and poetry. They should participate in spontaneous and creative art works, creative movement, meditation, and creative writing.

As an instructor or parent, you might encourage creativity by asking John and students like him to write various stories on imaginative topics. Try telling students to imagine this: "You are the last person left on earth and you have a choice of taking a spaceship to another planet or having a flying machine that would fly instantly to any place on earth. Would you take the spaceship or the flying machine? And where would you go?" Ask students to write a story about their decision. These stories will help you determine how imaginative your students. Obviously, your students would need fairly good writing skills to do this task (it would depend on the age group of your students.)

For most children it is easier to determine creativity by watching their creative dance movements

or by looking at their art work. Try some spontaneous painting or ask students to glue pieces of scrap wood together into a sculpture. (Rhoda Kellog's book, Analyzing Children's Art, offers a method to determine a child's creativity; check Bib.)

Keeping the Chakras open is a major part of a person's creative connection (refer to the section on Chakras in this book for development tasks). In creative exercises children should have their chakras open as much of the time as possible and they have their chakras open already.

In the John Wayne Youngblood example, we supposed that John was five years old and I gave examples of possible tasks that could be used in conjunction with his number scope. This does not imply that only five year olds could benefit from numerology; rather, people of all ages can develop the positive characteristics given by their number scope. Teachers and parents can confer to determine what might be the tasks best suited for their children.

The profile for the birthdate numbers other than those used in the John Wayne Youngblood example are given below with several exemplary tasks that teachers and parents could share with their children.

Birth Number 2 is concerned with harmony, being , at peace with others and the environment. The two covenant should strive to be around a lot of people interacting in a positive manner, creating an air of friendship. The teacher and parents should make it possible for this child to interact with many children in order that he/she will learn communication skills. Group games offer an opportunity for this child to learn cooperation and sharing with other children. Some games that would stimulate communication and cooperation would be:

Feeling Pictures: Gather a group of young children (four and five years old) and show them pictures of different people with different emotions. Discuss the pictures and the emotions portrayed. Have the 2 covenant child take part as much as possible. He needs to recognize how other people feel and initiate setting up some kind of relationship with as many people as possible.

Mirror Feeling: The same pictures used for the "feeling pictures" task can be used for this task, along with small mirrors for each child. Go through the pictures again and each time have children try making faces in the mirror to match the face on the picture card. Have the children come up in front of the group and act out each emotion - especially the 2 covenant child.

Older children should be involved in creative dramatics to sustain the natural creativity we possess as children. Try asking each student to act out for the group various simple situations. Simple props are useful in this exercise to stimulate ideas about possible events to act out. Hats, books, dishes, etc. spur creative possibilities. While the student is acting, ask the reminder of the group to guess what is being represented. Encourage your students to be creative and uninhibited. For further suggestions, some good books to refer to are Let's Playa Story, by Elizabeth Allstrom, Playmaking with Kindergarten, by Winifred Ward, and Storytelling and Creative Dramatics, by

J.H. Chambers.

The 5 covenant child needs to learn "letting go, " having freedom and little structure. The 5 covenant child should be taught to share things and to be independent, especially in decision making. All children, of course, need to learn to share because of the egocentric tendencies of the lower self evident in childhood, but 5 covenant children need more practice in this area than most children. These children should have as many opportunities as possible to give things to other children and to decide what to give.

A task to promote sharing could be set up in which each child is asked to do an art project and give it to another child in the class. The holiday season provides a perfect opportunity for this kind of project. This task could incorporate decision making by allowing students the freedom to choose from several different projects or to create a gift project of their own.

The 6 covenant child has two tendencies, the first being that of the homemaker, and the second showing artistic tendencies for either music or colors. The covenant of the homemaker is home-centered, caring for family members and accomplishing household chores. This does not imply that this kind of individual should be limited to staying home all the time. Rather, the home-centered child should learn to feel comfortable in his or her preferences, but should also be encouraged to explore beyond the realm of the home where their talents of caring and tending might be useful.

As a teacher, you could help the 6 covenant child by providing cleaning tools in the classroom and encouraging their help in keeping the classroom neat. Witnessing this, the other students might be prompted to join in and help out, which is a good lesson for any child. Be careful, however. Children should not be put in the position of doing overly difficult work, taking on adult responsibilities, sacrificing the natural learning trials and tribulations of growing up. In the 1880's children were thought to be "little adults, " thinking and working as adults. People then had a different understanding of how children think and learn. Recently, these trends have been reversed and children today are encouraged to play out the "child" in them.

The creative aspects of the 6 covenant child can be motivated in the home by allowing children such choices as how their room will be decorated and what they are going to wear. Of course, some guidance will be necessary. This guidance encourages interaction between parent and child. I will remind you, however, that your guidance may be questioned. Be open to the possibility that children can playa role in teaching adults. 1

In the classroom the teacher can also promote creativity and decision making by asking students to help decorate the room. Teachers might also help students use their musical talents, especially the 6 covenant child, by teaching music basics and having some instruments in the classroom for the students to experiment with. If there is a piano in the room, children could be directed to it during free time.

There are many ways of teaching music to children. Asking children to create and construct instruments is an excellent way to encourage music appreciation. Anything that will make sound makes good instrument material potential. One idea comes to mind: gather a bunch of boxes of all shapes and variously sized rubber bands. Have students put the rubber bands on the boxes, starting with one and adding more, and experiment with the sounds emitted while plucking the rubber bands. Allow the children to experiment with combinations of other shapes and sounds. The Elementary Science Series (ESS) has a great book on how to make musical instruments with things around the house.(check Bib.)

The 8 covenant child should pay particular attention to manifesting his/her creative ideas all the way through to completion. These children should strive to complete all work started and also be stimulated to manifest their creative ideas, possibly through art works or structured situations on a large scale using their creative ideas. Maybe the eight covenant child could organize an activity to be taught to the other children. The personal power that they possess needs to be used in a positive and constructive way. The eight child finally needs to learn structure and organization.

9 covenant children should be encouraged to extend themselves beyond very familiar things, events and people, such as the home, family, etc. To keep this covenant, these children should be introduced to large groups of people and places away from the home and should be encouraged to be aware of the way their communities work. For younger children, walks through the community, local stores, businesses and services will fulfill this covenant. Or try role playing in the classroom by asking students to portray different service people in the community: fIreman, policeman, waitress, nurse, doctor, etc. Be careful here and make sure girls and boys have a chance to try each other's traditional roles.

For older children, roles such as class officers - president and secretary - might be used. Send students out of the classroom to poll other students on things happening in the school. You might want to hold group discussions every day and have students report on events in the school and community. Use games about the community and events happening outside the community. Stories, media, artistic projects about the local community and the larger community would come under the 9 covenant.

Number 22 children keep their covenant by manifesting their visions into 3-dimensional reality. These children should be given considerable freedom and urged to bring their ideas into form. They are capable of creating and doing great things with their abilities. When these individuals are lazy, they tend never to put their ideas into reality. This attitude goes against their covenant and impedes their unfolding growth and development.

Twenty-two's are the constructors and builders in both idea and form. They should be stimulated to construct large and grand projects that strengthens their limitations. Nothing is too difficult for this vibration. He/she is a true leader if given the chance. Refer to the outline on 22 number characteristics for a fuller understanding of the 22 individual.

In the final analysis, working with children on a cosmic consciousness universal level would be enhanced if the parents took part in supporting their children's learning. This support would facilitate the teacher's role, consequently leading into experiences which would teach the child how to cope with life experiences. Once they have minimized the problems in their lives, they would be able to increase their concerns for creativity. Their parents are critically important in this process.

It might be of help to the teacher to give parents a questionnaire to ascertain the child's likes and dislikes (within the context of activities supportive of creative problem solving): his/ her moods, the type of toys with which he/she often plays, what are his/her favorite TV programs, how many hours he/she watches these programs, the type of discipline used by parents, self-help skills (does he/she dress themselves, etc.) and what are his/her sleeping patterns. The knowledge of these likes and dislikes will better support positive behavior in the child's world.

POTENTIALITY

Numerology can potentially shed light on aspects of your students' personalities and inner wishes, as well as possible future directions.

1. It will give you a chance to know your students better as individuals.

2. Knowing students innermost desires and their lessons to be learned could shed light on possible curriculums to benefit each individual child. A truly individualized program could be devised for each child.

3. Numerology provides a diagnostic tool that takes into account the nature of the child's total being.

4. It offers a holistic view of the child and adult.

5. Numerology, of course bridges many more particulars than talked about here. Seek out your own numbers and experiences, learn about a different perspective of yourself.

SUMMARY/CONCLUSIONS

Both the Pendulum and Numerology channels are systems that were designed to function as diagnostic tools, at least in my mind, for individual soul development — as a way to know of the progress of the soul and its individual lessons. Numerology is explained from a historical focus and from the point of view of how challenges for each individual can be utilized in the classroom and other environments.

I have included a breakdown of the numbers first, as they are interpreted in most numerological systems, to acquaint the reader with the basic system. (This approach is of the Pythagorean systems of numbers.)

Numbers are one of the coordinates that establish three-dimensional reality. With numbers, you can figure out anything; and the occult meaning of numbers (symbols) can be determined if one is familiar with number meaning. This is not the intent of this channel, however; numerology's practical application in the classroom, and an increased awareness of the provable individual natures in each of us, is what makes this process relevant. This is a beginning look at the individual soul, in its limited form, from a holistic perspective.

I have studied personality theory and practice in children, and the knowledge I bring to the subject using other systems to determine the characteristics of individual personality's, from a holistic/synergistic approach, helps us to start understanding the multidimensional aspects of human consciousness. It is not until we understand the uniqueness of each individual soul and personality that we will be able to maximize the learning process, and even our place in the cosmic scheme of things. More fundamentally, medicine and the healing process could better be understood from a holistic perspective as well.

I don't think that numerology is complete in itself as a diagnostic tool, so I have combined a few diagnostic systems, hopefully to round out the picture of the individual soul, by utilizing three other scales — the four temperaments of Hyppocrates and Galen (choleric, sanguine, phlegmatic and melancholic); a personality pendulum chart; and a breakdown of introvert-extrovert characteristics. These tools serve as an in-depth look at the individual personality to date (located in the Numerology and Pendulum channels in this book).

BIBLIOGRAPHY

Books:

Butler, Chris. Number Symbolism. London: Routheage and Kegan Paul, Ltd., 1970.

Campbell, Florence. Your Days Are Numbered. Marina del Rey, CA: DeVorss and Company, 1958.

Ellis, Keith. Number Power. New York: St. Martins Press, 1978.

Hall, Manly. Masonic Hermetic Qabbalistic and Rosecrucian Symbolical Philosophy. Los Angeles, CA: The Philosophical Research Society, Inc., 1973.

Jordan, D. The Romance in Your Name. Santa Barbara, CA: J.K. Rowny Press, 1973.

Petitpher, Dr. Grace. (One of the leaders of the Order of Melchizedek) "Numerology: The Practical Guide To Numbers"

Miscellaneous:

Workshops in numerology by Dr. Grace Petitpher, California Hotel, San Francisco, CA, 1974-1975. 161

PYRAMID ENERGY

Pyramid energy is the energy associated with pyramidal shapes, concentrated at the apex and other locations. No one really knows what comprises pyramid energy, but researchers have suggested that it is similar to orgone, od or bio-plasmic energy which are combinations of electro-magnetic or magnetic-cosmic radiation.

"There is also talk about Tachion energy prevalent in the pyramid."

One of the first persons to realize that there was an energy associated with pyramids was a French doctor named Bovis. (He also did many pendulum experiments.) While visiting the Great Pyramids of Giza, he discovered animal carcasses (unwrapped mummies) within the confines that were dehydrated and showing no signs of decay. This fascinated the French doctor, so he started researching the phenomenon by experimenting with smaller pyramids, small animals and perishable foods. He found that after storing normally perishable foods within a pyramid, they would dehydrate without decay, like the carcasses he saw in the Egyptian pyramid. His experiments provided the impetus for many others. Numerous researchers began studying the unusual characteristics of the energy associated with pyramids.

In 1949 a radio engineer named Karl Drbal started experimenting with sharpening razor blades under a pyramid. He found that he was successful in restoring a used blade's crystalline structure by sharpening it under a pyramid. Over a ten-year period, he applied several times for a patent on a pyramid that would sharpen razor blades of soft, pliable surfaces, like the Wilkinson Sword Blade or the Gillette Blue Blade. Drbal was finally awarded the patent in 1959.

Max Toth and Greg Nielsen have also had success with sharpening Gillette Blue Blades. In fact, they have used a total of only 68 blades between them in the past 25 years. In their book, Pyramid Power, they report that razor blades are subject to environmental changes of magnetic flux on the earth's surface, making them cut better on some days than others.

The professed uses for pyramids and their associated energies run the gamut from being resonant cavities for electromagnetism (similar to hi-fi speakers), to being capable of purifying water and healing plants. There are also some references by other authors and a particular secret KGB video files (through the sci-fi channel) that the pyramid is an energy generator that helps keep the planet align properly. In the video it shows a generator captured by a x-ray or microwave machine underneath the great pyramid of Giza, about a mile down. They closed their inquiry shortly after its discovery for unknown reasons.

Some conclusive evidence has been compiled testifying to the claims of pyramid energy. Bill Schul and Ed Pettit in their book, The Psychic Power of Pyramids, claim that milk can be kept from spoiling and made into yogurt by being suspended above the apex of a six-foot pyramid. Also, plants appear to grow better when rotated inside a pyramid. This was confirmed by time-lapse photography - the growth of plants grown inside pyramids was compared with the growth of similar control plants not exposed to pyramid energy. Pettit and Schul purified water with pyramid energy. For best results in the treatment of water or milk, the height of the pyramid should be at least sixteen inches high; eight gallons of liquid requires a six-foot pyramid.

Patrick Flanagan, author of Pyramid Energy has developed a process for electroplating pieces of steel and copper and using them to make pyramid grids which he claims attract pyramid energy, like larger energy systems. Eighteen small pyramids are joined together onto a rectangular metal sheet through electroplating. Setting a plant on top of this grid or spraying a plant with water placed on top of such a grid can supposedly keep bugs away. Water can be purified by placing it in a container resting on a grid or by running water over the grid for irrigation of fields of crops. Later in this section I will give directions for purifying water and dehydrating milk contacted by pyramid energy.

Another understanding of pyramid energy comes from Dean and Mary Hardy in Michigan. They have written a book, Pyramid Energy Explained, in which they describe the alien visits they have experienced while dreaming, in pre-sleep trances and in waking consciousness. They also tell how they have built a pyramid for their dyslexic son. Much of the information gained by the Hardys comes from Ken Killick, a self-made scientist and clairvoyant, the Kaballistic-Hermetic philosophy, Prophecies of Melchizadek in the Great Pyramid of Seven Temples, by B. Landone, and The Secret of Light by W. Russell.

From this information and their own observations, the Hardys say that a pyramid is like an antenna which tunes into different energy frequencies. The pyramid, therefore, acts to "tune" the user into various energy frequencies. Tachion or light energy accumulates within pyramids and the understanding or "tuning into" (creating a resonant frequency) this light energy is a prerequisite for evolving into the spiritual world.

The Hardys have built special pyramids as large as 24 feet high to concentrate, meditate and contemplate within. Silva Mind Control techniques play a part in their meditative and psychic experiences. The Hardys have also built a pyramid for their dyslexic son-John. The reason for this is best explained by an excerpt from one of Mary Hardy's letters to me.

Dyslexia is caused by a difference in brain wave frequency. John's brain wave frequency was not changed by pyramid energy. However, he has learned to tune into physical frequencies by using the pyramid. The pyramid is a tuning device a frequency-resonance device. We can use an analogy of a radio station to explain differences in frequencies. If you were tuned to WKZO and most people were tuned to WKMI, it would be hard to relate to people around you. This is John's problem. The pyramid has helped him to tune into WKMI without losing his ability to tune into WKZO.

In less than 20 years, the world's frequencies will change to WKZO, so we will have to change or lose our ability to function. The pyramid helped John adjust to a physical world he does not normally perceive.

Tuning into different energy frequencies has been a theme of this book. The Hardys, along with many others, believe that within 20 years we will all have to tune into a frequency different from the current frequency; that is, we will have to adapt to a mental plane. It is somewhat difficult to predict or judge what it will be like in the mental plane, even though we move in and out of this level all the time. It seems that when we totally resonate with the mental level, any thought we have will be transformed into existence instantaneously.

Our thoughts will truly be both our weapons and defenses of the future. Learning to see with the middle eye (clairvoyance) is a prerequisite for mental manipulation and will also be necessary for adapting to the mental plane? It is not clear what will happen to those who do not acquire the ability to resonate with the mental plane, nor have any real questions been answered about this mental existence. I have heard this concept before, but no one seems to know the details of our supposed future existence.

The Hardys have some interesting specifics on pyramid energy, stemming mainly from the research done by Brown Landone. He describes the geometry of the Great Giza Pyramid and its relationship to energy.

A discussion of pyramid energy would not be complete with out mentioning great researches like Dr.Ibrahim Karim of French radiestheists, and the Russian researcher Scariatin (known as Enel).Thanks to the excellent reference, Egyptian and European Energy Work by Dr. Robert J. Gilbert, Ph.D. Research on the negative energy effects in the Great pyramid (further on), will be discussed as we proceed to understand the incredible energy within the Great Pyramid of Giza. It is truly the eighth wonder of the world.

A set of proportions, called Teleois proportions, were used in ancient times by the Egyptian priesthood to build pyramids and by the Greeks to build temples. Teleois proportions are based on a geometric series of numbers which express relationships found throughout the universe, i.e., in the structure of plants, the design of snowflakes, and in the distance between the sun and planets. The Teleois is proportional to the electromagnetic fields of atoms, which means that systems based on Teleois proportions can be built to receive electromagnetic and other frequencies.

According to Chris Hill, knowledge of the Teleois gave ancients the tools to create an "electromagnetic/cosmic energy antenna system like the pyramids to stabilize and maintain the whole structure of the universe." Some people also have said that the pyramid stabilizes forces of the Earth as well. In some references Telesis proportion is described as the" Golden mean" or section 2/3-1/3 ratio. Or in number sets, the Fibonacci numbers if you prefer one side of the great pyramid of Giza is longer than another side; this is the ratio.

The geometric proportion of a pyramid is pi. The height of the ancient pyramids is proportional to the perimeter of its base in the same ratio as pi, which is also the ratio of the circumference of a circle to its diameter, or 3.13159265+.

Phi is another mathematically derived constant related to this proportion. It is equal to 1.6180334+, which is known as the sacred cut or golden section. This proportionality constant is found throughout the universe and was repeated by the ancients in the proportions of their pyramids and other buildings. i.e. Greek Temples.

The ancient pyramids, therefore, because of these balanced proportions, establish an energy field which resonates to the frequencies of the physical world (from the atomic constituency of matter), and which also resonates to the mental/thought frequencies and the spiritual/higher mind frequencies. As a result of the capacity to resonate to various frequencies, areas within each pyramid are associated with different frequencies. The King's Chamber resonates to the spiritual plane, the Queen's Chamber resonates to the mental plane and the Subterranean Chamber resonates to the physical plane.

Through modern studies of pyramids, using lasers and mirrors, researchers have found that pyramids reflect energy to different locations within the pyramid. Important in the studies of

Schul and Pettit was the finding that the walls of the pyramids were slightly angled towards the center of each side, helping to reflect energy into the King's Chamber. We are beginning to determine that proportions and materials used in the ancient pyramids were purposely chosen to concentrate energy by reflecting energy in certain areas of the pyramid.

We are also learning, through work by Brown Landone that the proportions of the pyramid act like an historical clock. According to Landone, every 25, 827 years, the time it takes the universe to rotate once around its center, the vibrational frequencies of all things will advance to the next vibrational level. But with new knowledge (or is it) where does the concept of speeding up the time come into play here. With the earth progressively speeding up, or is this reflected in the pyramid structure or is Dr. London just referring to a galactic movement of time, itself. (Referred to time studies in the concentration, meditation and contemplation channel.)

Chris Hill, author of Energy, Form and Matter, examines the qualities and characteristics of these energies. He says that pyramids have both positive and negative energy. Positive pyramid energy is associated with promoting healthy, pleasant effects and negative energy creates unhealthy effects.

According to Chris Hill, there is a spiral of energy flowing down into the pyramid, angling off to the left side. This energy functions in a way that dehydrates the life waters of organic substances and sometimes gives headaches to people sitting under the pyramid for any length of time. In contrast, Hill says that there is also a positive energy force which angles through the top side of the pyramid called the Pi-ray. This energy spirals down the right side of the pyramid. It gives an uplifting feeling and tends to alter or warp time, so that when one sits under a pyramid the experienced length of time can seem shorter than the actual length of time (there are studies using LSD that bare out this change in time perception.)

Through my research I have come to believe that there are two types of energy. This energy don't comes through the apex of the pyramid but being one energy, as we see in Dr. Gilberts book, at the angle of 85 degrees if his diagram is correct, coming down through the top side of the pyramid cumulating in the kings chamber. There is also a pulsating energy coming out of the pyramid apex. This is a positive energy that up lifts your spirit and be can used as a healing modality (do we have a 3rd energy here?)

This energy (top side) is Christopher Hills Pi wave. As mentioned above the wave breaks left and right; one direction is positive and one is negative as it comes down through the pyramid. Now I'm starting to understand that there was a basic misinterpretation of the energy between these two researchers. Dr. Gilbert's classical vertical wave-90 degrees was really a 85 degree vertical wave, one energy form, coming down into the king's chamber.

This wave form has two components positive and negative; one being the sub-component spiritual energy and the other is the negative Pi ray. This makes a big different in interpretation of how the energy functions in Dr. Gilbert's sub-component energy , "spiritual energy" , and Dr. Hills two different energy's breaking left and right; being only one energy breaking in two directions and refocusing in the kings chamber.

I have talked to people who have experienced both the positive and negative effects of pyramid energy. Chris Hills doesn't make it clear why these experiences happen to some people and not to others or why they are sometimes negative and sometimes positive. Some researchers believe that these effects are closely related to atmospheric conditions: sun spots, magnetic field changes, and planetary influences. Nothing, however, is conclusive at this time.

And then we have the influence of the French and Russian researchers, especially Enel that may shed some light on this issue. The effects of negative/noxious energy's have there origin in the Negative Green ray (-G ray, and Hills Pi ray) having both negative and positive components, focused on the horizontal and vertical wave forms (the negative effect is the vertical wave-electrical magnetic frequencies and the positive effect is the horizontal wave-magnetic energy according to Enel.

The interesting thing is that the negative green energy has a sub-component wave "the spiritual carrier wave" that is critical to spiritual work. They also talk about the higher octaves of Ultraviolet "the Angel ray" and the higher harmonics of Gold (the Christ-atomic energy). Resonance plays a major role in the energy's of the Great Pyramid. There is an interesting sighting of the vertical wave being an energy akin to comic energy that traverses through solid matter- could this be the much discussed scientific molecule, the neutrinos? On the other hand the –G energy (electro-magnetic energy) brings on cancer according to Enel. This discussion goes beyond the scope of this publication but you may want to seek out this discussion your self (refer to Bib.)

I would like to mention Verne Cameron at this point because he was an expert dowser. He was instrumental in examining the frequencies and strengths of energies associated with pyramids using the Aura Meter. He developed an aura meter, one of the most sensitive dowsing instruments known today to conduct his research on pyramids, (over a 50 year progression) as well as using it for map and water dowsing.

In Vernon Cameron and Bill Cox experiment with a model pyramid that showed the intensity of energy in the pyramid by dowsing the pyramid with there new aura meter, that yielded results that the pyramid apex shows a 100% raise in energy level, 1/3 of the pyramid from the bottom, the Kings chamber showed an 85% level on a side panel, and along the edges are about 5% of the energy levels; and the center is about 75% effective energy level. Nothing was said about the negative or positive energy's in the pyramid.

We're talking subtle energies here that act upon substances that mummify organic matter as well as other effects inside the pyramid. It has been termed tachyon by the Hardy's.

It has always been my contention and research results that a lot of the concentrated energy resides in the upper half of the pyramid. At one time I used my garage to string together a copper wire pyramid about 5 feet high. Copper is an excellent conductor of subtle light energy. After securing the last line to the two by fours suddenly a indigo flame danced from the apex of the magnificent structure; I was delighted an intrigued. Reichenback may have been talking about this phenomenon when he experimented with color emanations filtering down a copper wire from tests with sunlight. Wilhelm Reich saw the bluish energy around Orgone cells. And when I read about psychics seeing colors in the aura it all brings me back to that image of the indigo flare exuding from atop the wire copper pyramid.

Without thinking my hand moved to correct the angle of the pyramid (for its angle was off center and unbalanced, I thought), delivering a blow to the top portion of the wire pyramid, righting it back to the center. This was the worst thing I could have done because the beautiful indigo flame disappeared. I tried to move it back off center to no avail. I swore up and down and dance around like a crazy man, I couldn't get the flame back; I was livid. After calming down I thought about the consequences of my actions, and I gleaned an insight about pyramids that hadn't occurred to me. I realized that the golden mean or section was validated here, when one side of the pyramid is longer than the other, being off center was the right location for the apex.

I kept the pyramid up for a while but the indigo flame never returned (I have often thought that an invisible hand had moved my own – I guess I wasn't ready to receive this information at that time). What was the indigo flame? Does it have a relevance to the mathematics of the pyramid and thereby the energy of consciousness of the great pyramid of Giza? Has anyone cited this phenomenon in their research? These are questions I have yet to ascertain?

There was a reference, of a magnetic incandescent flame that I ran across in my research called the Odic force from the famous German scientist Baron von Reichenbach (I also talk about Reichenbach in the Radonic/Psychotronic channel). Basically Od energy is a natural terrestrial force in all objects especially concentrated in magnetic fields. He had extensive research where he cites studies on the Odic flame. Od energy manifests as different colors depending on the materials and the conditions. Reichenbach's research revealed that copper Od color is reflected as Red surrounded by a green flame.

So, I have a blue flame in my sights, and as I look for evidence of this strange energy, I continue my research references onto Wilhelm Reich and Orgone energy. Reich speaks of orgone being utilized as energy forced to run an engine and to heal the sick, and cure psychological and sexual problems. There is a reference to a colored flame – could this energy create an etheric flame? Reich does mention the energy as being bluish. I speak more about Wilhelm Reich in the Radionic channel.

As I continue my research, I find myself reading from notes taken when I visited Marcel Vogel's lectures at the dowsing conference. When Marcel is talking about Orgone and Od energies he relates that thermodynamics for these energies are reversed; blue as etheric energy is warm and red, as etheric energy is cool and blue (some out of body experiences have mentioned this phenomenon). Could this be the reason copper has a blue energy flame? Are we talking about an etheric energy being perceived in this dimension by way of the pyramid structure, but keeping one foot anchored in the next dimension; the fourth dimension?

We know Eloptic or Fine Media (as Hieronymus would say) energy changes colors in different magnetic fields, polarizes, so it is not too far of a leap to characterize changes of colors in different mediums and conditions. Unfortunately I have not run into any research that talks about this energy interacting with sacred energies/golden mean or Fibonacci numbers of the Great Pyramid.

SUNSPOTS

Sunspots are believed by some researchers to have an influence on pyramid energy. Some background information on sunspots is necessary to the understanding of this research.

Sunspots are dark spots that appear periodically on the sun's surface. They move in complete cycles of 23, 28 or 33 years. Within these yearly cycles are detectable half cycles of 11.5, 14 or 16.5 years. These cycles are characterized by the size of the sunspot's umbra or shadow, which increases in size at the half cycle and decreases at full cycle.

Presumably, the increased size indicates increased activity (which also has a cycle, a monthly cycle akin to bio-rhythms). Dominant sunspot activity is surrounded by less pronounced sunspots called faculae and flocculi, which have their own rhythms. Little is known about these types of sunspots, but speculation is that they influence humans in subtle ways.

Sunspot activity is correlated to the effectiveness of pyramid energy, increasing when sunspots are large and decreasing when sunspots are smaller. Schul and Pettit have determined through their studies and experiments that pyramid energy is enhanced during high sunspot activity and is less effective during low sunspot activity.

Scientists speculated that highly charged particles (moving faster than the speed of light) are carried on solar winds and interact with pyramid energy fields. Slower particles, such as magnetic and electromagnetic particles, are also carried on solar winds interacting with the earth and pyramid energy. Particle size determines travel time of the particle between the sun and earth. Light energy particles reach the earth in 15 minutes; other slower particles (traveling slower than the speed of light) may take as long as eight to ten hours .

There are several ways to teach students how to construct a pyramid, depending on the age group you're working with. Children under eight years old could cut out their own pyramids, but the outline would have to drawn for them.

Given the dimensions of the base of the pyramid, the formulas for determining the remaining dimensions, proportional to those of the Great Pyramid, are:

Base measurement x .636009825 = height

Base measurement x .951056519 = edge length

(all measurements are based on the English system of

Choose a base size for your students and plug that measurement into the above equations to find the height of the pyramid and the length of one edge or use the chart on the next page. Of course, your students will not be able to measure to the accuracy given by the above equations. This is given just to indicate the kind of accuracy possible. Schul and Pettit in The Psychic Power of Pyramids (p. 212) have an even more accurate proportional breakdown for pyramid dimensions.

CONVERSION OF ENGLISH MEASURING UNITS

TO METRIC UNITS

CONVERSION OF ENGLISH
MEASURING UNITS TO METRIC
FOR TECHNICAL DRAWING

Inches		mm	Inches		mm
1/16	=	1.5	7/8	=	22
1/8	=	3	15/16	=	23.5
3/16	=	4.5	1	=	25.5
1/4	=	6	2	=	51
5/16	=	8	3	=	76
3/8	=	9.5	4	=	102
7/16	=	11	5	=	127
1/2	=	13	6	=	152.5
9/16	=	14.5	7	=	178
5/8	=	16	8	=	203
11/16	=	17.5	9	=	229
3/4	=	19	10	=	254
13/16	=	20.5			

In measuring pyramids, the side measurement on one side is always slightly longer than the edge length of the other side. The difference is very small, less than one decimal place, but it is significant when very precise measurements are required to study how energy accumulates within a pyramid. BASE 7.8X 3.0)(25.9# 1;2. Ii, , ' These are possible measurements to use. millimeters for easier measurement.

In mearsuring pyramids, the side measurement on one side is always slightly longer than the edge length of the other side. The difference is very small, less than one decimal place, but it is significant when very precise measurements are required to study how energy accumulates within a pyramid.

BASE	SIDE	HEIGHT
25.9"	24.7"	16.5"
18.8	17.9	11.9
12.0	11.4	7.6
10.0	9.5	6.3
7.8	7.3	4.9
3.0	2.8	2.0

These are possible measurements to use. You may to convert the inches in this chart to millimeters for easier measurement; just count the marks on a millimeter ruler and you will the dimension you need.

The height chosen for the pyramid, is based on proportions of the Great Pyramid, but doesn't make that much difference, except in making it easier to determine the pyramid angle.

To take height proportions, find the middle of your square by drawing an X from corner to opposite corner. Where the lines cross is the center. A line drawn from any side to the center of the square represents the height of the pyramid. This method is not exact for precise pyramid measurement, but it is an easy way to make a basic pyramid side. You should end up with one side of a pyramid. Check the length of each angle line to see if you used correct measurements. Cut out four sides, making sure you remember which side is the bottom, and tape together to make your pyramid. If you plan to make an accrete size pyramid you will need to measure the accrete size of the bottom and longest side. It would be easier to use the charts or equation that I have provided you in order to make the pyramid.

It might be a good idea, while the kids are making their pyramids, to make a 32" base pyramid to experiment with different pyramid sizes. While having your students do experiments with their pyramids, you could conduct the same experiment with a larger model.

Try making different types of pyramids to see what effects you can achieve. Use different materials. Try different sizes. Try combining a number of pyramids to see if you can increase the pyramid's power. Try constructing them at various times. A 12 inch period has always yielded great results for me.

PYRAMID EXPERIMENTS

Before trying to use your pyramid, check to see if it is up to its full capacity. I have found that pyramids of the same size, cut differently', will have different intensities. Cutting the sides of a pyramid out of a single piece of material and then scoring the edges to fold them creates a pyramid which is less effective than one made of sides that have been cut separately, then pieced together.

The material composition of a pyramid also affects its capacity. Tin foil, cardboard or wood seems to be the most effective, but don't let that dissuade you from trying other materials. Myself, I built pyramids from all materials above as well as from galvanized metal, plastic and copper sheet. In fact I put a group of pyramids together, one over the other, tinfoil/cardboard, copper and cardboard on the sides; and to be effective as a dialectic. I still wear it on my head as an effective shield from noxious energies some times; it also has an energy field that totally relaxes me. I read of an artist that put animal fur on the pyramid and it heated the surface to hundreds of degrees. Can you believe that boys and girls.

Before using your pyramid, check to see if it is up to its full capacity. I have found that pyramids of the same size, cut differently, will have different intensities. Cutting the sides of a pyramid out of the single piece of material and then scoring the edges to fold them creates a pyramid which is less effective than one made of sides that have been cut separately, then pieced together.

The material composition of the pyramid also affects its capacity. Tin foil, cardboard or wood seems to be more effective, but don't let that dissuade you from trying other materials.

Before using your pyramid, hold your hand over the apex and feel the energy emitted from the top (if you have trouble feeling the energy, turn to the Radionics chapter and follow the lessons on feeling different energy fields). Besides using your hand to feel pyramid energy, different receptor devices can be used. Verne Cameron, mentioned briefly in the Radionics chapter, uses an Aura Meter he made out of copper, coil, and balanced weight to detect different types of energy and the distance and direction from their source. From the apex of some pyramids, he could follow a line of energy hundreds of feet up to a mile. He believes that the energy emitted is within the range of ultraviolet (and Dr.Gilbert says that the higher harmonic of ultraviolet are contained within the pyramid.) or x-ray frequencies. It is possible that these rays are harmonious with cosmic energy in the gamma ray frequency.

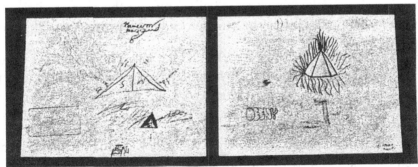

Elementary school age children's drawings from feeling pyramids with their hands.

EXPERIMENTING WITH MILK AND WATER

Place a container of water inside your pyramid about a third of the way up from the bottom, slightly off center towards the southeast corner or suspend the water container over the apex of the pyramid at 16, 30 or 32 inches. I have had success dehydrating some perishable foods using a 12-inch base cardboard pyramid. I have found that the way in which pyramid energy works in this process is dependent on the type of substance (for example, water or milk) which is placed in or over the pyramid.

For the milk experiment, have the children keep a journal of daily changes apparent in the milk, noting such things as the date, pyramid size, and any observations of environmental changes, i.e. sunny or rainy. They might also make drawings of their observations for their journals. Fluctuations in atmospheric or solar conditions can be determined by contacting the National Geographical and Solar Terrestrial Data Center in Boulder, Colorado. They will provide information about sunspots, magnetic and electromagnetic activities. Children should record these daily changes to determine how they affect changes in pyramid performance. Keep a record of the observations for three weeks to see what happens. You may want to present these findings to the class at the end of several weeks. Try making a flow chart of the changes.

Experimenting with water, you should follow the same directions as those for the milk, with the exception that in order to test pyramid water, have each child or group of children try their water on small plants. Obtain two plants: 1) a control plant watered daily with ordinary tap water and 2) an experimental plant watered with pyramid water. Place the plants in identical environments. Observe both plants for several weeks, asking the children to keep a record of plant size. This is a perfect time to teach your class about experimental methods, use of a control and experimental groups, and recording of such things as unit measurement and other distinguishing characteristics. You can also have the children taste the water to see if it has a different taste (there have been reports of water tasting different when treated with different energies.)

A journal can also be used in keeping a record of changes in the characteristics of perishable foods placed under a pyramid. Follow the same procedures as with the milk observations.

Another possible experiment would be to select containers of shapes other than pyramidal and compare their effects in relation to the pyramid. Try placing perishable food under these different shapes, i.e., a square, rectangle, or trapezoid and see which shapes, if any, affect the food.

Taking this experimental method a step further, you may want to build a model of the King's Chamber, an energy-intense area of the Great Pyramid. It should be placed inside of the pyramid, one third of the way up from the base with one of its walls butted up next to an imaginary center line on the southeast side.

"dehydrated 1 inch piece of fish".

Here is how you construct the King's Chamber:

Use cardboard to make a king's chamber. The height of the chamber should be 2/3 of the distance from the base of the pyramid up to 1/3 the distance up to the apex. Divide the height of the pyramid by three, and then take two of those thirds to get the correct height of the chamber. As shown, the King's Chamber has five slabs, each smaller than the next, with even smaller slabs in between. The Great Pyramid's King's Chamber was built from huge' slabs of limestone and granite, each weighing hundreds of tons to develop the additional power within the pyramid (referred to as piles or a battery). They rest on top of the rectangular room in which the King's coffer resides.

According to Schuls and Pettit, these slabs serve no structural purpose, so there must be another reason for why the Chamber is designed as such. Some say that the chamber design accumulates energy, that it once contained gold and other metal combinations which established a resonance frequency which added to the chamber's accumulated energy field. Above the slabs is a roof angled at 60 degrees. It is also claimed to be an energy accumulator, giving the entire chamber unusual energy potential. (this is quite a difference perspective than previously mentioned from the research done by the French radiesthesists, concerning the type of energy inside the pyramid.)

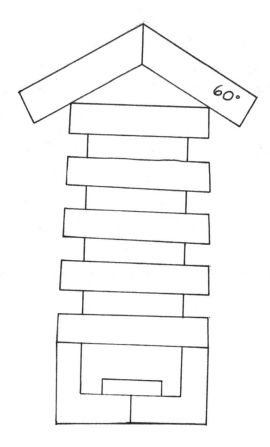

RAZOR BLADE EXPERIMENT

If you are interested in doing the razor blade experiment mentioned earlier, buy and use some Gillette Blue Blades. Build a 12 or 30 inch base pyramid with a King's Chamber and place one of the dull blades in the King's Chamber. Align it to magnetic north. Record what happens to the blade over several weeks. Test for changes in the blade's edges and sharpness.

Try other experiments with your pyramid. For example, recharging batteries; charging water for face conditioning or drinking; or try preventing food from spoiling by storing it in foil (and out) under your pyramid. Small pyramids, worn like a hat, could be used for meditation exercises; the energy feels really good when you where it. While leading a visualization session, have children wear a pyramid on their heads. Afterwards, hold a discussion about what each child experienced during the visualization exercise. This would be particularly effective if the children have gone through visualization before trying it with a pyramid hat.

Another possible exercise is to use the pyramid hats during study time, silent reading time or while the children are doing art projects. Look for changes in their attention span, and creativity during these exercises. The pyramid hat idea may even be useful while giving lectures during which attention is a prime factor in better retention levels? On the other hand we have learned that pyramid energy has a negative energy field as well. So, it is not advisable to wear the pyramid hat for long periods of time.

WHAT TO EXPERIENCE

Some possible results of working with a pyramid are:

1. Turning milk into yogurt.

2. Plants may grow bigger and healthier. Sick plants may revive after being watered with pyramid water.

3. Razor blades will stay sharper longer.

4. Perishable foods may be preserved longer, but not long enough to mummify.

5. Students' behavior and abilities might change under the influence of pyramid energy.

6. Different sizes will produce different effects . This list provides a limited range of the many possible results which can be gained by experimenting with pyramid energy. These effects should be recorded. along with associated observations and comments for future reference. 177

PYRAMID CHECKLIST

Here is a list of things to check when working with pyramids:

1. When constructing a pyramid, the more accurate you are in measuring, approximating the proportions of the Great Giza Pyramid, the better the results.

2. Place pyramids away from walls out lets, electrical appliances or any electrical equipment, it has the tendency to interfere with natural energy flow.

3. There seems to be some controversy as to whether or not pyramids should be aligned with magnetic north, true north, or north, at all when in use. Considerable information is now coming out about magnets and their ability to help stabilize and enhance psychic energy. Many researchers say that it proves to be advantageous in some experiments to align pyramids with the magnetic north.

   Therefore, in line with that thought, I would align pyramids with magnetic north. For razor blade studies, the blades were aligned to the magnetic north, which gave better results. For my own experiments with perishable items, aligning pyramids northward didn't seem to make a difference. You may want to try it, however, and see which way works best for you.

4. Some people say that pyramids work better with a bottom. It might be true. Try it. Some evidence has surfaced that says that placing a bottom on the pyramid creates a hoi zonal positive wave form;a magnetic field. Some people say that a red bottom facilitates pyramid energy flow.

5. Another important variable in attaining results under a pyramid is the possibility of concentrated energy spaces located within the pyramid. For example, the Great Pyramid has the King's Chamber, which is considered one of these high energy spaces. Try setting up a Queen's chamber and test what happens.

6. Under the Great Pyramid there is a river which is claimed to affect the pyramid's energy. Environmental conditions, therefore, may affect your pyramid. Sunny days are supposed to be more conducive to pyramid energy exchange than overcast days. Sunspot activity also alters the flow of pyramid energy.

A final topic of interest for you to explore is the possible futuristic uses of pyramid energy. There are some people who are so impressed with the power of pyramids that they have built their own pyramid houses. Pyramids and the Second Reality, by Schul and Pettit, shows several pyramid designed structures, located in different parts of the country, a pyramid church in Texas, a pyramid house in Okalhoma, and a pyramid office building in San Francisco. Within a few years, we will probably be hearing about some of the experiences these people encounter while living and working within these pyramid structures.

POTENTIALITY OF PYRAMIDS

There are several uses for pyramid energy. Besides the few I have already mentioned dehydrating food, purifying water, and stimulating concentration and creativity, pyramid energy could be used to help the mentally and physically handicapped. If the pyramid can help dyslexic children, why couldn't it be used to solve many other learning-related problems?

One might also question what possibilities the use of pyramid energy has for children of normal learning ability? Will pyramid energy enhance concentration, retention, and psychic abilities? Along with these things, supporters of pyramid energy claim that it can be used to control insect infestation and promote healing. With some consideration, you and your children could surely imagine many other possible uses of pyramid energy.

SUMMARY/CONCLUSIONS

The pyramid of Giza expresses a rich historical background, as one of the Eight Wonders of the World. There are reasons for everything that happens in the world, especially metaphysic, and I try to place this perspective in a realistic and practical context. The mysteries of the pyramids can be studied and understood if universal keys are applied in the process.

Pyramids become an interesting focus because they give us a perspective for studying alternative energies. Focusing on geometric form, I bring out the historical and contemporary ideas associated with form and energy in relation to ourselves and children. Lessons are integrated with current research on different types of pyramid energy and its function in a stable mass.

A few questions come to mind when thinking about pyramid energy: Does form play an important part in the stability of our mental and physical well being? Can geometric form enhance our well being? In a spiritually accelerating world, can pyramids help us experience our relationships with the whole, thereby clarifying our own individual directions in life?

For sometime now, my thoughts have focused on the forms that can be utilized to enhance a clearer feeling of euphoria, a connection with spirit and nature, and a feeling of total well being and centered-balanced spiritual consciousness.

Creating an environment that utilizes form to facilitate change in consciousness - an environment to make you feel good - can be created with the use of forms like pyramids, spheres, cones, geometric structures in nature, and animate and inanimate materials. Examples are Wilhelm Reich's orgone box and blanket, Robert Pavlita's bioplasmic generators, and Dr. Bell's specially designed wire-plated pyramids.

"Creative inspiration only comes to the prepared mind of relevant facts, impressions, and ideas", Authur Koestler

BIBLIOGRAPHY

Books

Bearden, Thomas. Excalibur Briefing. San Francisco, CA: Strawberry Hill Press, 1980.

Bentov, Itzhak, Stalking the Wild Pendulum. New York: E.P. Dutton, 1977.

Brunes, Tons, The Secrets of Ancient Geometry. Copenhagen: International Science Publishing, 1967. Capt, Raymond. The Great Pyramids Decoded. Thousand Oaks, CA: Artisan Sales, 1970.

Flanagan, Patrick, The Pyramid and Its Relationship to Biocosmic Energy. Glendale, CA: Pyramid Publishing, 1971.

Flanagan, Patrick. Pyramid Power. Glendale, CA: Pyramid Publishing, 1973.

Gallimore, J .G. Unified Field Theory, Mokelumne Hill, CA: Health Research, 1974.

Gallimore, J.G. Handbook of Unusual Energies. Mokelumne Hill, CA: Health Research, 1976.

Gilbert, Robert, J., Egyptian European Energy Work: Reclaiming the Ancient Science of Spiritual Vibration, Vesica, P. O. Box 27, Asheville, NC 28802, 2002 info@vesica.org

Hall, M.P. , Masonic, Hermetic, Kaabalistic and Rosecrucian Symbolical Philosophy, Los Angeles, CA: The Philosophical Research Society, Inc., 1973.

Halpern, Steve, Tuning the Human Instrument, Belmont, CA: Spectrum Research Institute, 1978.

Hardy, D., and Hardy, M. Pyramid Energy Explained. Allegan, MI: Delta-K Pyramid Products of America, 1979.

Hills, Christopher, Energy, Matter and Form, Boulder Creek, CA: University of the Trees, 1977.

Kerrell, Bill, and Goggin, Kathy, The Guide to Pyramid Energy, Santa Monica, CA: Fawcett Books, 1975.

Kueshana, Eklal, The Ultimate Frontier. Chicago, IL: The Stelle Group, 1963-1970.

Mann, W.E. Selected Writings: An Introduction to Orgonomy, New York: Farrar, Straus and and Giroux, 1951-1973.

Mann, W.E., Orgone, Reich and Eros, New York: Simon and Schuster, 1973.

Ostrander, S., and Schroeder, L. Psychic Discoveries Behind the Iron Curtain, Englewood Cliffs, NJ: Prentice-Hall, 1970.

Ostrander, S., and Schroeder, L. Handbook of Psychic Discoveries, Berkeley, CA: Berkeley Publishing Company, 1974. 182

Pol, Therese, The Sexual Revolution, New York: Farrar, Straus and Giroux, 1945-1974.

Puharich, Andrija, Uri - A Journal of the Mystery of Uri Geller. New York: Doubleday and Co., 1974.

Raknes, Ola, Wilhelm Reich and Orgonomy, Baltimore, MD: Pelican Books, 1970.

Stetson, W., Sunspots in Action, New York: Avon Books, 1947. Schul, Bill, and Pettit, Ed.

Schul, Bill, & Pettit, Ed, The Secret Power of Pyramids, Greenwich, CN: Fawcett Publishing, Inc., 1975.

Schul, Bill, and Pettit, Ed, The Psychic Power of the Pyramid, Greenwich, CN: Fawcett Publishing Inc., 1976.

Schul, Bill, and Pettit, Ed. Pyramids and the Second Reality, Greenwich, CN: Fawcett Publishing Inc., 1979

Tesla, Nikola, Assorted Tesla Articles, Mokelumne Hill, CA: Health Research, 1960.

Tompkins, P. , and Bird, C. The Secret Life of Plants, New York: Avon Books, 1973.

Toth, Max, and Nielsen, Greg, Pyramid Power. New York: Warner Destiny Books, 1974.

Publications:

Bilaniuk, Olexa, and Sudarstran, George

"Particles Behind the Light Barrier, " Physics Today, 1969, pp. 43-51.

Planetary Association for Clean Energy, Inc., Newsletter, Vol. 3, No. 1, June 1981.

The Pyramid Guide Newsletter, Life Understanding Foundation, 741 Rosarita Lane, Santa Barbara, CA 93105.

APPENDIX

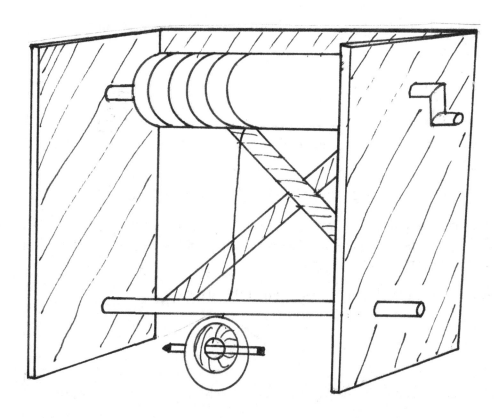

COIL WINDING DEVICE

Materials and Tools

- 1/16 - 1/4" plywood, two 12"xS" pieces (end plates)

- 1-1/4" wood slats, two pieces: 12" x 2" and 17" x 2"

- 3/8" x 13" wooden dowel

- 1/2" plastic pipe with threads on each end, no. 2 L-shaped piece of pipe with threads (if you can't find L-shaped pipe buy right angle pipes and 4 straight shorter pieces of pipe about 2" long with threads inside on both ends)

- 1/4 pound 8-penny

- rubber sheeting

- paper roll, from a roll of paper towels

- drill

1. Drill a hole in each plywood end plate 1/16" larger than the circumference of the plastic pipe and 2" down from the top.

2. Drill a hole a little larger than the dowel about 3" from the bottom of each end plate.

3. Stand each end plate on edge and nail a slat across the back on the top edge, as shown.

4. Then nail two more slats diagonally across the back, cutting off the overhanging edges.

5. Place the dowel through the holes near the bottom of the end plates.

6. Put a piece of plastic pipe through the paper roll and place the plastic pipe through the holes in the top end of the end plates. Wrap rubber sheeting around the plastic pipe to keep the roll from slipping.

7. Attach a right angle joint to each end of the plastic pipe.

8. Punch a small hole in the paper roll and attach copper or nylon cord through it.

9. Bring the spool of wire or cord under the wooden dowel and have one child crank the handle while another one holds a pencil placed through the hole in the spool. This child guides the wire around the paper spool (about 1/4" between each winding of the wire).

10. When the wire comes to the end of the paper role, again punch a hole and place the end of the wire through the hole, tucking it in so that the wire fits snugly on the roll.

ABOUT THE AUTHOR

Teaching and learning has been a challenge and inspiration for me for over 25 years. Working with children from the ages of two and a half to eighteen in public and private schools gave me the necessary experience to create the insights into curriculum design and research. Developing skills in photography as well as my consciousness has yielded a rich field of psychic phenomena that as yet to be explained by our scientific inquiry.

I have spent a lifetime developing innate abilities in Clairvoyance, Clairsentience, and Clairaudience – to clarify it in metaphysical terms, tweaking my interest in parapsychology. These interactions profoundly influenced my writing on these subjects, as did others. These are some experiences that also lead me into studies in Quantum Physics for a more scientific perspective.

Becoming an Art Teacher and an Early Childhood Specialist and masters student led me to researching how creativity functioned as a jumping off point for deeper exploration of the spiritual natures in all human beings, especially in children and young adults. I had the opportunity to open up the halls of higher academic learning and study great minds and understand what learned colleges thought of metaphysics and parapsychology. Delving into these fields with laymen was an exciting process as well; there's nothing like actual experience, including my own.

These studies stimulated me to continue to become involved in my own learning processes. I went to the source of spiritual experiences conducting my own research to answer some of the age-old questions. The more I experienced this arena the more my own childhood experiences came into focus as I learned that I had never been alone in the universe. Years later, being regressed by the late Dr. Jim Harder (one of the first academia to regress the famous abductee Travis Walton), I learned that I had been abducted at least twice in my childhood, and that I had a destiny to fulfill.

I soon learned that science was a necessary prerequisite for understanding the spiritual world bridging itself into our everyday lives. By now my metaphysical experiences were manifesting themselves (through my consciousness) in a more explicit way. I experienced channeling other consciousnesses that lead me to the study of this phenomena from expert channelers like Kevin Ryerson and academic researcher Jon Klimo, PhD, a conscious channel. I continued to bridge metaphysics and science developing a concept I call spiritual sciences. As I came into my adult life as a working professional I started to have some negative experiences around the study of consciousness.

For the first time I want to acknowledge the real threat of being in the metaphysical/scientific field for over 25 years. I have been a test subject, or guinea pig, of mind control experiments that span a decade. But I have to thank them, the proverbial "them", for their diligence on my behalf, because I was forced to develop techniques to counteract the psychotronic/psychic harassment they continue to throw at me to this day. This has helped me develop skills towards my own conscious enfoldment; escalating into a stronger communication with other intelligent beings in the universe, even now, as I write this bio. I feel more than one individual trying to disrupt my train of thought in the coffee shop where I'm writing. (I perceive the new disruptive signal coming from a laptop; they have created software?) They know that I know, and it has not deterred me in my quest to manifest my destiny. They have acknowledged this fact, indirectly, on several occasions over the years. There are no victims in this world, and there are no secrets any more; every thing can be known with our knowledge of mind dynamics; your thoughts can be read anywhere, anytime, thanks to Radionics/Psychotronics, E.L.F and radio frequencies, Remote Viewing, Astral Projection, and other psychic techniques. Welcome to the Twenty-first Century.

I currently live in Walnut Creek, after living in San Francisco for over 20 years. I'm single, but I had a profound experience when I met my twin flame (Summit Lighthouse has a excellent book on twin flames and soul mates). We had a great learning experience giving us the opportunity to purge emotions that we brought over from past lives holding us back from developing our consciousness. What I learned from our telepathic interaction you can't find in any book. We still continue to be in telepathic communication to this day, six years later. Our psychic senses have no boundaries (I have expressed a more in-depth story of our encounter in this book). Suffice it to say, you haven't LOVED until you have interacted with your twin flame; we all do at one time or another.

The concept of work no longer holds any validity for me, not because I'm retired, but the development of my consciousness sustains my life's passion in ways not limited to regimented routines or time schedule. (The concept of retirement has the same effect on me).

I'm involved in teaching workshops on Crystal and Crystal Healing, Dowsing, and Meditation classes (for adults). I do Numerology readings and occasional photo shoots, fielding any psychic photographs that reveal themselves in my work. I continue to develop my consciousness on a daily basis. I'm a metaphysician, parapsychologist, advanced dowser, numerologist, and art teacher.

My life quest has lead me into years of Buddhist practice, reciting the Lotus Sutra and chanting a daily mantra; meaningful interactions with The Order of Melchezedeck (Christ consciousness and great English spiritualist Dr. Grace Petipher) and various other consciousness groups; one being Cosolarology created by Gene Savoy, a world renown archeologist explorer of Peruvian ruins; years of looking at the sun using colored filters integrated with my biorhythm chart. This created an omni-present communication with my over-soul, archangels, and extraterrestrials, bringing my life to full spiritual awareness, realizing we are not alone in the universe; and our consciousness is limitless.

Jon Klimo, a professor at Rose Bridge Psychological College that I interviewed on several occasions concerning consciousness research, stated that during his entire travels he has never come across the information in my book integrated together in this way. He also confirms my concerns about psychic harassment (Jon wrote the book, "Channeling", one of the best scientific treatises on the subject, as well as others).

I continue to seek out synergistic experiences where ever I go! My life is a spiritual work in progress. I look forward to the next evolutionary step – 2012 hopefully will usher in higher spiritual consciousness. The universe continues to expand and our consciousness along with it. "It is done, it is finished."

Don Ellison, M.A. 10/5/2011